THE AUTHORS

James Hefley is a former Southern Baptist minister. He and his wife, Marti, are graduates of the New Orleans' Baptist Theological Seminary. Together, they have written more than thirty books on religious subjects.

THE CHURCH
THAT PRODUCED
A PRESIDENT

THE CHURCH THAT PRODUCED A PRESIDENT

«« »»

James and Marti Hefley

WYDEN BOOKS

Manufactured in the United States of America.
FIRST EDITION
Trade distribution by Simon and Schuster
A Division of Gulf + Western Corporation
New York, New York 10020

Library of Congress Cataloging in Publication Data

Hefley, James C
    The church that produced a President.

    Includes index.
       1. Carter, Jimmy, 1924- —Religion. 2. Baptists
—Southern States—Influence. I. Hefley, Marti, joint
author. II. Title.
E873.2.H43   286'.1'0924 [B]   77-16346
ISBN 0-671-22957-5

Contents

THE CHURCH
THAT PRODUCED
A PRESIDENT

1

«« »»

The President Is a Baptist

JIMMY CARTER has gone to a Baptist church almost every Sunday of his life. Before he became so busy in politics, he went twice on Sunday and once in the middle of the week, led home prayer meetings, called on the "unsaved" and other church prospects, and spoke at denominational functions.

Even when he was away from home—college, the navy, and later as governor—he taught a Sunday school class at a Baptist church. When at sea he led Sunday worship for his submarine crewmates.

But his most memorable church experiences took place in the Plains Baptist Church where he, his wife, his sons, his brother, his sisters, and his father and mother were all baptized. It was in the little white frame church with the stained glass windows that he learned to sing "Jesus Loves Me" and "Amazing Grace." Here he squirmed on pews when revival preachers waxed long, and learned to speak in public by taking "parts" in the Sunday evening BYPU (Baptist Young People's Union). And it was in the same Sunday school classrooms that he taught the upcoming generation what the older generation had taught him. In this sanctuary he had been ordained a deacon at thirty-eight, and had ushered, taken up the offerings, given lay sermons, and pronounced countless benedictions. Now on the last Sunday before boarding *Air Force One* for Washington to be inaugurated the thirty-ninth president of the United States, he followed his lifelong custom of attending worship services. Next Sunday he would "move his letter," as Baptists say, transferring his membership to the Baptist church nearest to his new home, the White House. But Plains, he declared, "will continue to be where my heart is."

In former days he and Rosalynn could walk the four short blocks along tree-shaded Paschall Street, catching up with neighbors they had always known, pausing under the familiar old oaks in the spacious churchyard to chat about children and crops before going inside. Today, as on immediate past Sundays, they cannot go alone. The omnipresent Secret Service must escort them: a station wagon loaded with clean-cut, short-haired agents in front; another trailing the president-elect's car. The bomb squad has already fine-toothed the church premises, prying apart the Communion table, lifting the trapdoor behind the pulpit and poking in the baptism tank, checking cabinets, closets, and anywhere else an explosive might be hidden.

Already the streets of "Peanut City, U.S.A." are thick with visitors. They are charmed with the little puddlejump town, the block-long main street of old-timey painted storefronts, Billy Carter's junky service station, the quaint little train station that served as campaign headquarters, the inviting wraparound porches, some with swings, and the plain "y'all come" country people. The eastern columnists may call Plains a throwback to the antebellum South and an anachronism that time has passed by, but Carter fans love it, especially the turn-of-the-century, twin-steepled "clapboard" church (that really has aluminum siding) to which they are heading today.

Tourists began coming to the church after the North

Carolina primary when the press finally realized that the peanut farmer running for president was serious about his born-again religion. The Sunday after the Democratic National Convention, seventy-six visitors turned up—a bicentennial omen perhaps. "Jimmy did right well on his trip up North," Deacon Theron Hobgood remarked dryly in Sunday school.

By November many church members were disgruntled. They couldn't park. Some were held back until Pastor Bruce Edwards or a deacon could identify them. Tourists were carrying off hymnbooks, offering envelopes, even rocks from the churchyard for souvenirs. Most galling for the segregationists of the church was black activist Clennon King's attempt to crack the race barrier for membership.

The November election results showed ninety-nine Plains men and women had voted against their neighbor Jimmy—about four out of ten whites in the town, assuming a solid black vote for the son of the town's chief "nigger lover." And with the Baptists being the largest of the three white congregations, many of the ninety-nine were likely in the president-elect's own church.

They hadn't liked him as chairman of the Sumter County School Board for trying to consolidate schools, which would have taken the elementary school out of Plains. They had disapproved of his politics in the state legislature. They had been displeased by his actions as governor. They had suspected he was a race mixer and he proved to be. Hadn't he and his family voted to let the "niggers" into the church back in 1965? They had pegged him with the liquor crowd and he had signed a law giving eighteen-year-olds the right to drink. They had said he wasn't the Christian he claimed to be and he had stopped the weekly worship service 'ole Lester Maddox had provided for employees at the governor's mansion.

Jimmy hadn't changed during his audacious presidential campaign, either, fraternizing with blacks, known drug users, and rock music stars and taking money from alcohol barons. Then giving that awful interview to the obscene *Playboy* magazine. There was no telling what he would do in the White House. What a hypocrite! And people were calling their church "his church." Every time they read about or heard someone say on television "Jimmy Carter's church," they winced with pain, exclaiming, "It's the Lord's church. Can't they understand that!" Especially after that rascal Clennon King had asked for membership in the church.

Following the highly publicized November 14 votes to "open" Plains Baptist to all races and to retain Pastor Bruce Edwards who had angered some of the deacons, scurrilous scuttlebutt had swept the town about the president-elect's family.

Miss Lillian's father, one story went, had been a whiskey runner for old Joe Kennedy. Old Joe was the real father of Jimmy Carter, who had been born five months after Earl and Lillian had married.

Carter relatives and supporters in the church weren't exempt. Rumors spread of extramarital sexual liaisons among some church officers. Worse were the frightening phone calls in the night and the stone thrown through the front window of Cousin Hugh Carter's spacious ranch-style home. Plains was "another Peyton Place," one Baptist declared.

All while the tourists and dignitaries flocked to Plains and the church.

On this last Sunday the churchyard is jammed with Carter admirers and the curious. The Secret Service estimates 1,500 are shivering in the cold. About 200 form a line at the side door facing Paschall Street, hoping to get into Sunday school. Only fifteen will be allowed in.

About 9:55 A.M. there is a shout and the crowd surges toward the side entrance. Children are boosted onto shoulders. Photo bugs lift cameras in the air. The Carter entourage sweeps up the driveway. "Mr. President, over here!" "Hey, Jimmy, I worked for you in Ohio." The middle car stops. The Carters alight amid a ring of protective agents. A smile and a wave and they are inside—Jimmy to the men's class in the basement of the annex, Rosalynn to her room on the main level, Amy bouncing up the steps to the junior girls' classroom.

Rosalynn's classroom is already full of women in their Sunday best. Her agent, whom they all call Steve, sits in a corner, failing to be inconspicuous.

The Bethany class gave her a silver bookmark as a good-bye gift last week. And a book to "another friend who will also be leaving us," class president Louise Shavers announced while Steve blushed.

Today they will say good-bye.

Teacher Margaret Whitley, who lives next door to the church, speaks for the group. "Our class has always been very close. We have worshiped together and shared our joys and sorrows. We've welded a chain, not of metal but of love and friendship, a chain that reaches out to encircle others. Rosalynn takes her link with her as she moves to Washington. But she'll always be a part of us."

The soon-to-be First Lady stands, clasping her green hardbacked *Living Bible* and Sunday school quarterly. She is wearing a light beige Ultrasuede jumper over a dark brown print blouse with a big bow. The gold circle pin she often wears shines from the jumper. She speaks in her soft southwest Georgia accent, but in the stillness of the room she can easily be heard.

"It gives me strength to know you all care. To know you pray for us. We need your continued prayers.

"Since the election the time has gone so quickly. There's been so much to do, so many plans to make. It's hard to say good-byes. Having to give away all my flowers. But we're leaving everything else just as is, because we will be coming back regularly. Once a month, Jimmy says. But he said that in Atlanta, too." She smiles. "He just worked all the time, so we didn't get home as often as we would have liked."

Downstairs in the cement-floored basement fellowship room every chair is taken. This is where the church suppers and Sunday school parties are held. For past months it has been taken over on Sunday by the Bible class for men in their forties and fifties. They had been meeting in a small cozy room upstairs, but the rise of Jimmy Now-everyone-knows-who forced the move. The old men's class still meets in the alcove back of the sanctuary. The president-elect's "Uncle Buddy," Alton Carter, spry at eighty-eight and on his third pacemaker, is in that group. Two floors up are the young married men.

The old men's and the young men's classes have never been transgressed by women visitors. Only since August 15, 1976, is the basement class no longer inviolate. The mixing of the class then made national news. The Sunday before, deacons had barred female reporters of the Associated Press and the *Washington Post* from the press pool assigned to cover the Democratic party's candidate in Sunday school. When it was reported that Carter had no objection to the banning, the Washington Press Club shot off a telegram to him, charging that he was acquiescing in the denial of equal opportunity for women to cover potential news. Carter then let it be known through his aides that he would not attend the class if women reporters continued to be excluded. He asked press aide Jody Powell to try and straighten the problem out.

Powell called teacher Clarence Dodson, who insisted the men were not "anti-women." The class, he said, had decided to enforce the tradition of separate classes for the sexes because families with small children were crowding into the basement. "Well, Jimmy has to have his press," Powell insisted. "Can't you do something?" Dodson allowed they could make an exception, and they did.

As the basement class settles down, children can be heard singing through thin walls:

> Jesus loves the little children;
> All the children of the world.
> Red and yellow, black and white;
> They are precious in his sight,
> Jesus loves the little children of the world.

Deacon Hobgood uncorks his long legs from under the banquet table at the front and stands up. "We welcome all visitors and especially the Atlanta Braves." The Braves came into Plains yesterday to play Billy Carter's baseball team. It was manager Ted Turner's idea they stay over and go to Sunday school with the president-elect. They were permitted in ahead of other tourists.

"How many read their Bibles daily last week?" the deacon intones. Jimmy Carter raises his hand. He reads a chapter in Spanish every night before going to bed. "It's more of a challenge that way," he says.

"How many brought an offering?" The president-elect lifts his hand again. "How many studied the lesson?" "How many staying for church?" The hands of the farmers and shopkeepers bob up and down in the timeless response to the Southern Baptist cradle-to-grave spiritual Brownie point record system. Each activity counts for percentage points. The class average is tallied by the secretary and passed along to the general superintendent of the Sunday school, who enters the figure in his book and figures the grade for the entire Sunday school. The same routine will be followed in 35,000 other Southern Baptist churches from Anchorage to Key West today.

The preliminaries are over. There is no suspense as to who will teach this morning. The president-elect taught last Sunday. "I wanted to teach one more time before going to Washington," he said. "I looked over the lesson for this Sunday and next, and next Sunday's is about how a prophet is without honor in his own country. (Laughter) So I decided to take this one."

Deacon Dodson now rises and stands behind a metal lectern. He is business manager at the South Georgia Technical and Vocational School in nearby Americus. A spare thin man, he lives across Paschall Street from the church in a white-columned house that his grandfather built. One of his ancestors was among the twenty charter members when the church was organized in 1848.

Clarence Dodson is a peacemaking pillar in the church, a man of no controversy, given to dark suits, minding his own business, and acceptance of what must happen. He and his wife Ann are friends with everybody, but their ties with Jimmy and Rosalynn Carter are especially close. Ann is a flower fancier whose yard is a showplace. The Plains Garden Club was organized in her living room twenty years ago. She was elected the first president and Rosalynn Carter the first secretary. A little over two years ago Rosalynn's husband spoke to the club and made the first public announcement that he intended to run for the presidency. Ann has been named to chair the committee to decorate the White House for the inauguration.

The lesson for January 16 is the third in a series about

the beginning of Jesus' ministry. Two Sundays ago Deacon Dodson talked about Jesus growing up in Nazareth. "Who would have expected the Messiah, our Savior, to come from such a little insignificant place, a common place that only common people would love? And who would expect that from the little town of Plains would come such a famous person as you see sitting before you this morning?"

"The third lesson," he now announces, "is about Jesus coming back to his hometown to declare his mission. A little town like Plains, where everybody knows everybody. As was his custom, he went to the synagogue in Nazareth that morning, where the men sat on one side and the women on the other just as people once did in this church. When the time came he stood up to read from the prophecy of Isaiah. Let us read in unison what our Savior read. Luke chapter 4, verses 18 and 19."

So they read: twenty-five Atlanta Braves; a dozen or so tourists; four Secret Service operatives; the press pool of six reporters representing the television networks, AP and UPI, and several large metropolitan newspapers; and thirteen class members, including the next president of the United States.

"The spirit of the Lord is upon me, because he hath anointed me to preach the gospel to the poor; he hath sent me to heal the brokenhearted, to preach deliverance to the captives, and recovering of sight to the blind, to set at liberty them that are bruised, to preach the acceptable year of the Lord."

In his soft drawl, Deacon Dodson picks up the story. "When they heard Jesus read this prophecy in the synagogue, they asked, 'Isn't he the one who grew up down the street, the carpenter's son?' Then when he disclosed, 'This day is this scripture fulfilled in your ears,' they judged Jesus guilty of blasphemy and worthy of death.

And when he said, 'A prophet is without honor in his own country,' they led him to the precipice and were going to push him over the cliff.

"We say, 'We wouldn't have done that.' But I wonder. I wonder."

About ten minutes later, the wiry, earnest deacon cuts the lesson short and walks in front of his lectern. He stands silently for a few seconds, gathering his thoughts, as he looks toward the center of the third row where the president-elect is sitting with his black King James reference Bible open to the lesson Scripture.

"This will be the last day before our distinguished, beloved, and most honored class member becomes president. The world will be watching to see how his love is demonstrated in diplomacy and politics. All Christians, and especially Baptists, will share in the spotlight cast on him. Let us as a class make a commitment to pray daily for Brother Jimmy and Rosalynn that they will find God the answer to all their problems, that Brother Jimmy can lead us in peace and unity.

"Now, Brother Jimmy, will you come up here. We have a little token of our love to give you."

Deacon Carter stands, looks around, smiles, excuses himself to the awed baseball player beside him, then threads his way through the closely wedged chairs. He reaches the front, turns, and looks shyly at his fellow deacon who hands him a silver bookmark that matches the one the women's class gave Rosalynn last week. "I'll promise to use it. Thank you," he responds.

Momentarily he seems at a loss for words. "Uh, I, well, I guess all of you know what this class and my hometown mean to me. I thank you for the little gift and for your prayers. As I undertake to serve my nation and the world, I hope I can order my decisions, commitments, and ideals that you might be proud of everything I do."

While the president-elect remains standing, Deacon Dodson calls on Cousin Hugh Carter, another deacon, to dismiss in prayer. Then the well-wishers press around the ex-peanut farmer, congratulating him, asking for autographs which he declines, saying, "The Secret Service won't let me." The deep voice of a uniformed Salvation Army officer booms above all others. "God bless you, Sir. God told me you were going to be elected and that Jesus will come back while you're in office. Hallelujah!"

Finally Deacon Carter breaks through to the short stairs with the others following. In the hallway he embraces an old friend, then turns and steps into the room where the small choir is rehearsing. There are tears all around as he moves about giving farewell hugs and kisses. He puts an arm around Sandra Edwards, the willowy, dark-haired pastor's wife and whispers, "You'll never know how much you and Bruce have meant to our family."

Outside the crowd has grown larger. A deacon peeks out the side door. "We can take fifteen more for church," he says.

A buxom woman breaks line and runs to the doorstep, extending a legal-looking paper. "My great-granddaddy was a Carter. Here's the proof." She is inside before the deacon can think of something to say.

The worship service is ready to begin in the high-ceilinged old sanctuary that dates to 1906. It is a short rectangle with alcoves around the two front entrances that are now locked for security. The sun streams through the stained glass windows depicting biblical scenes. The three sections of solid oak pews resting on cranberry red carpeting curve slightly toward the pulpit. The aged pews squeak under the weight of the capacity crowd.

The choir loft with organ and piano is at the left of the front, with a velvet curtain along the railing. At the center of the platform is the pulpit with the Communion table directly before it. A spray of fresh flowers brightens the scene.

Behind the pulpit are two ornate chairs with soft cushions and high, hand-carved backs. Cousin Hugh, a state senator, bespectacled with thinning hair, sits in the one beside the choir. Pastor Bruce Edwards occupies the other. Slightly stocky with smooth squarish features, Edwards looks expressionlessly toward the audience. On his left, just off the platform, is a single pew and some extra chairs. The press pool is jammed into this area with seven or eight lucky tourists.

This is a smiling, friendly congregation. Almost a revival atmosphere prevails, perhaps because the malcontents who were angry about the November votes to declare the church open to all races and to retain Pastor Edwards are absent. They are not here to wish Jimmy Carter Godspeed. After opposing him politically, they now blame him for attracting the troublemaker Clennon King, the pushy reporters, and the television cameras that turned their quiet Sundays into holidays and embarrassed them before the world.

Far fewer tourists can be accommodated today than on previous Sundays, for the close friends of Jimmy and Rosalynn have invited out-of-town friends and relatives for this historic occasion. These guests, many of whom are long-time friends of the Carters and hold tickets for the "Peanut Express" going to the capital for the inauguration, were allowed in with the Atlanta Braves.

Jimmy and Rosalynn Carter are in their usual spot, third pew from the front in the right section. When the sexes were separated in worship, this was the women's side. Miss Lillian has been ill and isn't here today. Lively Amy, pigtails bobbing, wiggles in the next pew up with a friend.

The maroon-robed choir is now entering. Another change from the old days when robes would have brought a revolt. Widowed Carol Anderson, tall and thin, is at the organ. Her late husband Elliot worked for the Carters and died unexpectedly while Jimmy was governor. Jimmy came to Plains for the funeral, which was on Valentine's Day. Before leaving he took time to help Carol get Elliot's business affairs in order. She has never forgotten the kindness.

There are other widows in the congregation who love and admire their president-elect. There is "Miss" Jewel Turner, seventy-eight, sitting in the third pew center front. Her late husband Dennis ran a grocery store in Plains and played Santa Claus every year at the church Christmas party. He served with Jimmy as a deacon and Jimmy was a pallbearer at his funeral. When Jimmy first ran for governor Miss Jewel had stopped him on the church steps one Sunday and told him, "I wish I could contribute some money to your campaign, but you understand my situation as a widow. But if you will stay humble, and keep serving the Lord, I'll pray for you every day."

Jimmy flashed her a bright smile and took her hand. "Miss Jewel, there is nothing that would mean more to me." When he announced that he was going to run for the presidency, the two renewed their covenant.

And the vivacious little woman everybody calls "Mimsy." She is mother to Carol and has a son George who is a doctor in Atlanta. Dr. Mims, who grew up in Plains, went to New Hampshire to campaign for Jimmy. And "Miss" Ida Lee Timmerman, who has been a member of the church for sixty-seven years. Her husband had the first peanut warehouse in Plains, later going into partnership with Oscar Williams. They were Earl Carter's competitors, as the Williams boys, Frank and Albert, are now Jimmy's and Billy's. "Miss" Ida Lee is another "prayer supporter" and fan of the president-elect. And "Miss" Maude Dodson, Clarence's mother, ninety-three, the oldest person in the church. She has been a member for seventy-nine years. And "Miss" Lilouise Sheffield. Her husband was superintendent of the Sunday school for over twenty years and superintendent of Plains High School for longer than that. He taught Jimmy math.

Carol is playing as the prelude "I Would Love to Tell You What I Think of Jesus." She has carefully chosen Jimmy's and Rosalynn's favorite hymns for this service. When she stops, Pastor Edwards steps to the pulpit to welcome the visitors and make necessary announcements. Dr. Winston Crawley, an area director of the Southern Baptist Foreign Mission Board, is in the audience. But Edwards calls no names.

"We'd like to ask that there be no moving around and that no cameras or tape recorders be used" is all he says to indicate that this service will be different from any other. There is not even a notation in the bulletin that Deacon Carter will be sworn into the nation's highest office on Thursday. Only once during the past year has Deacon Carter made the bulletin: congratulations for winning the Democratic nomination for the presidency. The pastor knows his most prominent member prefers it this way. He is also thinking of the members who resent any attention being given to the next president.

Today he has only three brief announcements. It is "good news" that the Christmas foreign mission offering has reached $662.97, past the $650 goal; "bad news" that the church is $540 short on its commitment to buy a freight car load of corn for farm livestock at the Georgia Baptist Children's Home. The third notice is that the Cherub Choir will not practice on Tuesday "because a lot of our people will be going to something more important." This brings a ripple of laughter.

"More About Jesus" is the first hymn, then "America the Beautiful," a song usually reserved for the Fourth of July.

Without anything being said, it is obvious that the congregation is deeply moved. During the first stanza the president-elect is seen to draw an arm closer about his wife. In the press group, CBS's Betsy Aaron wipes away a tear.

After the second hymn comes the children's worship, an innovation of Bruce Edwards. Amy and her friends suddenly come alive, skipping to the front, where they gather in a circle around the pastor. Today his mini-sermon is about how Jesus was friendly to the Samaritan woman at the well, somebody everybody looked down on but Jesus. "This week, boys and girls, let's try to be friendly with everyone. Okay?" "Yeah," they reply. "Yeah."

"Let's all join in singing 'Amazing Grace,' number 188," Cousin Hugh announces. This has always been a favorite among Southern Baptists, though few know that its eighteenth-century author, John Newton, trafficked in slaves before his conversion.

The ushers pass the offering plates. The choir sings their "special," a medley of Gospel choruses sure to stir the memories of Jimmy and Rosalynn: "Jesus Is the Sweetest Name I Know"; "Jesus, Oh How Sweet the Name"; "Oh, How I Love Jesus"; and "To Me, It's So Wonderful . . . That Jesus Is Mine." Simplistic, sentimental Jesus rhymes to cynics perhaps, but the words enshrine the faith that Jimmy Carter says is the lodestar of his life, "at the bottom of everything I do."

Bruce Edwards begins reading his sermon Scripture. He has chosen this text, Rom. 13:1-7, especially for today: "Let every soul be subject unto the higher powers. For there is no power but of God; the powers that be are ordained of God. . . ."

He begins his sermon rather stiffly, his voice betraying the anxiety he feels. "Paul is instructing us in man's relationship to government and government's relationship to man. Government is deemed to be good in verse 3: 'For rulers are not a terror to good works, but to the evil.' But government is allowed to exist only by God.

"We know that Paul wrote these statements when Nero was Caesar, an evil man who persecuted Christians. Yet Paul said we should 'be subject unto the higher powers.'

"Those who seek leadership should recognize they are allowed to receive power by God. Thus they are to seek to be good and do right. We who are governed by them are to render tribute, the apostle says in verse 7. It is our Christian responsibility to pay our just taxes; to render that tribute to our Caesar.

"We are told to render honor to government. It's so easy for us to criticize when we don't know all the problems. Most of us can't even manage our own households, let alone the government.

"We are instructed to pray for our leaders that they may be blessed and have wisdom. While doing that, we should also pray to be good followers.

"Finally, the Bible does not mean that we are to follow government blindly. When the disciples were released from prison for preaching the resurrection of Jesus and ordered to remain quiet, Peter declared, 'We ought to obey God rather than men.' If this rare time should come, we must accept responsibility for our own actions. In following our conscience to do what is right, we must be willing to accept punishment for the law we are breaking."

After more sermonizing on the Christian's responsibility to government, he pauses and tries hard to look historic. "This week a very distinct honor will come to our church. One of our own will become leader of our nation. We the members of this church have the responsibility to pray for our leader and his family as they go to Washington.

"Jimmy and Rosalynn, we are today covenanting to pray

for you and the tremendous responsibilities you will be accepting as our president and First Lady."

The minister lifts his hand in a blessing. "Our Father, we realize government is not always good, not as decent as it should be. But we can participate in government and make government good. So we ask your blessings upon Jimmy and Rosalynn, and Senator and Mrs. Mondale, and our congressmen, senators, Supreme Court, cabinet and all areas of government. Help us by the way we live to be supportive of the decisions made by government. Give us wisdom never to act out of self-interest. May our thoughts be pure. And may we enter into a covenant to pray without ceasing for those who go out from among us today. Help them, we pray. In Jesus' name, amen."

The president-elect has been leaning forward, his head cupped in his hands. He and Rosalynn now stand with the congregation to sing the hymn inviting "commitments to Christ":

> A ruler once came to Jesus by night
> To ask him the way of salvation and light;
> The Master made answer in words true and plain,
> "Ye must be born again...."

The hymn is over. A visiting Baptist prays in simple benediction, "Help us all, and especially Brother and Sister Carter, to be faithful to Thee in our vocations." At his "amen" there is a momentary hush, then Jimmy and Rosalynn step quietly to the front for tearful good-byes to their dear friends.

Four more days and Jimmy Carter, born-again Christian, Baptist deacon, Sunday school teacher, and lay missionary, will become the thirty-ninth president of the United States.

What will it all mean? Who are the Southern Baptists and how did they come to be what they are?

2

«««   »»»

Where Baptists Come From

WHATEVER ELSE Jimmy Carter is, he's a Baptist, as were most of his American ancestors.

On his mother's side, his second-, third-, and fourth-generation Gordy grandfathers were all Baptists. His first grandfather, Jim Jack Gordy, had the "misfortune" to marry a Methodist. But one of Jim Jack's daughters, Lillian, married Baptist Earl Carter and then joined Plains Baptist Church.

On his father's Carter side, the Baptist line runs back at least six generations in Georgia, and perhaps another generation or two in North Carolina and Virginia if the facts were known.

Baptists are also thick on the trees of the president's collateral ancestries. His Aunt Jeanette Carter Lowry reports: "My mama's family were Baptists as far back as we can know. My grandfather is buried in the cemetery of one of the oldest churches in South Carolina, Little River Baptist in Due West."

It is known that the Carter line came from England. A Carter pushed a cart, just as a Smythe (Smith) pumped a bellows.

But the earliest Carter in the great genealogy hunt that

began when one became president was no cart pusher, nor was he likely to have been a Baptist. John Carter, Sr., thought to be the ninth-generation grandfather to President Jimmy, was a prominent merchant of Christchurch in the early seventeenth century. When the White House staff was planning the president's first trip to England in May 1977, they considered a Carter reunion and checked with genealogist Silas Lucas, Jr., in Easley, South Carolina. Lucas, who is a distant twig in the Carter ancestral tree, has done more research on the Carter lineage than anyone. "Wait for another time," he advised. "We are pretty sure John Carter, Sr., is the one, but we don't want to say 'absolutely' at this point."

In any case, merchant Carter of Christchurch had to have been aware of the commotion that the Puritan forebears of the first Baptists were causing.

Olde England was then being rocked by tornadic winds of political and religious change coming from Calvin's Geneva. The main body of Puritans was calling for purity in politics, simplicity in religion, and divestiture of the crown's control over church affairs. They demanded that every ritual and action of the church follow Scripture. They asked that clergy be stripped of robes, vestments, and candles and that other liturgical trappings be swept from the altar. But what struck at the heart of royal privilege was the assertion that the monarchy must give up its power over the church.

James I, who, according to contemporary accounts, "slobbered and staggered like a drunken buffoon," listened to their "ravings" at the Hampton Court Conference, then made a few concessions. The major one was to commission a newly revised translation of the English Bible. But he adamantly refused to give up control of church appointments and revenues.

The Puritans were not appeased, but they were themselves divided over how the national church should be structured. Most wanted a strong central church government, as Calvin had set up at Geneva, but free from the reach of the crown. The most radical, called Separatists, said that each congregation should be free to run its own affairs by democratic vote. They also declared that Christianity wasn't hereditary and only believers should be baptized.

The king and the Puritan bishops were squabbling over who would control the church. The Separatists were, in effect, calling for a plague on both houses and demanding that religion be wholly voluntary. This was treason to both majorities. "If this [Separatist] sect prevale," moaned a royal adviser, "we shall have no Monarchie in the State, nor Hierarchie in the Church, but an Anarchie in both."

James's scholars described the Separatists in the preface of the new Bible as "self-conceited Brethren, who run their own ways, and give liking unto nothing, but what is framed by themselves, and hammered on their anvil. . . ." This harangue is still being printed at the front of King James Bibles, the most popular Bible version ever published.

The most vociferous Separatist congregation was at Gainsborough, led by John Smyth. He was a graduate of Cambridge, had taught at Christ College, and been ordained in the Church of England. A branch of the Gainsborough group met at Scrooby. Their pastor was John Robinson, also a graduate of Cambridge and ordained in the state church.

In 1607 King James began a crackdown on the "impure and carnal . . . schismatical rabble." Several Separatists from Gainsborough and Scrooby were carted off to York Castle. "They will conform . . . or else I will harrie them out of the land," vowed the king.

To avoid imprisonment, the Separatists fled to Holland. Robinson led the Scrooby group along with William Brewster and William Bradford from Gainsborough. Once in Holland they negotiated with English merchants for a land charter and passage to Virginia. But as they neared the American coast, a fierce storm drove them north and they landed at Plymouth Rock. The landing of these "Pilgrims," as Carlyle would later write, marked the "beginning" of the "soul of America."

John Smyth's group decided to stay in Europe. A lawyer among them, Thomas Helwys, felt they had made a mistake in leaving England. He vowed to return "where Satan's throne is" and oppose the king publicly.

While in Holland the Smyth-Helwys group was influenced by a flock of Mennonite Waterlanders, one of many Anabaptist* sects that had taken refuge there from intolerant church-state regimes. The Waterlanders told the English Separatists chilling tales of executions by courts and massacres by mobs, Protestant and Catholic.

Smyth wrote: "Do not the Papists call the Protestants heretics and call for fire and fagot? Do not the Protestants call the Separatists schismatics and heretics and judge them worthy of the gibbet?"

The Mennonites confirmed the English Separatists' belief that infant baptism was invalid and that only believers should be baptized. "Considering what baptism is," Smyth then said, "an infant is no more capable of baptism than is any unreasonable or insensible creature."

The English Separatists hadn't really been baptized, then. But who would baptize them, since they had renounced the authority of their state church? After long discussion, they decided that Smyth should first baptize himself, then administer the rite to the others. This he did by pouring water from a pitcher first over his head, then over the others' heads.

Most modern Baptist historians cite this event as the

*Re-baptizers: *Ana* is Greek for "again, anew."

beginning of the denomination. A minority differs and regards the Smyth group only as a link in a chain of physical succession running back to the "First Baptist" church of Jerusalem in the first century, when new converts were baptized in the "name of the Father, the Son, and the Holy Spirit." For this reason, they say, Baptists cannot be called Protestants; they never arose from the Reformation.

Dr. Walter Shurden, associate professor of church history at Southern Baptist Theological Seminary in Louisville, knows of no Southern Baptist seminary historian holding to this theory. Shurden believes Baptists should pattern their congregational life from the first-century churches, instead of trying to bend history to conform to successionist orthodoxy.

Whether the Gainsborough Separatists organized the first Baptist church or not, all Baptists agree on what happened next. They split, something Baptists have been doing at a remarkable rate ever since.

The division started when Smyth had second thoughts about their baptism. He decided they should have let their Mennonite friends do the honors. "No," argued Helwys, "one baptism is enough." Smyth and Helwys also argued about returning to England.

Smyth and the majority had the Mennonites baptize them. They stayed in Holland and in time lost their "Baptist" identity. Helwys took a minority of ten back to London, where in 1611 they established themselves as "Ye Baptiste Church." Baptist historians call this the first Baptist church on English soil.

True to his vow, Helwys sent their beliefs to King James. "Heare, O king, and despise not ye counsell of ye poore, and let their complaints come before thee," he began. "The king is a mortall man, and not God, therefore hath no power over ye immortall soules of his subjects, to make laws and ordinances for them, and to set spiritual Lords over them.

. . . O king, be not seduced by deceivers to sin so against God whome thou oughtest to obey. . . ."

His Majesty's response was to order Helwys arrested and all copies of his writings burned. After refusing to recant, the lawyer was incarcerated in Newgate Prison and was soon dead from causes never explained.

John Murton, a member of the congregation, took Helwys's place as leader of the London congregation. In 1615 he sent a message to the king, declaring, "No man ought to be persecuted for his religion, be it true or false. . . ."

The Baptist "infection" spread, with congregations popping up across England like so many boils on the king's corpulent backside. Their chief resource and weapon was the newly translated Bible. James had ordered the new version to appease his critics. Now they were throwing it back in his face.

Following what they believed to be the New Testament pattern, each Baptist congregation was a democracy, electing one or more pastors, contributing voluntarily to pay expenses. They made no assessments, charged no pew rents.

When a new believer asked for baptism, the congregation decided on his sincerity. If a member erred from the straight and narrow, a committee talked to him and recommended action to the church. But strict as they were with their own, they did not try to make outsiders conform.

Baptismal methods varied among the English churches. Most immersed, noting that the Greek word *baptizo*, which King James's scholars had conveniently failed to translate, meant "to plunge under." They further contended that only immersion was a true picture (or symbol) of conversion, depicted as a death, burial, and resurrection in the sixth chapter of Paul's epistle to the Romans. A few churches continued to pour or sprinkle.

They also differed over the relationship of man's freedom to God's sovereignty. General Baptists said God's grace and forgiveness were for all who freely chose to receive it. Particular Baptists held that only an elect few, known only to God, would be saved.

Whether Particular or General, the English Baptists were an outlawed minority. Preachers often had to hide during the day, surfacing at night to hold illegal services in members' homes. Many were caught and jailed.

The most celebrated Baptist prisoner of the mid-seventeenth century was John Bunyan from Bedford, a poor tinker turned preacher. Bunyan was seized while holding services at a farmhouse and indicted for "devilishly abstaining" from attending "the church" and "upholding unlawful meetings—to the great disturbance of the good subjects of this Kingdom, contrary to the laws of our Sovereign Lord, the King."

Bunyan had a wife and four children, one of whom was blind, looking to him for support. His wife was also expecting another child.

The magistrate ordered him locked in the vermin-infested Bedford Jail, with the assurance that he would be released in three months if he promised to start attending the lawful church and never to conduct "unlawful" meetings again.

Friends begged him to concede. "You can just drop in the parish church occasionally," they said, "and continue preaching to one or two persons at a time." The pressure became greater when word came that his wife had lost her baby and his blind daughter was grieving that she would never feel her father's touch again.

Bunyan chose to remain in jail. He wrote: "The parting from my wife and poor children hath been to me as the pulling of my flesh from my bones . . . especially my poor blind child who lays nearer to my heart than all else besides."

He served twelve years, remained free for four years, then was sentenced again for another four years.

But the joke was on his persecutors. While in the squalid jail, he wrote fifty-eight books expounding his religious and political beliefs. One of his books, an allegorical novel titled *Pilgrim's Progress,* became, next to the Bible, the most popular religious book in the Western world.

It was inevitable that Baptist ideas would be carried to the American colonies, where Puritans had been given their own colony in Massachusetts.

The seeds were sown while Roger Williams grew up in England. Williams lived near Newgate Prison and saw ghastly executions of Baptists and other "heretics" for no crimes other than dissent. He also knew that the bloody conflict (the Thirty Years' War) then raging on the Continent was between church-state regimes, battling to gain control of subjects' minds. He was further influenced by Sir Edward Coke, the liberal jurist who sponsored his Cambridge education, to sympathize with Baptists and other Separatists.

A letter came from the Puritan congregation in Boston inquiring whether Williams would be interested in becoming their pastor. He knew the Puritans had gone to Massachusetts to worship God according to their conscience. He hoped he would be permitted to preach what he could not in England.

Williams was not long in Boston before he realized that the Puritans wanted religious freedom only for themselves. They were more intolerant of dissenters than their Anglican cousins. He refused their pastoral call, explaining, "I durst not officiate to an unseparated people."

Williams took the pulpit of the liberal Salem church, which was then in rebellion against the powers in Boston. The Salem Puritans agreed with him that civil powers shouldn't be used to control conscience.

Williams said all the things the English Baptists had been saying and more. He attacked the Puritan laws against violations of the first table of the Ten Commandments. Whether a man worshiped a god or no god, Williams said, swore or never took an oath, went to church on the Sabbath or went fishing was none of the state's business.

As if this wasn't insult enough to the holy common-wealth, Williams preached to the aborigines that God loved them as much as he did proper Englishmen. When he found what the Indians had been paid for their lands, he gave the back of his hand to the Puritans for cheating.

The wigged heads in Boston could tolerate his meddling with the Indians; they needed his influence in persuading the Indians not to attack. But calls for "absolute permis-sion of conscience . . . in what is spiritual" were intolerable.

They passed a law requiring all citizens of the common-wealth to take an oath of loyalty to the general court. Re-fusal was punishable by banishment. Williams thundered that the law was illegal and unjust. He was promptly arrested and put on trial.

Convicted, he was offered a chance to recant. He replied defiantly, "I shall be ready . . . not only to be bound and banished, but to die also in New England for my convic-tions and for the truth as I see it!"

The court pronounced sentence and gave him six weeks to settle his affairs and depart. While he was trying to de-cide what to do, a close friend brought a secret message from troubled Governor Winthrop. There was a plot to put him aboard a ship bound for England. He should leave immediately.

Williams packed what he could carry, kissed his wife Mary and baby good-bye, and fled into the face of a blizzard.

Indian friends kept him through the first winter and sold him land for a colony. He started laying out a village and summoned his wife and close friends. Providence Plantations, he promised, would be a "shelter for persons distressed for conscience." A democratically elected civil government would have no authority over spiritual matters. Citizens could worship in their own way or not at all.

While Roger Williams helped build the village of Providence, Mary Williams gave birth. They named their new son Freeborn.

Harrassed dissenters poured into the new colony. Most came from Massachusetts, but a flock of Jews and a shipload of Quakers arrived from Dutch New Amsterdam (later New York). The Quakers had first come from England, only to be told at New Amsterdam that they could not come ashore. After they sailed out of the harbor, the Dutch port master supposed they had gone to Williams's colony, "the receptacle of all sorts of riffraff" and "the sewer of New England. All the cranks of New England retire, thither," he said.

At Providence, Williams was free to set up his own church. After studying the writings of English Baptists, he had himself immersed by Ezekiel Holliman, who had come from the Salem church. Williams then baptized Holliman and about a dozen others. Thus was born in 1639 the first Baptist church in America, and it is still in existence.

The second Baptist church in America was organized a year later by John Clarke, a Puritan pastor lately of Boston. Clarke had taken all the Puritan intolerance he could stomach. After the hanging of the Quaker woman Mary Dyer, he had vowed to "shake the dust of Boston off my feet, and betake me to a new place . . . where there will be full freedom of thought and full freedom of conscience." Roger Williams introduced Clarke to friendly Indians, who sold him a small island in Narragansett Bay. There he and his friends started Newport settlement and organized a church like the one in Providence.

The Baptists' belief in soul freedom didn't dampen their evangelistic zeal. The settlements in Rhode Island, for which Williams wangled a charter from London, became a base for preaching forays into Massachusetts. Baptists would steal into a friendly community, post lookouts, gather a crowd, and start preaching. Before unfriendly magistrates knew what had happened they would be back in Rhode Island.

Some were not so fortunate. In 1651 Clarke and Deacon Obadiah Holmes walked eighty miles into Massachusetts to hold a service in the home of a blind Baptist friend. Suddenly two constables burst into the house and caught them with Bibles in hand.

Their prosecutor was John Cotton, the same lawyer who had convicted Roger Williams. To Clarke's plea that they had been merely reading Scripture to their blind host and his friends and that a home should not be invaded by civil authorities, Cotton snorted, "A home is not privileged when a crime is being committed."

Cotton demanded the death penalty, but the judge let them off with fines. If they did not pay up and leave the commonwealth immediately, he added, they would be soundly whipped.

Friends came forward with money, which Holmes and Clarke refused, saying they would take the whipping as a testimony for their cause. On the way to the whipping post someone slipped gold coins into the hands of one official and Clarke was released. Still defiant, Holmes bared his back to the lash, preaching to the crowd between every crack of the leather.

All the courts in Massachusetts couldn't keep the Baptist plague from spreading. Perhaps the most notable convert was Henry Dunster, first president of Harvard, which had been founded by the Puritan establishment to educate their ministers. Because of his popularity, Dunster was permitted merely to resign.

Roger Williams spent more time writing than preaching. He kept up a running literary duel with John Cotton, and also wrote a book containing his arguments for human rights and against state control of religion. A sample paragraph:

> It is the will of God that since the coming of his Soonne the Lord Jesus, a permission of the most Paganish, Jewish, Turkish, or Antichristian consciences and worships, bee granted to all men in all Nations and Countries, and they are onley to bee fought against with that Sword which is onely (in Soule matters) able to conquer, to wit, the Sword of God's spirit, the Worde of God. True civility and Christianity may both flourish in a state or Kingdome notwithstanding the permission of divers and contrary consciences, either of Jew or Gentile.

Williams never wavered on soul liberty. He went further than William Penn, the Quaker founder of Pennsylvania. Penn limited liberty to law-abiding citizens who "acknowledged one Almighty and Eternal God to be the Creator, Upholder, and Ruler of the world." Williams said that no restrictions of any kind must be placed upon the individual conscience.

In his later years he had doubts about the authority of his baptism. He left the church he had founded and became a "seeker."

Though he did not die a loyal Baptist, Roger Williams is honored as the founder of the Baptist denomination in America as well as the Apostle of Religious Freedom. Because of Roger Williams, Jimmy Carter was correct in telling a *Playboy* interviewer three centuries later: "The reason the Baptist church was formed in this country was because of our belief in absolute and total separation of church and state."

3

«««   »»»

Why Baptists Fight for Human Rights

JIMMY CARTER began his political career as a representative of the most conservative Senate district in Georgia,
where blacks had been locked out of the political process
since Reconstruction. His first speech in the Georgia Senate was an attack on the infamous thirty questions that
had been used, he said, "since the Civil War to keep blacks
from voting—questions nobody in this room could answer."

When he became governor eight years later, he jolted
the state with his inaugural address. "I say to you quite
frankly," he announced, "that the time for racial discrimination is over."

The following July he told students at Albany Junior
College, in the town forty miles from Plains where Martin
Luther King had been jailed six years before: "There's been
a change in the [South]. . . . It's an insistence on the part
of the average person who's not powerful, who's not rich,
who's not socially prominent, who's not involved in politics directly—to make his own decisions—to control his own
future—and to make his own impact felt on his own government."

During his last year as governor he angered the white

power structure by hanging portraits of Dr. King and two other prominent blacks in the state capitol. "We must be number one in honesty, openness, and truth," he said on the occasion. "We must be preeminent in idealism and hope and in the recognition of the worth of all human beings."

Upon moving into the Oval Office he launched a crusade for human rights, scoring the Kremlin and other regimes for inexcusable violations. The Soviets were incensed, and responded by arresting dissident Alexander Ginzburg and expelling an Associated Press reporter. Carter expressed regrets for these actions. The Communist KGB then grabbed physicist Uri Orlev, head of the unofficial watchdog committee monitoring Soviet violations of the Helsinki agreement. Skittish American diplomats fretted that détente was going down the drain. Carter paid them no mind, vowing to continue speaking out "strongly and forcefully whenever human rights are threatened. . . ."

Nobody familiar with Baptist history was surprised. Jimmy Carter was just acting in the finest tradition of his early American Baptist heroes. They fought for human rights against church-state regimes in some American colonies that were in some ways as oppressive as the modern Soviets. And when independence was won, they kept battling, refusing to accept a constitution that did not provide protection for precious liberties of conscience.

Roger Williams had the dream, but when he died only tiny Rhode Island—"Rogues' Island" as outsiders termed it—was a sanctuary for dissidents. Pennsylvania was a paradise compared to Massachusetts, but the Quakers looked askance at atheists.

The vision of Williams and other Baptists widened in the century preceding the Revolution as the heretical ideas spread across the colonies like a contagion.

Most Baptists were not heavy intellectuals. They were too busy evangelizing and dodging constables to bother with such European philosophers as Rousseau, Voltaire, and Locke.

When they did talk politics, they argued from the Bible. God had created man in his own image and given him the power to make moral choices. Government was divinely ordained for the collection of taxes and the punishment of evildoers. But government was not to legislate on matters of conscience. Man must be free and church and state made separate. No legislature, no judge, no bishop or pope could come between man and God. No human authority could force one to believe.

The Puritan fathers of the holy commonwealth saw it differently. They had been sent by God to build the New Israel in America. They were the agents of the theocracy, the enforcers of God's law, judge, jury, and executioner. So they could fine or whip a man for failing to attend the official church on the Sabbath, put a woman in stocks for gossiping, burn a witch for consulting with a familiar spirit, arrest anyone who dared question their authority.

But try as they would, they couldn't stamp out the Baptists. By 1677 there was even a Baptist congregation in sacred Boston. They had the audacity to build a meetinghouse without getting official permission. When the general court found out they were holding services in the illegal building, it immediately ordered the property confiscated. The minister, John Russell, jumped to his feet to object:

"Your worships, how can you legislate against an event of the past?" The justices were taken aback. They had to concede his point. They then ruled that the Baptists couldn't meet in it again.

The stir over the incident reached England, where a new king, Charles II, was more tolerant than his predecessors. Charles sent a severe reprimand to the Massachusetts court, ordering respect for "liberty of conscience." The justices tried to keep the order a secret, but the Baptists found out about it and began meeting again in their house. The court sent constables to nail the doors shut and notify the Baptists that they would be severely punished if they tried to use the building again.

William Screven and his Baptist flock in Kittery, Maine (then a part of Massachusetts), fared no better. After a magistrate threatened them with fines and imprisonment if they even attended a Baptist meeting, the congregation took a ship to the Carolinas; they had heard that less persecution prevailed there. About 1696 they organized the Baptist Church of Christ in Charles Town (Charleston), marking the first Baptist church in the South. When Screven died in 1713, the Anglican bishop eulogized him as "extremely ignorant," adding the compliment that "next to the Presbyterians, the Anabaptists are most numerous" in the Carolinas.

The year after Screven died the first Baptists arrived in Virginia, over a century after the first English settlers had come to search for treasure and gather the heathen natives into the bosom of His Majesty's church. The Baptists came also to convert the natives and anyone else who happened to be in need of salvation. The latter, by the Baptist view, included Anglicans who were depending on their church ties to keep them out of perdition.

Jimmy Carter's ancestors were now in the New World. The first to arrive had been Thomas Carter, the profligate son of the merchant of Christchurch. After squandering his father's fortune, this Carter had to bind himself to servanthood to pay for his passage. Upon completion of his term, he had moved on to the West Indies, where the Spaniards took him prisoner. Escaping back to England, he married into a wealthy family that was descended from Alfred the Great, then returned to Virginia around 1650. He put down roots in the Old Dominion, prospered, was elected to the Virginia House of Burgesses and appointed a vestryman of Christ Church in Caroline County. He left a sizable estate at his death in 1669.

His son, Thomas Carter, Jr. (1648-1710), next in the Jimmy Carter line, was a less solid citizen. He joined Nat Bacon's abortive venture to drive the Indians back and expand the colony—against the clear command of the royal governor. Only by throwing himself on the mercy of the king did he escape execution. But like his father, he regained public favor by marrying well. His bride was Magdalen Moore, daughter of one of the richest politicians in Virginia.

Moore Carter (1680-1741), next in the presidential line, was living when the first Baptists arrived. He, too, participated in a revolt—for the lowering of taxes. Then, his mission accomplished, he moved his large family to Bertie County, North Carolina, where he owned a large plantation at his death. There is no record that he ever became a Baptist in Virginia or in North Carolina (where Baptists had been since 1660).

The first Baptist Carter likely came from a line descended from John Carter, Jr., a brother of the president's direct ancestor, Thomas Carter. Unlike Thomas, who arrived penniless and bound to servanthood, John Carter was granted 4,000 acres of land in 1665 for bringing eighty immigrants into the colony and was awarded the titles of Colonel and Counsellor of the State. From five successive wives he received only two sons, John Carter III and Robert.

Son John died unmarried, leaving Robert to inherit an estate of 18,500 acres. Robert was the famous "King" Carter, one of the most colorful figures in Virginia history. He was speaker of the House of Burgesses, treasurer, president of the council, and acting governor of the colony. A strong member of the establishment church, he built at his own expense Christ Church in Lancaster County, and reserved one pew for his descendants for all time to come. He died owning 300,000 acres and 300 slaves.

"King" Carter's grandson, "Counsellor" Carter, was the Baptist, converting to the hated sect a few years before the American Revolution. Then to heap insult upon insult on his family, he freed his hundreds of slaves. "The toleration of slavery indicates great depravity of mind," he wrote a friend in London.

"Counsellor" Carter probably lodged every Baptist preacher in Virginia at one time or another and kept some of their families from starving. When a preacher stopped to visit, the "Counsellor" invited the countryside into his famed Nomini Hall mansion for meetings. Crowds of 200 to 500 attended.

Being a Baptist couldn't have helped his social status among the landed gentry to which his Carter cousins belonged. They were the vestrymen of the established Anglican church, who strutted like peacocks before the small farmers who tended to be Baptists and Presbyterians.

The landed gentry were colorful dandies. They sported lace collars, embroidered doublets, silk trousers, hose lined with crinoline, steeplechase beaver hats with a feather in the brim, shoes with silver buckles, and gilt belts. At cockfights and horse races they were joined by their tax-supported clergy, who, when they were not at sporting events, were likely to be sipping tea with the lords and ladies of their parish, clucking over the crudeness of the lawless Baptists.

By 1760 the Baptists were a major concern of the ruling class in Virginia. During the Great Awakening revivals of the past two decades, an estimated one-sixth of the population had been converted, and many of these had been immersed by Baptist preachers. It was a common saying that the chickens of George Whitefield, the most prominent evangelist of the Awakening, were all turning into Baptist ducks.

Baptists were now blessed by the Acts of Toleration. The English Parliament had finally conceded that dissenting churches could exist. But taxes still had to be paid to support the state clergy, and Baptist preachers had to get licenses and register with the courts in the places where they preached. And there were still laws on the books demanding attendance at the official church.

The first Baptist preachers in Virginia had complied, but now a new breed of Separate Baptists were ignoring the license law and exhorting their people not to pay the hated church tax. They were demanding nothing less than complete separation of church and state.

After a period of leniency, the authorities began cracking down in 1768. Three Baptist parsons, John Waller, Lewis Craig, and James Childs, were arrested in Spottsylvania County. They were charged with "preaching the Gospel contrary to law" and "disturbing the peace." "May it please your worships," the prosecutor told the court, "these gentlemen cannot meet a man on the road without cramming a text of Scripture down his throat."

The fiery Patrick Henry rose to their defense: "May it please the court, what did I hear read? Did I hear it distinctly, or was it a mistake of my own that these men are charged for preaching the Savior to Adam's fallen race! Great God! What law have they violated?"

When Henry finished, the judges were willing to let them go for security and a pledge not to preach in Spottsylvania for a year and a day. The trio refused and were jailed. They took turns preaching through their cell window to crowds gathered outside.

A more troublesome Baptist lawbreaker was James Ireland, a Scotchman from Edinburgh. After several close calls, he was grabbed from behind while preaching without a license and hustled off to trial in Culpepper. Eleven magistrates pronounced him guilty and deserving of a prison term. The jailer pitched him in with the drunks.

A crowd assembled outside to hear him preach through the bars. The enraged jailer came running and threatened to strip and whip the slaves in the crowd if Ireland didn't stop. "Keep on, Massa," the blacks shouted. "Tell us about de Lawd." The jailer turned away in disgust.

A day or so later a charge of gunpowder was set off in his cell. The dust settled and he went right on preaching. Tormentors then stuffed Indian red peppers and brimstone in an open place below the door sill. The tough Scot had to put his mouth to cracks in the walls to draw in fresh air and keep from suffocating.

The doctor whom the jailer brought gave the Baptist poisoned food. This made him ill, but he went right on preaching. When his voice grew hoarse he wrote letters to friends, heading each one "From My Palace in Culpepper."

The authorities in Culpepper were glad to see him released. A Baptist church was later built on the site of the old jail. "To the memory of James Ireland" was engraved on the steeple bell.

The parsons were also subject to mob violence. Vigilantes would break up baptizings by plunging their mounts into a river where a preacher was dipping new converts. Then they would seize the preacher and plunge him into the muddy water until he was almost drowned.

The persecutions of Baptists continued in Virginia, the Carolinas, Georgia, and New England well into the 1770s. In 1774, when the first Continental Congress was meeting in Philadelphia to discuss worsening relations with mother England, they took the offensive against their tormentors. In October Reverend Isaac Backus led a Baptist "grievance committee" to petition the Congress for relief. They represented the newly organized Warrenton Association of Baptist churches in New England.

The church-state establishment in Massachusetts and their political representatives considered Backus "the most contentious man we ever knew." John Adams, who had led the Massachusetts congressional delegation to Philadelphia, was visibly irritated to see Backus and his committee. He inferred they had come to embarrass him.

"You have full religious liberty in Massachusetts," he told Backus when the Massachusetts congressmen met with the committee.

"You are in error, Sir," Backus retorted. "For one thing, there is the matter of the Baptist property at Ashfield that has been seized for payment of taxes to one of your ministers. And he doesn't even reside in the Ashfield parish."

The heated conference ended four hours later with tempers frayed and Adams only promising they would do the best they could. Then, as Backus told it later, the flinty Adams snorted, "Gentlemen, if you mean to try to effect a change in Massachusetts laws respecting religion, you may as well attempt to change the course of the sun in the heavens."

Backus gave up on Adams and put a stronger petition for religious liberty to John Hancock, president of the Congress. Hancock got a resolution passed expressing a "sincere wish" for "the establishment of civil and religious liberty to each denomination." But having no civil powers as yet, the Congress could only recommend that the Baptists take their grievances to the next general court assembly in Massachusetts.

Backus was at Watertown in July 1775 to read the congressional resolution. He got a bill introduced proposing that no person be punished for 'worshiping God in the manner most agreeable to the dictates of his conscience."

To Backus's exasperation, conservatives kept it from coming to a vote.

Massachusetts newspapers called the determined preacher a "fanatic" and a "treasonable scoundrel" who was trying to break up the union of the colonies. One editor said the gallows would be his "fitting reward."

The fight for independence was now on, and Baptists were rallying to the cause with strong sympathy from their brethren in England. The eloquent John Ryland, the leading Baptist light in the mother country, said, "If I were Washington I would summon all the American officers, they should form a circle around me, and I would address them, and we would offer a libation in our own blood, and I would order one of them to bring a lancet and a punch bowl and we would bare our ams and be bled; and when the bowl was full, when we all had been bled, I would call on every man to consecrate himself to the work by dipping his sword into the bowl and entering into a solemn covenant engagement by oath, one to another, and we would swear by Him that sits upon the throne and liveth for ever and ever, that we would never sheathe our swords while there was an English soldier in arms remaining in America."

Support for the Revolution was by no means unanimous in the colonies. It was said that a third of the people were rebels, a third Tories, and a third on the fence. The Baptists were not so divided. Among their ministers, historian William Catchcart found only one Tory sympathizer, the "eccentric" but brilliant Morgan Edwards. He, Catchcart noted, was persuaded by his son, who happened to be a British officer.

The response at the Hopewell Meeting House in New Jersey reveals the Baptist temper. The Hopewell Baptists were in Sunday worship when news came of British victories at Concord and Lexington. At the sound of the last amen, Joab Houghton rushed outside the building and mounted a great stone block. "Men of New Jersey, the redcoats are murdering our brethren of New England!" he trumpeted. "Who follows me to Boston?" "There was not a coward nor a traitor in old Hopewell that day," it was later said.

For the Baptists the fight was not over when Cornwallis surrendered in 1781. Oppressive established churches remained in nine colonies. The Baptists feared that a central American government might continue in these nine. Baptists in the other four—Rhode Island, Delaware, Pennsylvania, and New Jersey—feared a loss of the freedoms they had gained. Rhode Island, which was estimated to be two-thirds Baptist, did not even send delegates to the convention that met in Philadelphia to draw up a federal constitution.

The Constitution, as proposed at Philadelphia, was a disappointment to most Baptists. They weren't appeased by the provision that "no religious test shall ever be required as a qualification to any office or public trust under the United States." They wanted guarantees of religious freedom in the individual states.

The Constitution had to be ratified by at least nine of the thirteen states. The most crucial tests were coming in Massachusetts and Virginia, where Baptists were the most vocal and were joined by Quakers, Presbyterians, and other groups. Supporters and opponents both knew that if the Constitution didn't pass in these heavily populated states, it would probably fail to get a majority or be unenforceable elsewhere.

In Massachusetts the minority of Baptist delegates held the balance of power between opponents who felt the Constitution favored special interests and supporters who feared anarchy if the document wasn't accepted by the states. When the contentious Backus called for firmer guarantees of religious freedom, it appeared that ratification was doomed in this crucial state.

James Manning, first president of Rhode Island Baptist College (later Brown University), feared the worst if ratification failed. He begged his Baptist brothers to vote yes and continue their fight for religious freedom in Massachusetts after the nation was secure. He swung enough Baptist votes, and the Constitution was ratified in the Bay State 187-168. Governor Hancock, who was presiding, gratefully asked Manning to lead in a prayer of thanksgiving—an epochal honor for Baptists in Massachusetts.

In Virginia a Baptist parson named John Leland was the key figure in the fight for ratification. A native of Massachusetts, Leland had become the most influential Baptist in the Old Dominion. He was a close friend of "Counsellor" Carter. They served on a committee to "forward the business respecting a seminary of learning."

Leland's burning concern was to win religious liberty. He was good friends with Thomas Jefferson, Patrick Henry, James Madison, and George Mason. Jefferson occasionally came to hear him preach and sought his counsel on legislation for church and state. The man from Monticello, however, would not accept Leland's belief in Bible miracles; Jefferson held to a piecemeal collection of Scriptures on ethics that he called "my religion."

Leland's passion was tempered by a sharp wit, which his friends in the fight for religious liberty came to rely on. The following exchange occurred in the 1784 Virginia Assembly between Leland and an Anglican clergyman over state support of the ministry:

ANGLICAN: "I suggest that tax support will make a minister's sermon preparation easier."
LELAND: "I don't need any special preparation to get up my sermons."

ANGLICAN: "So you say, Sir. How, pray, would you handle a text such as Numbers 22:21, which reads, 'And Balaam saddled his ass?' "

LELAND: "I find a sermon here with three points: First, Balaam, as a false prophet, represents the state-hired clergy. Second, the saddle represents the tremendous tax burden of their salaries. Third, the dumb ass stands for the people who bear such a burden."

A short time later the Assembly passed Jefferson's Statute for Religious Freedom; the law cut the last bond between church and state in Virginia. It provided that no one could be compelled to attend or support any church, and that everyone should "be free to profess, and by argument to maintain . . . religious opinions" without civil restrictions. Jefferson later acclaimed the passage as one of the three great accomplishments of his life.

Then a new compromise bill was introduced that would in part nullify Jefferson's great accomplishment. Taxpayers could designate their church taxes for support of their individual faiths. But the Anglican church would continue to be recognized as a state corporation and Anglican ministers would hold life tenure.

The Baptists stood bitterly in opposition, declaring "the Gospel wants not the feeble arm of man for its support," and that such taxation "will be restrictive to religious liberty."

James Madison was impressed. He wrote his friend James Monroe that several denominations were for the assessment bill, but the Baptists were standing firm for complete church-state separation. Under Madison's leadership, the bill was defeated.

Madison's work on the federal Constitution was another matter. John Leland, acting as agent for Virginia Baptists, had wanted him to write three guarantees into the document: (1) no taxation for any religion, (2) no government control of any religion, (3) no government favoritism of any faith. They were disappointed when he said the federal government would hold only delegated powers and could not pass laws on religious liberty.

Leland published "Ten Objections" as part of a campaign to prevent ratification. The first began:

"There is no Bill of Rights. Whenever a number of men enter into a state of society, a number of individual rights must be given up to society, but there should be a memorial of those not surrendered, otherwise every natural and domestic right becomes alienable, which raises Tyranny at once, and this is as necessary in one Form of Government as in another."

The fiery preacher concluded his tenth objection:

". . . Clearest of all—Religious Liberty, is not sufficiently secured. No religious test is required as a qualification to fill any office under the United States, but if a majority of the Congress with the President favour one system more than another, they may oblige all others to pay to the support of their system as much as they please . . . it is very dangerous leaving Religious Liberty at their mercy."

Leland was now ready to play his trump card. He knew that Madison intended to run for Congress from a district that was heavily Baptist. He would need Baptist support both to get elected and to get the Constitution ratified in Virginia. Accordingly, Leland sent word that he would like to have a talk with Madison.

Madison likely had a copy of Leland's "Ten Objections" in his pocket when he reined in his horse at the parsonage gate. Leland came out and they walked over to a grove of oak trees to talk. What they said was never recorded, but Leland's success became obvious a few days later. Standing on a hogshead of tobacco, Madison announced his candidacy and promised that "if elected, I will introduce

the amendments suggested by Mr. Leland and other public citizens."

The Baptists made Madison their candidate and he won
handily.

Ratification of the federal Constitution was more difficult. Patrick Henry and George Mason vigorously opposed
the Constitution on the same grounds as the Baptists:
There was no Bill of Rights. Madison repeated his promise
made to Leland that he would seek to add the protective
amendments. Ratification finally passed 89-79.

Madison kept his pledge and presented his first amendment as a tribute to the Baptists and other fighters for
religious liberty: "Congress shall make no law respecting
an establishment of religion, or prohibiting the free exercise thereof; or abridging the freedom of speech, or of the
press; or of the people peaceably to assemble, and to petition the Government for a redress of grievances."

Still the battle was not won, for church establishments
continued to cling to power in some colonies after the Bill
of Rights was added to the federal Constitution. In Massachusetts, Backus, along with Quakers and Unitarians,
kept fighting for separation. Finally, in 1833, that state
added a bill of rights to its constitution, effectively di-
vorcing itself from ties with the Congregational church.
The Massachusetts bill of rights became the seed of the
Fourteenth Amendment to the federal Constitution,
adopted in 1868, which gave further protection in individual liberties.

After Massachusetts acted, other appendages of religious legislation remained state law. The North Carolina
Constitution of 1776 had specified that no person denying
God or "the truth of the Protestant religion" could hold
office. In 1835 "Protestant" was changed to "Christian." In
1868 a new constitution still disqualified atheists from at-
taining office in that state.

Many of these laws have been declared unconstitutional. Many more, especially Sabbath or "blue" laws, still remain on state books. For example, Sunday fishing is illegal in Georgia today.

Baptists, of course, are now joined by many other groups with an interest in religious liberty, notably the Seventh-Day Adventists and the American Civil Liberties Union. They continue to take a strong leadership role through their Baptist Joint Committee on Public Affairs, which monitors church-state issues and makes recommendations from offices in Washington. The Joint Committee, for example, opposes an amendment to the Constitution that would permit "official" prayer and Bible reading in public schools.

Unfortunately, historians have largely overlooked the role of Baptists in ensuring and maintaining religious liberty. The part that Virginia Baptists played in lobbying for the Bill of Rights to the federal Constitution is given little notice. John Leland is not accorded a mention in the *World Book Encyclopedia*, the *Columbia Encyclopedia*, and several other standard references.

But Leland and his determined colleagues are remembered and honored by Baptists. Jimmy Carter was regularly exposed to the ideals of Leland, Backus, and Roger Williams in the Baptist Training Union at Plains Baptist Church. On July 4, 1976, then presidential candidate Carter reminded reporters in his Sunday school class at Plains that he subscribed to the principles of human rights for which Leland and others fought. In the ensuing worship service Pastor Bruce Edwards appeared in costume as John Leland and related what Leland and other Virginia Baptists had done to have the cherished Bill of Rights added to the federal Constitution.

4

«« »»

Missionary Baptists at Work

CARTOONIST John Lawing of the *National Courier* showed a smiling Jimmy Carter behind a pulpit emblazoned with the presidential seal saying to reporters, "And now as we close the press conference I'm going to ask Jody Powell to hum 'amazing Grace' while those of you who wish to repent...."

Jokes aside, Jimmy Carter is not only a Baptist but a missionary Baptist who talks about his missionary travels as naturally as a sportsman might recall a fishing trip to Bermuda.

He related this experience the last time he taught his Sunday school class in Plains, just sixteen days before he was sworn in as president of the United States:

"My partner and I knocked on a door. A nice lady invited us in after we told her who we were. She served us sweet bread and cold milk and we had a good time talking about the plan of salvation until we got around to the sin part. Her attitude really changed when I quoted from the third chapter of Romans, verse 23: 'For all have sinned and come short of the glory of God.' 'You mean to tell me, I'm a sinner?' she said. 'Yes, ma'am,' I replied, 'we've all sinned and need Jesus to forgive us. That's what it's all about.'

"She looked at us real hard and then said, 'Get out! Leave! Right now! Nobody's going to come in my house and tell me I'm a sinner.' She looked pretty mad so we left and went on to see somebody else.

"The point I wish to make," he told the class of old friends, tourists, and reporters, "is that it's very difficult for us to admit we're sinners and need God."

Without doubt, Jimmy Carter speaks more openly about his faith than any president in American history. By comparison, the two previous Baptist presidents, Harding and Truman, were rank backsliders.

Carter's outspokenness about his born-again religion has raised this question among Jews and other nonevangelicals: Will he use what Teddy Roosevelt called "a bully pulpit" as a missionary platform?

Not in the sense of being a Billy Graham in the White House. He has said, "I am the president of all the people. I will not have special services in the White House. I will worship at the nearest Baptist church."

Because of his adherence to the Baptist position on church and state, he can be expected to keep these promises.

But he will remain no less a missionary Baptist. He will keep sharing his faith in speeches to such groups as the National Prayer Breakfast and his Sunday school class in Washington. And when he "feels the Spirit moving," he will talk with individuals about "the One who comes first in my life." He did so one evening in Plains Baptist Church during the campaigns when a reporter confided that he would like to know how to find God. Candidate Carter took him aside into a Sunday school room for a private conference.

This type of sharing of one's faith has been a normal activity for Christians since the birth of the church. Even when persecuted, the early Christians went "everywhere preaching the Word." During the first, second, and third centuries hundreds of thousands were killed by Imperial Rome for their persistent evangelism and disavowal of the deity of emperors.

Then Constantine reportedly saw his cross in the sky and proclaimed Christianity as the official religion of the empire. The "born again" conversion experience was shortly reduced to baptism, often with a sword hanging over the pagan head. This institutional blight continued until the "morning light" of the Reformation flooded dark Europe in the sixteenth century. Then, once more, becoming a Christian became a vital, personal experience.

The early English Baptist churches spread the message of this "new birth" Gospel throughout England. What their persecutors could not do they almost did to themselves by falling under the influence of extreme Calvinism. Particular Baptist preachers began saying that evangelism wasn't necessary.

They were rescued in the late eighteenth century by a remarkable cobbler-turned-preacher named William Carey. When Carey first presented his "obligations of Christians to use means for the conversion of the heathens" to a minister's meeting, he was answered with head shakes. "Sit down, young man," an older pastor scolded. "When God wants to convert the heathen, he'll do it without your help or mine."

Carey wouldn't sit. A year later, in June 1793, he packed his wife, five children, and sister-in-law aboard a Danish trading ship bound for India.

Carey's troubles began immediately after landing in Calcutta. His home supporters, the "British Society for the Evangelization of the Heathen," didn't send enough money. His children languished at the point of starvation. After one child died, Mrs. Carey went mad and tried to kill her husband. She had never wanted to come in the first place.

Carey took a job managing an English indigo factory and hung on. Seven years after arriving he had his first convert. Then a year later, his physician colleague Dr. John Thomas went berserk and had to be confined. But Carey kept at it—preaching, translating the Bible, compiling grammars and dictionaries.

Because he was a true Baptist, Carey was a tolerant man who respected the customs of other religions. But the Hindu barbarity of burning widows upon the funeral pyres of dead husbands was too much. He collected evidence proving that in one six-month period nearly 300 widows had been burned to death in Calcutta, 10,000 in all of India, many of them young brides still in their teens. He bombarded British officialdom with protests until London forbade the rite.

His preaching and translating produced results. He baptized thousands. He also started the first paper mill in India, set up a printing plant, printed the first newspaper in the Orient, translated the Bible into forty-two languages, and became recognized as one of the Orient's leading scholars and educators.

There had been sporadic Protestant missionary thrusts before Carey, but the missionary society he initiated was the first in modern times to call for the evangelization of the whole world. Protestants were stirred as far away as New England to join in this task.

In Massachusetts five young students from Andover College, a Congregationalist school, met in a maple grove to talk about the challenge Carey and his friends had laid down. A heavy rain drove them to seek shelter under a haystack, where they prayed earnestly for the heathen abroad.

The students in the "haystack prayer meeting" organized a group called "The Brethren," with each member pledging to "hold himself" ready to go "when and where duty may call." The leader of the group, Adoniram Judson, persuaded Massachusetts Congregationalists to set up an agency "for the support of missionaries to foreign parts." This was the American Board of Commissioners for Foreign Missions, the first missionary society in America.

In 1812 the board sent its first missionaries abroad, four of the young men and their wives along with bachelor Luther Rice, whose fiancée had been unwilling to make the voyage. They were welcomed in Calcutta by Carey.

On the voyage, the Judsons and Rice had studied the New Testament on baptism and had begun to doubt Congregationalist practice. Carey convinced them that only believers should be baptized and they became Baptists. "We are . . . confirmed Baptists," Ann Judson wrote her sister, "not because we wished to be, but because truth compelled us to be."

They knew their Congregationalist sponsors would cut off financial support. They would have to look to American Baptists who, as Ann Judson wrote, "were yet a feeble folk. . . . The hand of every other denomination was against them."

To compound their difficulties, America and Britain were now at war and shipping was cut off with their homeland. They were ordered on board a ship bound for the Isle of France in the Indian Ocean. There they decided that the Judsons should remain in Asia while Rice returned to the homeland and raised money from Baptists.

By a roundabout way Rice finally got back to Massachusetts. Happily he found that news of the new Baptist missionaries had already reached Baptists there and backers had formed "The Baptist Society for Propagating the Gospel in India and Foreign Parts." They encouraged Rice to travel among Baptist churches soliciting donations for the mission cause.

Rice rode out of Boston on September 29, 1813. He stopped in Northborough to see his family and preach in his home church on the topic "I am not mad." Then he galloped on to New York and from there to Philadelphia, where he found Baptists who had already sent money to Carey in India. The Philadelphia Baptists had also organized the first local association of Baptist churches in America and were keenly interested in Rice's idea of a national Baptist missionary society.

From Philadelphia, Rice took the stagecoach to Washington and Baltimore and lined up Baptists in those two cities for the cause. Hurrying on to Richmond, he strode into First Baptist Church and found a young businessman teaching illiterate blacks to read and write. Two of the blacks in the class would later become the first American Baptist missionaries to Africa. The Richmond Baptists also pledged to cooperate, as did Baptists in Charleston, Savannah, and other cities Rice visited.

The following May 14, thirty-three of the leading Baptists of America met in Philadelphia and organized The General Missionary Convention of the Baptist Denomination in the United States of America. Rice was the only one present who knew all the others. The convention would have no authority over individual churches. Rather, representatives of local churches would elect an executive committee to receive contributions, appoint and assign missionaries, and pay salaries. Richard Furman of South Carolina was elected the first president, attesting to the growing strength of Baptists in the South. Adoniram and Ann Judson were employed as the first foreign missionaries. Rice was named a home missionary at large "to excite the public and more generally engage in missionary exertions . . . ." Because they decided to meet in Philadelphia every three years, this first national Baptist organization became popularly known as the Triennial Convention.

Thus missionary work brought American Baptists together for the first time. This same challenge, Southern Baptist scholars agree, holds their giant denomination together today.

"We are 'missionary' Baptists," they say. "That is how we can find a oneness in purpose among our diversity."

The 2,715 Southern Baptist foreign missionaries of today pursue the same goals as their early-nineteenth-century predecessors. They are mostly preachers and religious education workers, but they are also doctors, dentists, nurses, artists, engineers, agriculturists, even veterinarians, and many other specialties. The ministers and religious education workers must have college and seminary degrees plus proven practical experience in Baptist churches at home. At seminary they study Bible, theology, and church history, but they also take courses in counseling, group therapy, church recreation, ethics, and community development.

Before final appointment, foreign missionary candidates prepare an autobiography, present a battery of personal references, and are interviewed in great depth by Baptist psychiatrists and other authorities. After appointment they receive six to eight weeks of orientation at a regional retreat (one is at Callaway Gardens, only sixty miles from Plains). Then they are off to language school for a year or more before taking up field assignments.

In the various fields they join together in democratically governed missions, selecting their own officers and committees for projecting budgets and submitting requests for funds and other recommendations to the foreign mission board offices in Richmond, Virginia. As long as they conform to broad policy outlines, each field mission is free to determine its own program of work.

They do not start "Southern Baptist" churches, but give fraternal support to national Baptist bodies in the countries where they serve. In nations where they initiate Baptist work, they assist converts in setting up churches and church-related organizations.

Take Malawi, a small Pennsylvania-sized agricultural country of five million in southeast Africa that became independent in 1964. The first Southern Baptist missionaries arrived in 1959 and began evangelizing Bantu tribesmen. Three years later the first Baptist church was organized and a Bible training school was opened in Lilongwe, the capital. Eight years later, in 1970, the Baptist Convention of Malawi was organized. By 1970 it included 215 churches, all self-supporting, with 11,020 members, and had sent a foreign missionary to work with gold miners in South Africa.

The twenty-seven Southern Baptist Convention (SBC) missionaries assigned to Malawi include preachers, teachers, agriculturists, broadcasters, and electronic specialists. Missionary Charles R. Middelton reports great success with cassette tapes, radio programs, and Bible correspondence courses. "Malawi has been eager to hear the Gospel," he says.

Southern Baptist missionaries, along with colleagues of other denominations, are often the last to leave a trouble spot when war breaks out. Dr. Bill Wallace, considered one of the finest surgeons in China, stayed too long after the Communists took over. Though he pleaded, "I am only a missionary engaged in healing the suffering and sick in the name of Jesus Christ," they arrested him, forged a confession, and beat him to death in his cell.

Many Southern Baptist representatives have been arrested by unfriendly governments coming to power. Dr. Herbert Caudill and his son-in-law David Fite were abused and tortured in Castro's dungeons before being released for medical treatment. More recently, Dr. Samuel R. J. Cannata was held sixteen days by the new Marxist government in Ethiopia, and three of his fellow missionaries, two veterinarians and an agriculturist, were detained for forty-eight hours.

Often Southern Baptist missionaries decide to sit out attempted coups and revolutions. Howard Shoemake, a former Texas Baptist pastor, remained during the fighting in the 1965 Dominican Republic civil war. He opened his house to refugees of all parties and remained politically neutral. The house was so jammed that many nights he had to sleep in a closet. When the war was over, Shoemake was named to the six-person National Civil Defense Board in the little Caribbean island country, the only foreigner ever so honored. Two of Shoemake's fellow missionaries, Paul and Nancy Potter, were not so fortunate. They were murdered in their beds by assassins who scrawled "Death to the Yankees" on their house and fled into the night.

The U.S. counterpart of the Southern Baptist Foreign Mission Board is the Home Mission Board. This board has responsibility for all fifty states, Puerto Rico, and U.S. territories. It employed 2,492 full-time missionaries in 1977 and gave salary supplements to hundreds more Baptist church workers. They drive pickups across the Western ranges, carrying the Gospel, and sometimes medicine and food, to isolated farm families. They serve on Indian reservations, helping people find spiritual balance amidst upheavals of culture change. They start new churches in suburban housing developments and reopen old churches in rural areas where reverse migration is occurring from the cities. They direct goodwill centers in ghetto areas. They assist downtown churches in drug rehabilitation for youth and fellowship programs for neglected senior citizens. They help urban ethnic minorities maintain their identities by establishing churches tailored to their traditions and culture. They serve as chaplains at prisons, industrial plants, and resorts. They minister to showpeople and employees of gambling establishments in Las Vegas. They hold interfaith conferences with Jews and Buddhists. They help black seminaries train ministers.

They pursue many other imaginative strategies to relate Jesus Christ to the multiplicity of spiritual needs in modern society. For example, Elias Golonka is a sort of roving Southern Baptist ambassador at the United Nations, and he is finding that diplomats from socialist countries have a "special interest" in Jimmy Carter as a Baptist.

While theologians in diminishing denominations bewail grass-roots disinterest during this "post-Christian" era, the Southern Baptist home missionaries are reaching out to a cross section of Americans searching for stronger values and more meaningful relationships.

Item: Missionary Elmer Whiten, director of Southern Baptist Social Ministries in the northwest, teaches a weekly Bible class and does personal counseling at the Oregon State Penitentiary. One of his counselees is prisoner "Duke" Mosebroten. "Elmer helped me get my head on straight. My attitude about religion changed. Three or four years ago when I heard someone talking about religion, I figured he was some spineless idiot who didn't have the courage to go another route. I'm not going to tell you I'm real heavy into the Bible right now. If things keep going at the rate they are now, I surely will be. And my wife and I are looking for a church to attend after my release in two months. If you had told me that four years ago, I'd probably have slapped you."

Item: Missionary Bill Sims roams Yosemite National Park talking to employees and tourists, then on Sundays conducts a worship service. One of his parishioners is Bob Metzler, a park construction worker who pans for gold on the side. "One day Bill wandered into my place and we struck up an immediate friendship. Even though I've had little to do with preachers over the years, we found something to talk about. He kept coming back, helping me move the muck out of the mine (Metzler works a claim during his off-hours) and doing some of the chores that take two persons. Finally, he led me to see that I needed a closer relationship with Jesus Christ. I'd gone to church when I was younger, but for more than forty years I'd done some rough living. I came to see that I needed a present life with Christ. I guess you might say I struck it rich, with the help of Preacher Sims. He now has me busy, doing some teaching and even leading the singing . . . ."

Item: Missionary Jim Reid patrols the Las Vegas strip: "Hi, I'm your friendly chaplain. Can I be of any help?" Winners and loosers, hookers, dealers, bartenders, and a variety of other non-Baptist types take him up on that offer. Besides strolling among his "flock," Reid has five therapy groups, three Bible study groups, two worship services, a television show, and a newspaper column. "I don't have a regular church, if you mean one that meets in a building," he says. "But if you mean a communion of believers, then I have that."

And what does a seminary-trained Southern Baptist preacher say to sinners in Vegas? "I just tell them about Jesus. The Holy Spirit will convince them of the kind of life they should lead."

Besides career missionaries like Jim Reid in Las Vegas and Howard Shoemake in the Dominican Republic, the Southern Baptist mission boards have taken a cue from the Peace Corps and now recruit recent college graduates for two-years stints. Many of these "Journeymen," who go abroad, and "US-2's," who serve in the homeland, later apply for permanent assignments.

The largest Baptist missionary corps of all is comprised

of laity who give a week to a year of their time and pay their own travel expenses. Sometimes a large church will send a hundred or more volunteers to assist missionaries with a special project. For example, the First Baptist Church of Pensacola, Florida, trained medical teams of six to eight persons around a doctor or dentist, then chartered a jet to take them all to the Dominican Republic for ten days. During the daytime they moved about the small country, giving inoculations and extracting teeth. At night they gave concerts in town squares. They left behind a vast reservoir of goodwill for the small Baptist minority.

The best-known Baptist lay missionary is, of course, Jimmy Carter. His journeys to the "pioneer" North were preceded by a time of wrenching religious self-examination.

He had suffered a humiliating defeat in his first run for governor. But it was more than the galling setback and the pain of seeing Lester Maddox in the governor's mansion that caused him to reflect. It was an awareness that he had only been playing at religion, going through the motions of serving God.

One morning he sat in church listening to Pastor Robert Harris preach a sermon on the apostle Peter's imprisonment by King Herod. The thin, diabetic, dark-haired minister reminded the congregation that Christians were still being imprisoned for their faith. He cited as examples two Southern Baptist missionaries, Herbert Caudill and son-in-law David Fite, who had been locked up in Cuba for alleged "espionage," "illegal currency transactions," and "ideological diversions." Then he looked thoughtfully at his congregation and asked, "If you were arrested for being a Christian, as Peter and Herbert Caudill and David Fite were, would there be enough evidence to convict you?"

For days and weeks afterward Jimmy Carter mulled over that question. He was a deacon and Sunday school teacher, a leader in the men's brotherhood, led "cottage prayer meetings" and made "soul-winning" visits for the annual revivals, and was always ready to help with special projects such as promoting the annual freight carload of corn that Plains Baptist sent every fall to the Georgia Baptist Children's Home for feeding farm livestock. Yet he still felt he was less a Christian than he ought to be. "I finally decided," he wrote in his autobiography, "that if arrested and charged with being a committed follower of God, I could probably talk my way out of it! It was a sobering thought."

A few weeks later he was asked to speak to the Baptists in the nearby community of Preston about "Christian Witnessing." When he sat down to write his speech, he reflected on his own record. Every summer, just before the week's revival, he had visited church prospects. He and a fellow deacon would make a couple of calls on neighbors, go in to read the Bible, give a short testimony of their beliefs, talk up the revival and other church activities, have a prayer, and leave. By figuring the average family size at five and visiting two families a year, Carter estimated that since coming home from the navy fourteen years before he had "witnessed" to a total of about 140 people.

He felt rather proud until he remembered that in campaigning for governor he and Rosalynn had contacted more than 300,000 Georgians. Three hundred thousand in a short political campaign and 140 for God in fourteen years. He was chagrined.

During this time he had a catalytic talk with his younger sister Ruth. They had both grown up in the Plains Baptist Church. She had made her profession of faith and been baptized in July 1940, five years after he and his other sister Gloria had been immersed "in the name of the Father, the Son, and the Holy Ghost" in the tank under the pulpit. Now she spoke of a second experience, of having come into a "fresh, intimate, personal, loving, caring relationship with Jesus Christ." They walked into the piney woods and sat under a tree. He questioned her about her newfound peace and purpose, finally asking, "What can I do to have this closeness to God?"

"You've got to be willing to accept God's will, Jimmy, no matter what he should want you to do," she said. "Look beyond yourself to his purpose."

"I see what you mean," he finally said, and they knelt on the pine needles. There he cried softly, promising that "from now on Jesus Christ will come first in my life."

He began praying and reading the Bible more and became more active in church work. Then, in 1969, a call came from the Southern Baptist Home Mission Board in Atlanta saying they had heard good reports of his lay leadership in Plains Baptist Church and the area Friendship Association of Baptist churches. They wondered if he would join a lay mission team for ten days of missionary work in Pennsylvania. "We hope a new Southern Baptist church will be the result."

Carter asked for more information and was told he and three other men would be assigned to Lock Haven, Pennsylvania, a mountain town of 37,000 where Piper airplanes were built, about halfway between Pittsburgh and Scranton. More teams would be going to other Pennsylvania cities, marking the first big assault of Southern Baptists on that target state. Each team member would be responsible for his own expenses.

From brotherhood meetings and Sunday night Training Union classes at Plains Baptist, Carter already knew about Southern Baptist advances into northern and western "pioneer territories." The first churches had been organized for migrating southerners who wanted to worship the back-home way. Now the emphasis was on reaching "natives," building churches indigenous to local communities.

"I'll go," he said.

Only one other Georgian was in his party, Hoyt Robinson, a dairy farmer from Dahlonega, in the mountains north of Atlanta. The other two, Claude Perry and Milo Pennington, were Texans.

Arriving in Lock Haven on May 27, the quartet moved into the local Fallon Hotel. Their battle plan was to go out two by two during the day, as Jesus sent out his first disciples, present the Gospel and tell about plans for the new Southern Baptist church, then invite new friends to the YMCA for services at night.

Carter's partner was Pennington, a rancher from Elkhart, Texas. In his seventies, Pennington had been going on lay missions for many years.

Pennington later recalled his week with Carter for W. A. Reed, religion editor of the *Nashville Tennesseean*, who did a series of follow-up articles when Carter became a presidential candidate.

"Jimmy and I would pray as we sat in his automobile before we went into a home. Sometimes he led the prayer and sometimes I led it." According to Pennington, Carter would then knock on a door and say, " 'I'm a peanut farmer from Georgia.' Every home we went into he would make a record of it in case we had to call back.

"Jimmy . . . acted all the time like he was on the mountaintop for the Lord. He was never one to talk politics. We were just witnessing for the Lord. We went into ten to fifteen homes each day and we were there ten days and Jimmy and I heard fourteen persons make professions of faith and accept the Lord."

Mrs. Thelma Farwell was one of about twenty-five who joined the new congregation during the ten-day crusade. She remembers that in the night services all the lay missionaries "stood and gave their testimonies. . . . Although

I can't remember his [Carter's] words, I do remember he knew the Bible well and all his talk was geared to the Lord."

The team took meals where invited. When Carter went to the Farwells for dinner, he told Mrs. Farwell that her daughter Lorraine, who played the piano for the services, was the age of one of his boys. "He was just like one of the family," Mrs. Farwell recalls.

The four lay missionaries departed Lock Haven on June 10. The following month the Home Mission Board rented an abandoned church building for the new congregation that had started meeting in the Y. The congregation is still active.

Carter's ten days in Lock Haven apparently marked a deepening spiritual commitment in his life. After becoming governor, he wrote the Farwells that their town would always have a "special place" in his life, because it was "where I first experienced in a personal and intense way the presence of the Holy Spirit in my life." He could still remember "almost all of those I visited to tell them about Jesus," and signed his letter, "Your Christian friend, Jimmy."

Carter was campaigning for governor again when he got a call from Elias Golonka, a Polish immigrant preacher, then on the language missions staff of the Home Mission Board. Golonka wanted him to help in a week's mission to Springfield, Massachusetts. About two dozen men would be going. Golonka explained, for a campaign among Spanish and other language groups, as well as native English speakers. "You have such a beautiful smile," he added.

Carter agreed to take the time off and go.

Besides his smile and previous experience in lay missions, Carter had learned a little Spanish in the navy and had vacationed in Mexico, where he and his family spent a week in a backcountry village speaking only the native language. This time he brought along his new pastor from Plains, Reverend John Simmons; fellow Sunday school teacher Jerome Etheridge, an agriculturist at the Georgia Agriculture Experimental Station near Plains; and Edwin Timmerman, a Baptist minister of music who had grown up in the Plains church. Dairyman Hoyt Robinson from northern Georgia also made the trip.

The Springfield project represented a new thrust in Baptist mission strategy that was already proving successful in Chicago, Los Angeles, San Francisco, and other large cities where Southern Baptists were about as well known as grits and hog jowls. The idea was to start a new church for each sizable ethnic or language group within a city, providing Sunday school classes and worship services in each language. The latest research in church growth indicated that this was more successful than trying to establish multicultural, integrated congregations.

They were counseled not to use southernized religious expressions such as "revival." They should speak of the project as a "festival of faith." And those going into homes where English was not spoken should attempt to communicate in the people's mother tongue. With all this, Golonka warned, they should expect many rebuffs.

The week began cold and rainy. Residents were putting up storm windows to be prepared for an expected cold wave. Pastor Simmons and dairyman Robinson, who were assigned to an English-speaking section, had doors slammed in their faces the first day. "Southern what?" people asked. "Are you from some black church organization?" One resident called the police, and a patrolman took them to the station house to verify the missionaries' identification.

Jerome Etheridge, the Plains agriculturist, and his partner were getting into about one of ten houses where they called. "Mostly, we just talked to maids," he recalled later. "I was so discouraged that I telephoned my wife and said I was wasting my time. I even cried over the phone.

"Then a couple of days later we spotted a head sticking out of a manhole in the street. We ran over and asked the man if he was a Christian. He was the first person who had listened to us all week. That one contact made the whole trip worthwhile."

Carter's partner was Eloy Cruz, a swarthy, muscular Cuban refugee preacher. He had been living in Brooklyn, but was planning to move to Springfield and become pastor of the Spanish congregation that he and the Georgian hoped to establish.

Because of Cruz's identification with the Cubans and Puerto Ricans, they were received warmly by almost everyone who answered their knock. Carter was deeply impressed by the Cuban and asked him, "How can a tough and rugged man like you be so sensitive and filled with love?" Cruz answered, "Our Savior had hands that are very gentle and he cannot do much with a man who is hard." In his autobiography Carter called Cruz ". . . one of the best men I have ever known. He had a remarkable ability to reach the hearts of the people in a very natural and unassuming way, and quickly convinced them that God loved them and we loved them."

Carter was also touched by the people they encountered in the shabby apartments and dingy walk-ups. In one "particularly poor home" they found an elderly couple keeping a small baby. After Cruz convinced them that they could trust him and Carter, the man confided tearfully that the child's mother had bled to death while having a tooth extracted in a dentist's office. Upon hearing the news, her husband had gone berserk. He had tried to commit suicide and threatened to kill the baby, then had relented and left the child with the grandparents.

Carter and Cruz knelt and prayed for the broken family. When they stood to leave, Carter pressed some bills into the old man's hands. "Buy something for the baby in memory of its mother," he suggested.

On the final visit of the last day, Carter and Cruz called on a landlord. As they walked toward his apartment, he pointed to a closed door and remarked that a young father lived there who had recently lost his wife in a freak accident at a dentist's office. "He will not come out or speak to anyone."

Cruz knocked on the door and was told to go away. When Cruz said, "We know your baby," the door opened and a sad voice asked if they were the ones who had given the baby money. When Cruz nodded, he invited them in. Carter later reported that the young father "accepted Christ. It was one of the most moving religious experiences of my life."

The week undoubtedly had a profound impact on Carter's life. Etheridge roomed with Carter and recalls how they would pray together at night. "The first time I just bowed my head, but Jimmy got down on his knees, and then I got down on mine." Another team member, Reverend Peter Miccoli, remembers that Carter "would actually cry during his prayers for the Spanish-speaking people." And Ed Timmerman, the church musician, tells of Carter feeling the need of the people so intensely that he declined to buy an evening meal at a Howard Johnson's on a special night out, settling instead for a sandwich at a hole-in-the-wall restaurant. Carter himself says that Springfield made him "uniquely aware of the Holy Spirit as an integral part of my life."

When the week was over, Carter drove Cruz home to Brooklyn and accepted an invitation to spend the night. Before going to bed he slipped into the bedrooms of each of Cruz's small children and kissed them goodnight. "That was when my heart really went out to Jimmy Carter," Cruz says affectionately.

There were times after Carter came home that his sister Ruth thought he might become a full-time missionary—especially when she would receive long-distance calls from persons telling how he had helped them. "Your brother Jimmy gave me his [telephone] credit card number," they would say. "He said you could tell me what to do."

But Carter resumed his campaign for governor, saying that politics was his "calling." His Springfield roommate and fellow church member, Jerome Etheridge, took the missionary route. Three weeks before Carter was inaugurated as president, Etheridge and his wife Joann left for French language school to prepare for agricultural missions in Togo, Africa.

Having one of their own in the White House is a bonus for Southern Baptist missionaries. For example, the week after the election the national news magazine of Brazil ran a photo feature on Baptist work. And in March 1977, lay missionary George Crisan, a retired attorney, went to Rumania and told large congregations that the new American president was not only a Baptist, but also a Sunday school teacher. Crisan added that he was the deacon who served Communion to the Carter family in Washington's First Baptist Church.

Even before Carter was elected, the Southern Baptist Foreign Mission Board set a goal of 5,400 full-time workers in 125 countries by the year 2000. The Home Mission Board is aiming to do no less than "evangelize and congregationalize" the nation by 1980. Twenty-two major cities are targeted for a Baptist blitz in three phases, with New York, Chicago, Los Angeles, Baltimore, Seattle, and Houston targeted for the first round.

Says Dr. William G. Tanner, newly elected head of the denomination's Home Mission Board: "Our agency's plans have been developed around two broad objectives under 'Bold Mission Thrust.' One relates to 'evangelizing' our nation—'let every person in our land have an opportunity to hear and accept the Gospel of Jesus Christ.' The second relates to 'congregationalizing' our nation—'let every person in our land have an opportunity to share in the witness and ministry of a New Testament fellowship of Believers' [a Southern Baptist church]."

Tanner's foreign missions counterpart, Dr. Baker J. Cauthen, speaks of doubling the foreign force to 5,400 by the end of the century and multiplying tenfold the number of overseas churches: "[We will] press forward . . . with the thrilling objective of enabling every human being upon the face of this earth to hear the Gospel of Christ before the year A.D. 2000."

The missionary thrust that unites Southern Baptists is the reason why they keep growing while membership of most other major U.S. denominations drops or increases only slightly. In 1976 Southern Baptists posted a 1.8 percent increase, with their preachers baptizing around 9,000 new members each week.

Contrasting membership statistics of other religious bodies are: United Presbyterians—down 2.4 percent; the Presbyterian Church in the United States—down 2 percent; Episcopal—down 1.2 percent; United Church of Christ—down 1.2 percent; and United Methodist—down 1 percent; Roman Catholic—up 0.4 percent.

Southern Baptists take their cue from Jesus' "Great Commission" to his disciples: "Go therefore and make disciples of all nations, baptizing them in the name of the Father and of the Son and of the Holy Spirit, teaching them to observe all that I have commanded you; and lo, I am with you always, to the close of the age" (Matt. 28:19, 20, RSV).

They proclaim that one must be "born again" to enter the kingdom of God. They use interchangeable euphemisms for this experience, such as "accept Jesus as your personal Savior," "commit your life to Christ," "repent of your sins and trust Jesus."

Jimmy Carter defined the experience while teaching his new Sunday school class at First Baptist Church, Washington. "What are some of the basic things Christians believe?" he asked. The answers came back: "A life of sharing," "caring for others," "an abundant life."

"How many of those things do you find in other religions?" he continued, and not waiting for answers, declared, "The point I want to make is this: There is something absolutely unique about Christianity. We have a personal relationship with a living God: Christ. Faith is union with the living Christ."

5

«« »»

To Be a Baptist in Georgia

LESTER MADDOX has called Jimmy Carter "a Dr. Jekyll and Mr. Hyde," "the most liberal man I ever knew," "a liar," and a few other choice labels. Carter hasn't been as verbose about Maddox, but he laughed when Jody Powell remarked, "Being called a liar by Lester Maddox is like being called ugly by a frog." Indeed, a croaker was given to Carter that Powell promptly dubbed "Lester."

But if the former governors of Georgia were being introduced at a Baptist meeting, they would properly be called "Brother" Carter and "Brother" Maddox. Both are Southern Baptists, as are the present governor of Georgia, George D. Busbee, and the two governors before Maddox, Carl E. Sanders and Ernest Vandiver. The one before Vandiver, Marvin Griffin, started out a Baptist, then switched to Methodist.

Busbee is a deacon at Second Ponce de Leon Baptist Church in Atlanta, where Attorney General Griffin Bell was also a deacon and chairman of the finance committee, responsible for a million-plus annual budget, before going to Washington. Busbee was more active back home at Sherwood Baptist in Albany, where he was chairman of all the deacons. When he ran for office, his pastor was kind enough to write a letter documenting his churchmanship.

Brother Carl "Cuff Links" Sanders, governor from 1963 to 1967, was as active in denominational affairs as the man who defeated him in his try for a second term in 1970. In 1966 he was the only layman to give an inspirational address at the Southern Baptist Convention when it met in Detroit. "I, for one, am willing to think that our chief business is religion," he said.

U.S. senators from Georgia tend to run about the same. Herman Talmadge, who got divorced in 1976, is from a political dynasty of Baptists. Sam Nunn, the junior senator, is (oops!) a Methodist.

'Ole Herman took the seat of Georgia's most distinguished statesman, the late Walter George, another Southern Baptist. It was Senator George who got Jimmy Carter out of the navy when Earl Carter became too ill to manage the family business. He served in the U.S. Senate for thirty-five years (1922-57) and wrote much of Roosevelt's New Deal legislation. Never touched by scandal, he "lived and led by the rule of reason," wrote Ralph McGill. George once taught the men's Bible class in Vienna Baptist Church, where Jody Powell and Mrs. Bruce (Sandra) Edwards were baptized.

George succeeded in the U.S. Senate the colorful Tom Watson, the most controversial political figure in Georgia history. A Southern Baptist, naturally, Watson enjoyed a revival meeting as much as he did a street brawl. Half-angel, half-devil, the fiery muckraking redhead fought the little man's battle against big business interests. He was the Populist candidate for the U.S. presidency in 1904.

Watson happened to be the political hero of Jim Jack Gordy, Jimmy Carter's maternal grandfather. Gordy named one of his sons after the man who schooled him in practical politics. Alton Carter thinks nephew Jimmy got his political acumen from Jim Jack via Miss Lillian. "The Gordys were all red-hot politicians," he says.

The new breed of Georgia Republicans are also more likely than not to be Southern Baptists. Howard "Bo" Callaway is probably the most pedigreed Baptist politician in the state. He claims thirty-one Baptist preachers in his lineage. One of his cousins, Royall Callaway, was Jimmy Carter's boyhood pastor at Plains. He baptized Jimmy, Gloria, and Ruth Carter, as well as several other Carter relatives. Another Callaway, Cason J. Callaway, Sr., set up the nonprofit foundation that operates Callaway Gardens, Georgia's most scenic attraction for nature lovers.

"Baptists in Georgia started out as an outcast minority," reflects Jack U. Harwell, editor of the Georgia Baptist Convention's weekly newspaper *The Christian Index*. "Now with over a million of us in the state, one of every three whites, we are the establishment. Almost every governor, sheriff, judge, ordinary [county clerk], and state legislator is a Baptist. It's the same in the other old Confederate states."

Harwell is a deacon and professional journalist, one of a growing number of laymen serving in Baptist staff positions. He has edited *The Index*, the second oldest continuing religious periodical in America, for eleven years; before that he was associate editor for eight years. From his second-floor corner office in the gleaming, white-columned, futuristic new six-million-dollar Georgia Baptist Convention headquarters in northeast Atlanta, he can look across to the new campus of Mercer University at Atlanta, a thriving branch of Mercer at Macon. Harwell's preacher father and thousands of other Georgia ministers are graduates of this oldest and most prestigious of Georgia Baptists' five colleges. Harwell has an interview scheduled with George Busbee on "how the governor is putting his Christian beliefs in action." Harwell didn't request the interview. The governor's press secretary called him.

The Index is one of thirty-two newspapers serving constitutents in the various state Baptist conventions. With 125,000 circulation, Harwell's paper is third only to Texas, which has 373,000 and Alabama, with 156,000. Like the other state papers, it is a house organ reporting on Baptist doings. But editor Harwell is free to comment on political and social issues and whatever else seems relevant to Baptist life in Georgia. "I believe in getting out of the church house," Harwell says.

During every gubernatorial campaign Harwell asks major candidates to present their views on "moral issues." For example, in October 1966 he asked Lester Maddox and Bo Callaway, who were contenders in the general election, to answer a ten-point questionnaire about gambling, pornography, nudist colonies, prostitution, legalized liquor, narcotics, prayer and Bible reading in the public schools, and other church-state issues.

Maddox replied immediately, agreeing with traditional Baptist positions. Sample: "As to legalizing nudist colonies in Georgia, I am OPPOSED, now and forever." Callaway did not respond, despite repeated requests to his aides. They claimed he was too busy campaigning to give proper thought to completing the questionnaire. Harwell reported this along with Maddox's answers.

The ink was hardly dry when a telegram arrived from Callaway begging "to sincerely apologize to those whom I may have offended" for failing to answer the questions. Still Callaway refused specific comment, citing only his Baptist lineage and assuring, "I stand as I always have for preservation of the highest morals in our state and among our people." Harwell published this along with an account of his difficulties in eliciting information from the Callaway camp.

Callaway got more votes in the general election than Maddox, but not a majority. This threw the contest into the Georgia Assembly, where the heavily Democratic majority put Maddox in the governor's mansion. Had Callaway responded to Harwell's inquiry and given the "right" answers, his vote margin might have been enough to give him a clear victory.

Of course, after election a governor stays on the hot seat with Harwell. For example, Harwell hit Jimmy Carter hard for signing legislation allowing eighteen-year-olds the right to drink. But Harwell, like other Baptist editors in the Southern Baptist Press Association (which he served as president of in 1977), will not endorse any political candidate.

In the year that America discovered and elected Jimmy Carter to the presidency, Harwell became the Baptist press contact for national reporters researching Carter's church background. Harwell gives their coverage low grades. "Except for *Time* and a few others, they didn't do their homework on us. Some referred to us as the 'Southern Baptist Church.' That's a fighting phrase for Baptists who hold to the autonomy of the local church. But their worst offense was painting us all one stripe—red-necked, fundamentalist, simplistic, close-minded, hyperemotional, snakehandlers. There are Southern Baptists who fit all those labels. But most of us don't and we resent being so classified."

For those willing to do their homework on how Southern Baptists came to be the largest and most influential religious denomination in the southern states, Harwell suggests that the history of Georgia Baptists is a good place to start. "You can see how our four levels of organizational life developed—the local church, the association, the state convention, and finally the Southern Baptist Convention, which was organized in Georgia.

"Then if you want to look at a single personality who might be called Mr. Baptist in our state and who helped make us as big as we are in Georgia, well, that would be Jesse Mercer. My preacher brother is named for him. He helped Luther Rice form the Triennial Convention. He was the chief contributor to *The Christian Index* when it was a national journal for Baptists, and later became its editor when it was moved to Georgia. He was the chief promoter and organizer of the Georgia Baptist Convention and then the leader for many years. He pastored some of our most historic churches. He helped found Mercer University, where many of our state's leading citizens have been educated. And in his time he was also a great power in state politics."

By consulting sources Harwell recommends, you find that the first Baptists came to Georgia with the first European colonists in 1733. But Baptist work didn't begin until the first preacher, Nicholas Bedgewood, arrived in 1751 to work in George Whitefield's Bethesda Orphan House, the first institution of its kind in America. Bedgewood came from South Carolina, where, according to one historian, he was sent packing by Charleston Baptists when they found he had two living wives. Bedgewood made a few converts, but not enough for a church, and he soon faded away.

Georgia's first viable Baptist congregation was organized in 1772 by Reverend Daniel Marshall at Kiokee Creek, about twenty miles northwest of Augusta. In 1973 Governor Jimmy Carter came—responding to a bicentennial invitation a year late—and memorialized the founding, noting to the pastor that his first Carter ancestors had come to Georgia about 1780 and had joined the historic church.

Daniel Marshall is a Revolutionary War hero and a monument stands over his grave at Appling, Georgia. He was one of six Baptist preachers among the eleven Georgia chaplains in the American army and the only preacher of any denomination who did not flee when the British occupied the state. He directed a corps of lay preachers who roamed the wilderness, keeping up the spirits of embattled settlers.

In 1784, the year Marshall died, messengers from five small churches organized the Georgia Baptist Association at the Kiokee Meeting House. By 1790 there were forty-two Baptist churches with 3,211 members in the state. By 1824 there were 264 churches organized into ten associations, with 18,108 members. Many of these were converted after the frightening 1812 earthquake. And by 1832 there were 486 churches in eighteen associations with 37,072 members.

Jimmy Carter's forebears were among these early Georgia Baptists. The first to arrive was Kindred Carter, great-great-grandson of Thomas Carter, Sr. Kindred's father, Isaac, son of Moore Carter, had first moved from Virginia to Bertie County, North Carolina. Then when a devastating drought hit the Carolinas, Kindred and his brother James headed for Georgia. Kindred settled on a 307-acre farm in then Richmond County. He grew wheat and cotton and raised livestock with the aid of ten slaves on land from a huge tract ceded by the Cherokees for debts they had run up to Augusta merchants.

Some historians think Kindred Carter might have come to Georgia as a Quaker. There is no record that he was ever a Baptist convert. But his son James, fourth-generation grandfather of Jimmy Carter, was on a Baptist church roll, as was another son, Jesse. When this James Carter died at age eighty-four in 1858, *The Christian Index* reported that he had been a Baptist for "many years" and on his deathbed was "ready to converse about his hopes beyond the grave."

His brother Jesse was the more prominent one in Baptist affairs. A well-to-do slave owner, as was James, he was frequently a church messenger (delegate) to associational and state Baptist meetings.

There were many other Carters in Georgia during this time, some closely related to the president's line, others only distant cousins. Carter names appear frequently on the fading roll books of old Baptist churches. Reverend Joseph A. Carter, a great bear of a man with flowing white hair, for over thirty years pastored the Hephzibah Church in Lincoln County, near where the president's direct ancestors lived. Josiah Carter, a lineal descendant of "King" Carter, was a leading citizen of Gainesville. Two of his granddaughters, Morning Irene and Lelah Mae, later went as missionaries to China. A second Josiah Carter settled with his wife Violator in Stewart County.

Still another Josiah Carter bore a son named James Carter. Though a biographer describes him as "not brilliant," he became one of Georgia's most famous Baptist preachers. One of the many churches he organized was Carter's Grove, a church that still flourishes.

Once this James Carter was riding to a church when he discovered a deck of cards in his overcoat. Wheeling his horse around, he galloped back home to find who had played such a dastardly trick. After the culprit confessed that he was merely trying to hide the forbidden deck, the preacher forgave him. Then he washed his hands of the pollution and rode back toward his pulpit appointment.

Reverend James Carter's spiritual mentor and close friend was the famous Jesse Mercer. His father, Silas Mercer, emigrated from North Carolina and was baptized in Kiokee Creek near the church in 1774. The elder Mercer subsequently became a preacher, organized several churches, and started the first Baptist school in Georgia, a venture that was short-lived. When Silas died in 1796, his son Jesse was fast becoming the biggest Baptist power on the frontier.

Jesse Mercer left his stamp all over Georgia. But his main stomping ground was in the rolling countryside of Wilkes County, where so many of Georgia's greats were born and reared.

A history buff can keep himself entertained in old Wilkes indefinitely. The ghosts of Revolutionary War heroes Elijah Clarke, John Dooly, and Nancy Hart haunt the gently rolling meadows and woodlands. Eli Whitney perfected his cotton gin at Mount Pleasant Plantation, seven miles west of Washington, the Wilkes county seat. The last cabinet meeting of the Confederacy was held where the county courthouse now stands. The wagon train bearing the last of the Confederate treasury, a half million dollars in gold and silver, stopped in Washington. Legend still persists that quantities of the lost gold remain buried in the area.

The list of firsts in Washington and Wilkes seem endless: first town named for the first president, first woman hanged in Georgia, first woman newspaper editor in the United States, first Methodist church in Georgia, first Presbyterian minister ordained, first cotton mill, first stamp mill for gold.

And the white-columned antebellum homes of such departed southerners as General Robert Toombs excite *Gone-With-the-Wind* nostalgia, attracting thousands of tourists.

But the chief Baptist interest remains Jesse Mercer. Driving in from Atlanta on state highway 44, you pass a historical marker beside the Phillips Mill Meeting House, home church of the Mercer family. A few miles on, just inside the city limits of Washington, is another marker specifying the site of Jesse Mercer's home. A few blocks beyond is a vacant lot where he had the publishing establishment that informed and educated Baptists all over the South.

The local Mercer authority is Reverend Waldo P. Harris, III. A quiet scholarly man whose ancestors came to Wilkes around 1780, Harris is director of missions for the Georgia Baptist Association, oldest among the ninety-three associations in the Georgia Baptist Convention. His bailiwick covers forty-eight churches in eight largely rural counties, twelve of which were organized before 1800, including old Kiokee. He travels constantly among the churches, preaching missionary sermons, consulting with committees, and advising pastors. "I have no authority to tell any church or pastor what to do. I am their servant. Baptists don't have bishops, you know."

Waldo Harris is one of three preacher brothers; another brother is chairman of the Wilkes County Board of Supervisors. The three preachers all attended Mercer University and Southern Baptist Theological Seminary in Louisville. Robert, the youngest and now deceased, was Jimmy Carter's pastor at Plains Baptist Church from 1955 to 1967.

Waldo Harris pursues Baptist history like a detective, sifting and savoring each clue to the past. He and some friends in the Georgia Baptist Historical Society recently relocated the grave of Silas Mercer in the Phillips Mill churchyard. "When we examined his skull, we found he had probably been kicked in the head by a horse or cow. We never knew that."

From Waldo Harris and other sources a profile of the famous Jesse Mercer emerges. He was tall and in later years corpulent, with a strangely elongated egg-shaped head, small piercing eyes, a thin, reedy voice, and a nervous affliction that caused his neck and shoulders to twitch as he was getting into his sermon. Once warmed up, he would shout and cry while holding a congregation transfixed.

Though he studied Greek and Hebrew under an eminent Presbyterian divine, and knew philosophy and history, his sermon illustrations were from the daily life-style of the frontier people.

Many of Mercer's minister contemporaries believed the Bible was the only book learning preachers needed, that formal schooling only made a preacher vain and print-proud. One complained, "These larn'd preachers will git all the pay, leavin' us to work or starve." They were also wary of any kind of organization that might take away their independence. Mercer disagreed on both counts. In 1803 he got eighteen ministers to form a "general committee" that would sponsor regular preaching in new settlements, establish a Baptist college, and provide a school for Creek Indians living in the vicinity. This committee evolved into the Georgia Baptist Convention, which was formally organized in 1822. Jesse Mercer was elected moderator (chief presiding officer), a post he held for many years. This was the second state Baptist convention in America; South Carolina was only a year earlier. The organizational framework was typically Baptist. Churches gave voluntary gifts to finance programs set up and carried on by their elected representatives. In 1976 the combined giving from Georgia Baptist churches to programs of their convention ran over $9 million.

Mercer was also a power in Georgia politics. He often preached to the legislature and might have been elected governor had he accepted requests to run.

At twenty-six he was a delegate to the 1798 state constitutional convention and was asked to write the section on religious liberty. When someone moved to bar ministers from serving in the legislature, Mercer promptly proposed that the motion be amended to exclude doctors and lawyers instead of ministers. That threw the convention into an uproar and Mercer rose again to offer to withdraw his amendment if the original motion would be withdrawn.

After getting a new constitution, Georgia became bitterly divided between the parties of John Clark and William H. Crawford. Families split. Men dueled. Tavern brawls erupted. All because of state politics.

Mercer held a personal grudge against Clark for an unforgettable incident. Clark had run off with the fifteen-year-old sister of Mercer's wife Sabrina, leaving her to freeze to death in a cabin while he hunted for a minister to marry them. Mercer could never forgive Clark for that.

Clark's big chance came when Governor William Rabun died, Mercer's "dear and pleasant friend" and the leading layman among Baptists. The governor was then elected by the legislature in Georgia. Rabun's body was still warm when Clark maneuvered successfully to get the post. But Mercer would have his revenge, for he had been invited to eulogize Rabun before the assembly.

The preacher drank a bitter toast, spouting a prayer from Psalm 109: "Let his days be few and let another take his office." Then striding into the Assembly, he mounted the rostrum and gave Clark hell and damnation.

"The Lord has taken a good and righteous man on account of the sins of the people," he declared in his jeremiad. "Now he will bring judgment by putting wicked rulers over them. Georgia has reason to tremble." Clark was in the audience.

Clark could not succeed himself. When his term was over in 1822 he put forth Matthew Talbot to run against George Troup, the candidate of the Crawfordites. The campaign was one of the bitterest in the state's history. Some churches had to cancel services to prevent quarreling and fighting in the churchyard afterward.

When the legislature met to vote, every balcony and

window was jammed with people. A fiery Irish Methodist preacher, Daniel Duffy, vowed aloud that though he hated Baptists as he hated the devil, he would be willing to go to heaven with Jesse Mercer if the Crawfordite candidate could be elected.

The ballots were collected in an old black hat and handed to the clerk to count. He called the names as he drew them out. "Talbot. Troup. Talbot." The count was tied at sixty, then again at eighty-two. Only one ballot remained. The clerk turned the hat over, shook it, and picked up the last paper. "Troup!"

The Methodist danced about, shouting, "Thank Thee, Lord! The state is delivered from the rule of the devil and John Clark!" Mercer, according to one historian, "waddled from the chamber waving his hat above his great bald head and shouting, 'GLORY! GLORY!' until he was out of sight."

But for all his success, Mercer suffered his personal tragedies. He and Sabrina lost two young daughters, their only children, to illness. Then in 1826 they went to Philadelphia where Jesse was to preach the main sermon at the Triennial Convention. During a business session their dear friend Luther Rice was accused of mismanaging Baptist funds and fired. Rice had founded Columbian College in Washington, which he hoped would become a great national Baptist university. President Monroe, his cabinet, and leaders of Congress had attended the first commencement. Rice had also started a national Baptist newspaper, which he called *The Columbian Star*, and appointed a friend, Baron Stow, as editor. It was Stow who had gotten Rice fired. After that the Triennial Convention had severed all connections with the college and newspaper, leaving both in deep financial trouble.

Mercer was almost in despair as he and Sabrina began the long journey home. His friend Rice had been humiliated. The national Baptist convention was wracked by bitterness. But when they reached Andersonville, South Carolina, he forgot these troubles. Sabrina was sick with a "bilious fever" and they had to stay over. She died a few days later, leaving the grieving Mercer to return to Georgia alone.

Then a stroke of good fortune befell the "Father" of Georgia Baptists. Jesse Mercer struck it rich—materially.

He bought the newspaper Rice had founded and began publishing it as *The Christian Index* in Washington, Georgia. He made sizable gifts to the school that had been named for him. Mercer Institute (later to become Mercer University). He had money left over for other Baptist enterprises. Exactly how much he put into Baptist work is not known, but estimates run as high as $400,000—a princely sum in those days, far more than the Methodists and Presbyterians had at their disposal.

"Father" Mercer did not acquire his wealth dishonestly, but how he got it is a story that few Georgia Baptist preachers will tell their congregations even today.

The narrative begins with a friendship between the preacher and the biggest gambler, whiskey dealer, and sporting man west of Augusta. "Cap'n Abe" Simons, as everyone knew him, had fought at the Revolutionary War battle of Kettle Creek and afterward made his fortune by ways not acceptable to most Baptists. He belonged to the Augusta and Washington jockey clubs, raised and trained thoroughbreds on his private track, sold spirits, entertained gamblers and staged dances at his fancy two-story business-residence on a hill nine miles west of Washington. He also kept a team of mules and a couple of slaves outside the house to pull wagons through the bog at the foot of the hill. For this service he charged $2.50 and allowed travelers to stop and refresh themselves at his bar. It is also said that during dry periods he would order his slaves, who were mortally afraid of him, to haul barrels of water and soften up the bog for more business.

Jesse Mercer often stopped to visit with "my good and particular friend," who "had a peculiar faculty for the acquisition of property." Undoubtedly the preacher accepted libations of Abe's hospitality, for Mercer freely admitted that he partook of cognac brandy every day "for my stomach's sake." He did have an intestinal ailment. Most Baptist preachers railed mightily against strong drink in that day, and it galled them that their beloved leader imbibed. Mercer had a scar on the bridge of his nose, reportedly caused from repeated rubbing against the rim of glass fruit jars. A Methodist minister also told of how he happened to lodge with Mercer at a guest house. When the time came to retire, their host brought in two toddies. Mercer proposed that they give thanks and the Methodist dutifully bowed his head. When he looked up, Mercer was finishing off the second drink. The Methodist said that in the future he would pray with both eyes open when drinking with Mercer.

The nearest synagogue was then in Savannah. Cap'n Abe, like other frontier Jews, paid his respects at Protestant services. He was also an easy mark for a threadbare preacher and didn't object when his wife Nancy invited one home for Sunday dinner.

Nancy was a frontier belle who rode to the nearby Smyrna Presbyterian Church in a fine carriage, pulled by four prancing white bobtailed horses, with a slave running in front and another behind. When she alighted in the churchyard, a crowd would gather around just to admire her beauty and hear the swish of her multicolored petticoats.

During his frequent visits Mercer sought to persuade both Abe and Nancy that they should get ready for Judgment Day. Abe laughed, saying that his slaves had already made his coffin from hammered steel. "They are to bury me fully dressed and standing up with a loaded musket on each hip." When Mercer asked why, the Jew said, "So I can shoot the devil when I see him and get into heaven." But there came a time, as Mercer later wrote, when Nancy "found her soul was lost in sin, and she knew not how it was to be saved . . . . In her distress her mind was turned to Christ crucified, as the only way by which a condemned sinner could be justified and saved. . . . But this was interrupted by fears lest she might be deceived, which gave her excessive distress."

Then, according to Mercer, "she was called to a new source of trouble by the death of her husband." Abe's slaves, fearful of his ghost, dutifully buried him standing up in a clearing above his house. According to a tale told later, they locked the coffin and threw the key away so the devil could never find him. They reserved a spot for Nancy and built a foot-thick, neck-high stone wall around the grave, leaving only an opening for a wrought iron gate.

To continue Mercer's journal: "In her great distress she cried unto God, and made supplication to the widow's Judge, and found relief . . . ."

Mercer could commiserate with her widowhood, for he had just lost his own wife. Nancy moved into Washington and they became closer friends as he helped her settle Abe's large estate and successfully contest a claim from a woman who claimed to be his daughter. They married in December 1827, and the following year Mercer baptized his fifty-five-year-old bride at the Washington Baptist Church where he was now pastor.

Nancy provided Mercer the fortune he used to build a financial undergirding for early Baptist institutions in Georgia. Most of the money went to a school for ministers founded by Billington Sanders, whom Mercer had ordained. (Sanders's wife had been related to Abe's deceased first wife.) He knew that Nancy Simons Mercer had inherited a large estate. So he bargained with Mercer, agreeing to let the school be renamed, in exchange for a large endowment. Thus came Mercer University.

Besides making him a rich philanthropist, Nancy made a gentleman out of Jesse Mercer. She accompanied him to every fitting at the tailor's. She permitted the front of his waistcoats to be a pious black, but ordered that the backs be a worldly butter yellow. And she made sure that a house slave kept his ruffles starched, shirts pressed, and accompanied him as a personal valet everywhere he preached.

The Baptists got everything, except a few thousand dollars willed by Abe to his stepson from his previous marriage and to three children of close friends. Even the ornate, ten-foot-high floor-to-ceiling hand-carved cupboard where Abe had kept choice liquors. It now protects the Communion ware in the Nancy Mercer Annex of the First Baptist Church of Washington. Across the room a marble slab is set into the wall marking Nancy's grave.

Mercer's influence and Abe Simon's money helped keep most Georgia Baptists in a progressive stream. In the 1830s hardshellism—no ministerial training, no painted church furniture, no instrumental music in church, no Sunday schools, no missionaries—swept thousands of Baptists aside. Remnants of these Primitive Baptists still survive today in Georgia and other southern states, as does a related group called Two Seed in the Spirit Baptists. The latter believe that God created part of the human race, and the devil the rest. They argue that since God will save his seed anyway and the devil's are hopelessly doomed, nothing should be done to evangelize either.

Outside of Georgia, principally in Kentucky and Tennessee, more Baptists were sloughed off into a new sect called Campbellism. They sacramentalized baptism by immersion, saying it was essential to salvation, taught falling from grace, threw out their church organs, disdained multichurch organizations of any kind, and proclaimed themselves the pure and only true churches of Christ. In later years, a progressive movement called Disciples of Christ arose among them, restoring musical instruments to worship and conceding that there were true Christians in other denominations. The Disciples of Christ, or Christian Churches, claim 1.3 million members today; the more sectarian Churches of Christ, 2.4 million.

Still another Baptist breakaway in the 1830s was led by Reverend William Miller, a New York pastor. Miller convinced a large following that Christ would return on a date in 1843; when that didn't happen, he announced it would be on March 21, 1844. His people sold their property, donned white robes, and climbed to the top of a high hill to await the expected return. Miller had to admit that he was mistaken again, but maintained that Christ's return was still imminent. The Millerites later merged with other "Adventists" and formed the Seventh-Day Adventist denomination, which today lists half a million members —all tithers.

Mercer led the main force of Georgia Baptists past all of these defections, emphasizing cooperation, evangelism, and education. In his older years he even became a total abstainer; he published the first temperance journal in the South and one of the first hymnbooks, *Mercer's Cluster*.

As editor of *The Christian Index*, Mercer's influence extended far beyond Georgia. He was a towering influence on the national Baptist scene and served as president of the board of managers for the Triennial Convention from 1830 until his death.

He died in 1841 at the home of his good friend, Reverend James Carter, in Indian Springs. Friends put his body in a wagon and started toward Washington, intending to bury him beside his second wife. But the body began to decompose in the hot weather and they stopped at the Mercer University campus, then in Penfield, and buried him there.

Mercer's death left a huge vacuum. He was the glue that had kept Georgia Baptists together, the ballast that gave their institutions stability. He had also kept them in the Triennial Convention, even though he had no truck with the northern Baptist abolitionists who were making their southern brethren squirm. Slaveholding, Mercer felt, was a matter of conscience over which honest men differed. It shouldn't be made a test of Baptist communion.

Cotton was now king. The price of slaves rose and fell with the price of cotton. White planters traded slaves as they did other property and sometimes argued over ownership. Such an argument provoked Wiley Carter, who was a Baptist layman, James Carter's son, and President Carter's great-great-grandfather, to kill a man in supposed self-defense.

According to Warren County court records, Wiley Carter accused a man named Usury of stealing one of his twenty-nine slaves. When Usury refused to return the black man, Carter, the sheriff, and several other men went to get him. After an all-night standoff, Usury came out of the house with gun drawn and Carter shot him. The president's ancestor was acquitted in a trial and moved to a new plantation about twenty miles north of Plains. He was so wealthy in slaves and land when he died that he was able to will $22,000 to each of his twelve children.

Slavery had come to be an integral part of the southern society in which Baptists flourished. Spencer B. King, Jr., who recently retired as professor of history at Mercer University, notes that the portion of slaveholding families in the population of one region in Georgia increased from 25 percent to 70 percent between 1790 and 1850. In South Carolina two-fifths of the Baptist ministers owned slaves.

Abolitionist sentiment continued building among northern Baptists. Baptist churches and associations were passing resolutions condemning slavery. The northerners reminded their southern church fellows that Baptists before 1800, both North and South, had been largely opposed to the practice. John Leland in particular had waxed vehement against the "evil" institution as a violation of human rights.

In reply, Baptist voices in the South condemned the abolitionists and tried to defend slavery from the Bible. The Sarepta Baptist Association, meeting in Elbert County, Georgia, lambasted the abolitionists "as enemies to us and those whose condition they profess to commiserate . . . . We highly disapprove of their nefarious schemes, and view them as destructive to the cause of religion . . . . "

From this time on, separation from the North was inevitable. This would leave Southern Baptists in captivity to their slave culture, and guarantee their role as the establishment religion of the South. As Jack Harwell puts it: "This is part of our problem today. We are shaped by the culture instead of shaping it. We are creatures of our society rather than creators. The challenge of our leadership is to overcome this."

6

«« »»

The Noose of Slavery

WHEN DEACONS of the Plains Baptist Church decided to enforce an old rule barring "Negroes and other civil rights agitators" from services, Jimmy Carter's campaign for president was jolted and Southern Baptists were made to look like white racists before the world.

Ugly headlines screamed:

CARTER'S CHURCH BARS BLACK MINISTER

PLAINS CHURCH FACES SOUL-TEARING CRISIS

CARTER MUST ALTER CHURCH OR LEAVE IT

BAPTIST IN CONGRESS TERMS CHURCH AN
EMBARRASSMENT

Cartoonists had a field day. The *Los Angeles Times* showed an angry white deacon asking a trembling black at the church door, "Which J. C. you lookin' for?" The *Chicago Daily News* presented two haloed whites arriving in glory to find a couple of blacks floating on clouds. "I'm from the Baptist Church in Plains, Georgia," one white says to the other, "and this isn't my idea of heaven." The

90

Atlanta Constitution pictured church dropout Billy Carter balancing on a soda pop case in the door of his messy gas station, can of beer in hand, and remarking to a deacon and his wife coming from church, ". . . I see it don't do much for you either, Deacon!"

Even television's Archie Bunker got into the act when he came under fire for belonging to a segregated social club. "Why bother our little club, Meathead?" he demanded. "Go pick on President Carter's church."

The networks kept the issue hot on the nightly news. Americans saw black preacher Clennon King, the catalyst of it all, striking a prophetic pose at the church door, begging, "Please, open the church to me."

No Baptist church ever received so much angry mail in such a short time.

"How can you all call yourselves Christians?" demanded a southern white woman. "God loves MAN, not just the white man. I think your church is evil. You have shamed Jimmy Carter."

"What you did was stab a good man in the back," charged a Californian. "I shall drop out of the Baptist church."

"When are you and the other Ku Kluxers going to stop this racist nonsense! A racist Christian is nothing but a hell-deserving Satanic heathen idolater and whoremonger." This from a student at Baruch College in New York City.

And from Dallas: "Do you honestly think Heaven is 'lily-white?' If Jimmy Carter, who says he is against a segregated church, has no influence in his hometown, how can he possibly have a positive influence in Washington?"

Perhaps the sharpest cut of all came from Africa: "I'm a student at one of your Baptist mission schools. You have convinced me I should return to the religion of my fathers."

Prominent Southern Baptists effusively expressed regrets. James E. Sullivan, the SBC president, was "greatly disappointed." Representative John H. Buchanan, a Republican from Alabama and the only Baptist preacher in Congress, said it was "embarrassing" to him "as a Southern Baptist. They have wronged all of us." Jimmy Carter, on one of his last campaign swings, declared he intended to do all he could to change his church.

Then, as if the Plains debacle wasn't bad enough for the new image in race relations that Southern Baptist progressives had been building, news began leaking that hundreds of other southern congregations probably had racially prohibitive laws on their books. One was the First Baptist Church of nearby Americus, where Carter confidant (and now attorney general) Griffin Bell had been baptized and ordained a deacon. Another bit of upsetting news came from Alabama, where the Open Door Baptist Church claimed it had been rejected for membership in the Birmingham Baptist Association for no other heresy than welcoming blacks.

The civil rights battles had been won in the courts, schools, and restaurants, but blacks were still being excluded from churches in the South. An April 1977 Gallup poll confirmed the position of segregationist churches. Sixty percent of southern whites surveyed who attended churches said they would not like them integrated. Outside the South only twenty-eight percent of attendees at all-white churches wanted their services to continue this way.

Why not the churches, when blacks and whites were mixing elsewhere? "That's government," was the way one Plains deacon explained it to UPI reporter Wesley Pippert. "Church and state are supposed to be kept separate."

One denominational figure not taken by surprise was Foy Valentine, director of the Southern Baptist Christian Life Commission in Nashville. "I'm embarrassed, too," he admitted. "But I'm not astonished. We were born in slavery over a hundred years ago and we're still bearing that burden. The Plains thing just proves what some of us keep saying: We still have a long way to go with race prejudice. Some Baptists," he added in his laconic native Texas drawl, "will do almost anything to keep from doing right."

Southern Baptists have long conceded that slavery was one of the issues that led to their rupture from the national body, but only in recent years have establishment figures been willing to admit that slavery was the major cause as well as the catalyst. As Atlanta's Dr. Louie Newton, the eighty-five-year-old unofficial "dean" of Southern Baptists in Georgia put it, "Slavery was the occasion. I don't think we can deny that."

The conflict centered between resolute northern abolitionists and die-hard southern slaveholders. The question was: Could slaveholders be approved as denominational workers? The southerners saw northern demands as totalitarian, trampling of conscience, and violating the rights of white Christians. The northerners saw southern recalcitrance as maintaining the worst social curse of humanity.

Actually many Baptists in the South had strongly opposed slavery before 1800. The general committee of Virginia Baptists adopted John Leland's resolution to "make use of every legal measure to extirpate this horrid evil from our land." Georgia Baptists supported a provision in the 1798 constitution of their state to ban the importing of slaves. As late as 1832, Virginia's General Assembly debated a Baptist-backed plan that would send slaves back to Africa. It passed in the Virginia House 79 to 41, but lost in the Senate by one vote.

Proslavery advocates gained dominance after the southern economy fell captive to cotton. Slaves became necessary to maintain a way of life for influential Baptist planters, including preachers who supported their ministry by farming.

When antislavery agitation arose in Baptist associational

meetings, slaveholders loudly objected. In 1805 the Elk-
horn Baptist Association of Kentucky resolved it "improper
for ministers, churches, or Associations to meddle with
emancipation from slavery or any other political subject."
In the South, where Baptists were growing seven times
faster than in the North, the rule became neutrality.

Theological rationales for slavery developed. It was said
that blacks were under the curse of Ham, who had looked
on the nakedness of his drunken father Noah. As a result
of that curse, Ham's son Canaan became a servant. The
defenders of slavery claimed blacks were descended from
Canaan, and therefore condemned to perpetual servanthood.

A Georgia Supreme Court judge ruled: "The Negro and
his master are but fulfilling a divine appointment. Christ
came not to remove the curse; but recognized the relation
of master and servant. He prescribed the rules which gov-
ern, and the obligations which grow out of it, and thus
ordained slavery as an institution of Christianity."

A more common defense was that slavery as practiced by
Old Testament patriarchs and later in the Roman Empire
was never condemned by Christ and the apostles. To the
contrary, the slave advocates said, the New Testament provided a blueprint for good relations between masters and
servants. Along this line, Robert C. Howell, pastor of the
First Baptist Church, Nashville, argued that there always
had been and always would be three kinds of relationships
in the white family: parents and children, husband and
wife, masters and servants. Christianity, he said, "sancti-
fies" the relations of masters and servants, "and makes it
one of love, of sympathy, and a perpetual benevolence."
Slavery, he concluded, "is legitimate, benevolent, and
scriptural."

Pastors preached this to their congregations. It was

taught in a course at Mercer University. Christian slave-holders were told to treat their servants (always the preferred term) kindly, teach them the way of salvation as they would their own children, allow them Sunday off for rest and worship, and not break up black families by selling one spouse. Slaves, in turn, were commanded to respect, revere, and obey their masters; not to steal, lie, use profanity, or commit adultery. And slaves were advertised for sale in *The Christian Index* and other Baptist periodicals just like other property.

Slaves generally went to church with their masters. They sat in a gallery or in the rear, men on one side, women on the other. They could be members; males could even be ordained deacons and preachers and given spiritual oversight of black brothers and sisters.

Many churches had "lookout committees" to evangelize blacks and "promote love, obedience, and fear" among black members. A slave who desired membership had to have his master's consent before joining.

What was church life like for Baptist slaves before freedom? University of Georgia students wrote down recollections from aged blacks as part of a research project in the 1930s. Some examples:

"There was no lookin' neither to the right nor to the left in church. No matter what happened nobody could half way smile. I remember once an old goat got up under the church. Evertime the white preacher said somethin' real loud, that old goat would go 'Baa! Baa!' I almost busted I wanted to laugh so bad."

"My grandma was a powerful Christian. She loved to sing and shout. She would get to shoutin' so loud and make such a fuss nobody could hear the preachers. And she would wander off from the gallery and go downstairs and try to get to the altar where the preacher was. He was alwus lockin' her up for disturbin' worship. But he could never break her from shoutin' and wanderin' around the meetin' house after she got old."

"Colored folk weren't allowed to jine the church on Sunday morning. They had to wait till Sunday afternoon to come and 'fess their faith and jine. We didn't know there was any other church but de Baptist. All de baptizin' was done by the white preacher. First he would baptize de white folks in de pool back of de church, den he would baptize de slaves in the same pool."

"When white folk died, they were laid out the same as niggers. If it was a man they put a suit of clothes on him. A woman, they jist wrapped in the winding sheets. Dey alwus had de white funeral de day after buryin'. But we had to wait to have our funerals until Sunday or after de crops were laid by.'

There were a few all-black churches in the South. Most were holdovers from the previous century. The first black Baptist church in American was organized in 1773 across the Savannah River from Augusta, Georgia. Three other black churches were established in Georgia in 1778. But these and other black churches belonged to white associations, and masters could still keep an eye on them.

One of the black churches in Georgia, the First African Baptist Church of Savannah, asked the Georgia Baptist Convention for a recommendation on the remarriage of slaves who had been sold away from their spouses. The convention advised they could remarry if there was no probability of reunion with previous spouses, and "on no other condition."

The first black Baptist preacher to be ordained in America came from the old Kiokee Church in Georgia, where, according to Jimmy Carter, his ancestors belonged. Until 1831 black preachers were permitted considerable free-

dom in officiating before black congregations. But after
Nat Turner, a Baptist preacher, incited a slave insurrection
in Virginia, laws were passed requiring that black pastors
could only lead a service when a white was in attendance.

All in all, most Baptist slaveholders felt they were treat-
ing their slaves in a Christian manner. Blacks were better
off in their households and churches than in Africa where
they would never hear the Gospel, they reasoned.

The theological mindset of northern abolitionists on
slavery was poles apart from thinking in the South. The
curse of Ham was not a divine order, just a prediction. Nor
was there any proof that blacks descended from this son
of Noah. Christ never approved of slavery, but did not
directly oppose it because there was no way, short of ter-
rible violence, that slaves could gain freedom in the totalitarian Roman Empire. What Christ did was to break down
walls between peoples, and open the way for a new humanity to emerge. On this score, they frequently quoted
from Eph. 2:16, 19: "That he might reconcile both [Jew
and Gentile] in one body by the cross. . . . Now therefore
ye are no more strangers and foreigners, but fellow citizens
with the saints, and of the households of God." And from
Gal. 3:28: "[In the Christian family] there is neither Jew
nor Greek, there is neither bond nor free, there is neither
male nor female: for ye are all one in Christ Jesus." A few
abolitionists even said women should be granted equal
rights on this basis!

The abolitionists then went on to condemn slavery as
an inhuman moral evil that could not be justified on any
grounds.

The abolitionist movement had flamed from a powerful
religious revival led by Charles G. Finney, a Presbyterian
lawyer, that had swept across the North in the 1820s. The
revival had incited a moral fervor resulting in marches,

pamphleteering, and petitions to Congress that slavery be outlawed. The South in particular was inundated with abolitionist literature.

As much as Baptists in the South hated the abolitionists' ideas, they respected their right to speak. But a takeover of the national convention and its mission societies by Baptist abolitionists was something else. This, they feared, was coming.

They felt a dangerous precedent had been set in England, where the British Baptist Missionary Society had been torn apart by an antislavery crusade in Jamaica led by a Baptist missionary.

The young missionary, William Knibb, had been inflamed by what he saw in the colony. "The cursed blast of slavery has, like a pestilence, withered almost every moral bloom," he wrote his mother. "For myself, I feel a burning hatred against it as one of the most odious monsters that ever disgraced the earth."

When Knibb aroused fellow missionaries, enraged planters had him thrown in prison. Upon release he hurried back to England, vowing to walk barefoot "throughout the length and breadth of the United Kingdom to make known to Christians of England what their brethren in Jamaica are suffering."

Leading Baptist pastors tried to dampen his fervor. When he persisted, they forbade him to speak on the subject at the annual meeting of the missionary society. He leaped to his feet and shouted, "No! I will not desist till this greatest of all curses is removed." Eustace Carey, nephew to William Carey, helped him rally support, saying that slavery was just as bad as the Hindu barbarism of burning widows which his uncle had fought. Two years later the British Parliament abolished slavery in all colonial possessions, to become effective at midnight July 31, 1833.

Knibb went back to Jamaica and was there to count down the minutes before a roaring crowd of blacks. When the clock struck twelve, he screamed, "The monster is dead! The Negro is free! Thanks be to God!" When he died of yellow fever shortly thereafter, 8,000 grateful blacks attended his funeral.

Just as the American southerners feared, the antislavery virulence reached the missionaries of their denomination. To show what was happening and raise an alarm, Robert C. Howell, who also edited a [Baptist journal] for Tennessee, published a letter from a missionary in Burma named Mason.

"I have an invincible hatred to slavery, and I shall say so," Mason wrote. "It is the foulest blot on the American flag. . . . I believe it to be the greatest sin ever to clothe itself under Christianity, that was ever attempted to be defended from the Scriptures. . . . If it be right to run away from persecution as our Saviour taught, surely it is right to run away from slavery. . . . I have therefore the pleasure to enclose an order for ten dollars on our treasurer . . . to assist in the escape of runaway slaves."

Howell editorialized: "If we send money [his missionary salary], we thereby indirectly contribute the means by which our own slaves are kidnapped and dragged off. Brethren, will you do this? We know you will not." Howell was echoed by other Baptist editors in the South.

For several years Southern Baptist voices had been complaining about the way the denomination operated. Philadelphia was too far to go for the national meetings, they said. Because of the distance, their churches, which had more members (59 percent), had never had equal representation with the North. The South was being slighted on home missionaries because northerners wouldn't work in slave states. The organization of the national convention was too loose. The home and foreign mission societies were allowed too much independence. Missionaries like Mason in Burma should be reined in.

Leading northern Baptists weren't happy with the way the denomination was going for different reasons. They suspected that some home missionaries owned slaves and demanded that the head of the Home Mission Society, Benjamin Hill, either confirm or deny. Hill replied that none did.

Hill's answer disturbed the southerners. Did he then mean that a slaveholder couldn't be employed by the society as a missionary? Such a denial could render the denomination "asunder," advised *The Christian Index* from Georgia. Caught in the middle, Hill would only say the society was neutral on slavery.

The 1844 national convention featured a passionate debate between abolitionist Nathaniel Colver, pastor of Tremont Temple Baptist Church in Boston and Richard Fuller a leading South Carolina divine. It settled nothing. After a vote reaffirming neutrality, the delegates went home more divided than before.

The Georgia Baptist Convention decided to smoke out the Home Mission Society on the issues of appointing slaveholders. They presented a slaveholder for appointment. James E. Reeves came from a well-known family of Baptist preachers. He had started up many frontier churches and was obviously well qualified. And he was a godly slaveholder who read Scripture and prayed with his servants.

The Home Mission Society turned him down.

Now it was Alabama's turn to ask the Foreign Mission Society for a "distinct explicit avowal" that slaveholders could be employed as foreign missionaries. The answer: "We can never be a party to any arrangement which would imply approbation of slavery." Southerners who couldn't agree, they suggested, should withdraw from the national convention.

Virginia Baptists called upon churches to send delegates to meet in Augusta, Georgia, in May 1845 to organize a new convention "for the propagation of the Gospel." The largest number of the 327 delegates came from Georgia.

The preamble to the new Southern Baptist Convention declared that "a painful division has taken place in the missionary operation of the American Baptists. . . . Fanatical attempts have indeed been made, in some quarters, to exclude us of the South from Christian fellowship. . . . The few northern brethren to whom we allude must take what course they please. . . . The first part of our duty is to show that its [the split] entire origin is with [them]."

The southerners set up a denominational body, responsible to the churches, but holding firm control over its agencies through elected boards. The first two agencies named were the Foreign Mission Board at Richmond and the Home Mission Board at Marion, Alabama. The latter was later moved to Atlanta.

About the same time the national Methodist Episcopal Church divided over a demand that Bishop James O. Andrew of Wilkes County, Georgia, cease official duties until he disposed of slaves obtained through marriage and inheritance. The Georgia Methodist Conference rebelled, seceded from the parent body, and joined Methodists in other southern states in forming the Methodist Episcopal Church, South.

The same issue of slaveholding split the Presbyterians.

After their breakaway, Southern Baptists launched a missionary blitz. New stations were opened in China and Africa. Home missionaries moved into western territories of the United States. And in every southern state, itinerant preachers, many not yet ordained, stepped up efforts to plant a church in every settlement. The latter didn't have to have seminary training or approval of a hierarchy. All they needed was a "go ye" from their home congregations. Most were self-supporting farmers.

The result was faster growth than before the division. To compare: Georgia Baptists in the decade before schism increased about 28 percent. The decade after, 1845-55, they expanded almost 50 percent, and established 362 new congregations.

Many of these new churches were started in southwest Georgia where colonists had settled on lands inveigled from the Creek Indians by the federal government. One of these congregations was the Lebanon Baptist Church of Christ, established December 1, 1848 with twenty members. It continues today as three congregations: the all-white Plains Baptist Church, the new Maranatha Baptist Church, and the all-black Lebanon Baptist Church, also in Plains.

The founders of the church that would produce a president 128 years later "called" as their first pastor thirty-five-year-old Jesse Stallings, who had recently lost his wife and one of his two children. This was his first pastorate, for it is stated in the minutes that he was ordained only the next day.

The eleven males and nine females from six families subscribed to a typical Baptist covenant of that time.

> We whose names are hereunto subscribed having, as we trust, first given ourselves to God, by faith in the Lord Jesus Christ, and having from our hearts solemnly agreed to come under the laws of the New Testament for the government of our lives, and believing that it is our duty and privilege to live soberly and righteously and piously in this ungodly world, and in every manner to show forth glory of God, who has called us with a holy

calling from darkness unto light, and that it is also
our duty to commend the same by secret, family,
and public prayer; by the faithful worship of God
on the Sabbath day; by the support of the Gospel, and of the ministry, and in every other way
ordained of God, for the perpetuity of His worship, and for the glory of His name—do now
solemnly covenant, before God, to give ourselves
in the constitution of a Christian Church in the
name of our Lord Jesus Christ.

They adopted articles of doctrine standard to Baptist
churches of that time. The Bible, they said, is "the Word
of God, and the only rule of faith and practice." Man is a
sinner, impotent "by nature . . . to recover himself from
the fallen state." Sinners are justified by "the imputed
righteousness of Christ, through faith in Him." Believers
shall be baptized by immersion. The saints shall "preserve
in grace and never finally fall away." At the "great and
general judgment of the last day," the "punishment of the
wicked shall be everlasting and the joys of the righteous
eternal."

They scheduled preaching every third Sunday (Stallings
pastored other churches), business conference on the Saturday before, and Communion quarterly.

They agreed to strict rules of discipline. A brother "continuously and repeatedly" missing business conference
without a good excuse "shall be considered as walking dis-
orderly." (Women were allowed only to attend Sunday
school and worship.)

A member "speaking in an angry or unkind manner" or
failing "to use the endearing appellation of 'Brother,' when
speaking to or of another," shall be reproved.

No member "shall make or sell ardent spirits" or permit
his rent houses to be used for "such purposes."

Other breaches of faith, understood though unwritten, included dancing, sexual immorality, drinking, profanity, and lodge membership.

A committee was appointed to visit and "labor with" accused persons. If guilt and repentance were expressed, the violator was forgiven, though sometimes put on probationtion. If he held to his sin, his name was stricken from the roll.

The Lebanon congregation worshiped in a "brush arbor" while completing their first building at a cost of $300. It was located on a rise about a mile west of the present town of Plains, a few hundred yards from "Miss" Lillian's "Pond House" where Democratic leaders met to confer with Jimmy Carter after his election. The first member to die was interred beside the church, starting the burying place known today as Lebanon Cemetery. As time passed, a settlement of the living grew up around the church. Thousands of other communities began this way across the South.

Baptists often built beside a stream. Since Lebanon did not, they probably baptized about two miles away at Magnolia Springs, where clear water gushed from subterranean limestone rock. Here were located the hardshell Phillipi Baptist Church and Tabernacle Methodist Church. Magnolia Springs developed into a community also.

Baptists and Methodists were not the only denominations represented in this sandy, loamy area of piney woods in west-central Sumter County. There was a Lutheran settlement named Botsford about two miles east of Lebanon. Rosalynn Carter's Murray ancestors grew up in this community.

The fourth community in the area was the most unusual of all. A company of Universalists from the northeast, probably Massachusetts, staked out lots where two Indian trails crossed about halfway between Lebanon and Magnolia

Springs. They named their town Plains of Dura, after the Babylonian plain where Nebuchadnezzar built his giant golden image and commanded everyone to fall down and worship or be thrown in a fiery furnace. Plains of Dura had a post office as early as 1839 in a store operated by Arthur Turner.

The Universalist Church was an oddity in southwest Georgia. The members were considered heretics because they didn't believe in hell, although they acknowledged other basic Protestant doctrines. George Harper, a deacon at the present Plains Baptist Church, says his great-grandfather was a pastor of this congregation, which Alton Carter refers to as "that infidel church."

The Plains of Dura Universalists probably differed with their Protestant neighbors at Lebanon, Magnolia Springs, and Botsford on slavery. Universalists in New England were known to be zealous abolitionists.

Fifteen years of separation from northern Baptists had not made Southern Baptists any less defensive on slavery. In February 1860 *The Christian Index* editor E. W. Warren castigated the most famous Baptist preacher in England, Charles H. Spurgeon, for his abolitionist views. Warren quoted Spurgeon as saying, "I do from my inmost soul detest slavery anywhere and everywhere, and altho' I commune at the Lord's table with men of all creeds, yet with a slaveholder I have no fellowship of any sort or kind . . . the erring sin of a manstealing people shall not go unrebuked. . . ." Retorted the Southern Baptist editor: "Our Southern Baptists will not hereafter, when they visit London, desire to commune with this prodigy. . . . We venture the prophecy that his books in future will not crowd the shelves of Southern book merchants. —THEY WILL NOT, THEY SHOULD NOT." Today no books of sermons are more popular with Southern Baptist preachers than Charles H. Spurgeon's.

The great majority of Southern Baptists approved secession from the Union and the resulting war. The first state convention for secession met in the First Baptist Church of Columbia, South Carolina. The editor of the *Alabama Baptist* declared secession was the only alternative left to the South. His Texas counterpart branded Lincoln and his "Black Republicans" as the implacable foe of both constitutional government and good religion.

But there were a few thoughtful leaders who refused to beat the drums. The *Virginia Baptist* editor begged readers to pray for a peaceful resolution of the crisis. The North Carolina editor warned against hasty action and hoped for reconciliation. The Kentucky editor, Joseph Otis, said no Baptist ought to crusade for secession and war. Two months after fighting started, he declared: "SINK OR SWIM, LIVE OR DIE, SURVIVE OR PERISH, WE ARE OPPOSED TO THIS WAR."

By this time the voices of moderation could not be heard. Some Southern Baptist preachers pronounced the god of the Yankees to be the biblical Antichrist, personified by the demonic Lincoln. The Georgia *Christian Index*'s editor termed Lincoln "His Satanic Majesty, Commander-in-Chief of the Enemies of the Confederacy."

Baptist meetinghouses were turned into recruiting stations, and preachers marched off with their men to fight the evil foe. Thirteen Baptist ministers served in one Alabama regiment. The clerk of the Lebanon Baptist Church recorded in August 1864: "There was no preaching or conference today. All the male members of the church, except two, being absent in the Army."

The Southern Baptist Home Mission Board threw all its funds into war ministries. Chaplains were commissioned and thousands of tracts and New Testaments printed for the "moral and spiritual well being" of the men in gray. The Lebanon Baptist Church joined hundreds of Southern

Baptist congregations in collecting sacrifice offerings for missions to the military.

Foreign missionaries could not come home and were stranded for a time without support. Desperate board officials shipped bales of cotton on Confederate blockade runners to Nassau, where the cotton was sold and the money sent on to missionaries in China and Africa.

Dozens of interesting side notes about Southern Baptist involvement in the war clamor for telling.

A Confederate prison was planned at Magnolia Springs, but the Phillipi Baptist Church objected that they would lose their baptizing pool. The stockade was built at Andersonville twenty miles away, where water was less healthy and uncertain. Once during a drought there was no water for days and hundreds died from thirst. Altogether, over 12,000 Union prisoners succumbed from wounds, hunger, and privation at Andersonville. Had the camp been put at Magnolia Springs where there were eight to ten springs feeding an artesian pool, many might have survived.

In another incident Sherman reached Columbia, South Carolina, after scorching a path across Georgia, and ordered a squad to "destroy that Baptist church where the first secession convention was held." The Yankee soldiers located a white-columned building and asked an old black standing nearby if this was the Baptist sanctuary. "No, Suh," the caretaker replied. "It's that one over there." According to the story, the troops blew up a church of another denomination, leaving the Baptist structure unharmed.

When Lee surrendered, the Confederate cabinet fled to Washington, Georgia, with Federal troops hot on their heels. After holding one last meeting in the historic old courthouse Jefferson Davis walked out into the town square where a crowd had gathered. He spotted Reverend Henry Allen Tupper, pastor of the Washington Baptist Church. "It's over," he told Tupper in resignation. "There's nothing more we can do." Then Davis took the hand of his good friend and whispered a quote from Job: " 'Though he slay me, yet will I trust Him.'"

Davis rode away, his head held high. The next day the Federals arrived in Washington and strode into the courthouse. According to local legend, the courthouse clock stopped at that instant. The Confederacy was forever dead. But Southern Baptists stubbornly continued to believe that their cause had been right. Robert Howell, the leading Baptist in Tennessee, was thrown into prison for refusing to take the oath of allegiance to the Federal government. "I'll rot in my cell before I do," he vowed. He almost did.

The Georgia Baptist Convention pronounced the defeat a judgment of God upon southerners for their sins. Slavery was not a sin they had in mind.

The war's end brought freedom to three and a half million slaves, almost all illiterate. Many begged their former masters to hire them back in their old jobs at any wage. Others roamed the countryside, homeless, jobless, resorting to stealing just to stay alive. Some murdered and raped, spurring frightened, angry whites to take vigilante action.

In this atmosphere northern "carpetbaggers" and southern "scalawags" moved in to take control and make the freed men their vote pawns. Georgia, admitted back into the Union, reacted by refusing to ratify the Fifteenth Amendment to the Constitution that was to give every male citizen, regardless of race, the right to vote. The Federal government then expelled the state and would not readmit it until July 1870, after it had accepted the amendment.

Northern Baptist missionaries and teachers were sent by churches to start schools for the former slaves. Southern Baptists did not distinguish them from carpetbaggers and refused to cooperate. Northern Baptists made overtures for reunification. The southern churches angrily refused.

Condemnations flew back and forth, and southerners threatened to open mission work in the North. Both sides finally agreed to stay out of one another's territory.

On the political scene a tacit compromise was reached between the old ruling class of the South and the Democratic city machines in the North. The South would support the machine bosses if they would call the carpetbaggers back home. The white power structure took control again in Dixie.

Blacks were hardly better off than before. They worked at starvation wages. They were kept from voting by devious laws that circumvented the intent of the Fifteenth Amendment. They were excluded from public schools. They were kept in fear of lynch mobs and night-riding Klansmen.

Relationships between blacks and whites changed in Southern Baptist churches. Now that they were "free," the blacks didn't want to worship with whites who still saw them as inferiors. They also felt inhibited and couldn't express themselves as they wished.

For their part, the whites didn't want to associate with blacks socially. White women were terrified of rape, and also worried that their daughters might be drawn into sin.

But the bonds between the races, fostered originally by the church, were still strong and there was a caring that did not exist elsewhere. A white man could hardly pray in the presence of blacks without feeling kindly toward them. And many whites still looked upon the blacks as children to be led in the way of the Lord.

Yet separation of white and black Baptists was certain. Among the thousands of Southern Baptist churches with former slaves, only a scant few remained "integrated" past 1900.

The pattern that developed at Lebanon Church was repeated all over the South.

By mutual consent the whites began training black pastors and deacons. When the blacks left, the whites wanted to ensure that they remained Baptists. At Lebanon two "colored brethren," Macklin Biggins and Scott Maynard, were "licensed" to preach. Then the church appointed a committee "to look up our missing colored members and to investigate their physical welfare and spiritual condition."

October 24, 1871, was a momentous day for the Lebanon blacks. Sixty-nine were given "letters of dismissal" to form their own church. The list of charter members reveals that many bore the same last names as white members—Champion, Chapell, Jenkins, Cato, Jones, Lowery, and others. One black member was named Ann Stallings, presumably for the first pastor's deceased wife.

The year before, the Lebanon congregation had built a new building "above" the cemetery. The whites gave the black congregation the "right" to worship once each month in the building on a Sunday when they were not having services.

In 1884, the Americus, Preston, and Lumpkin Railroad began surveying a right-of-way for a narrow-gauge track. There was a bitter tug of war over which town the railroad would pass through. Company officials compromised and ran it across Milton Hudson's farm, making a stop about equal distance between Lebanon, Botsford, and Plains of Dura. Several stores and a cotton gin soon opened for business beside the stop.

Families from Lebanon, Botsford, Plains of Dura, and Magnolia Springs began moving in. The new town took the name Plains from Plains of Dura.

In 1888 the Methodists left Magnolia Springs and located in Plains. The next year the Lebanon white Baptists built a new sanctuary in Plains behind the stores. They soon changed their name to Plains Baptist Church. The black Baptists got to keep the old building and the original name,

Lebanon. Later they moved to a black housing section on the south side of Plains.

The Botsford Lutherans kept their church in the old community until 1966 when they merged with another Lutheran congregation in Plains.

Today the four communities that coalesced to become Plains are practically ghosts of the past. A few houses still stand at old Botsford. Only the Lebanon cemetery, now the Plains burying ground, remains where the first Baptist church was built. The grave plot of Jimmy Carter's parents lies between the stumps of two trees that shaded the front of the old Lebanon church.

Magnolia Springs recovered to become a health spa after the turn of the century. Now the tourist hotel is gone and the large swimming pool is partially filled with sand. The hardshell Phillipi Baptist Church disbanded long ago. It never believed in a missionary outreach. The Methodist cemetery at the top of the hill is overgrown and no longer visible to passersby.

The site of Plains of Dura is least obvious. A new residence has been built at the crossroads. In the woods nearby, only depressions mark the graves of the Universalists whose church also died. The gravestones from the "infidel church" cemetery have been carried away by vandals. The site is now known as "Devil's Half Acre."

The Lebanon Baptist Church and other black split-offs from Baptist congregations dominated by whites formed their own conventions. The largest, the National Baptist Convention U.S.A., claims 6,300,000 members today. The National Baptist Convention of America lists 2,700,000 members. A smaller black Baptist group, the Progressive National Baptist Convention, Inc., reports 522,000 members.

After a century the pattern of separate, segregated churches for blacks and whites largely persists in the South.

During the last decade there has been a slight though steady movement back to Southern Baptists; several hundred Southern Baptist churches now have one or more black members. And 374 all-black churches have affiliated with the Southern Baptist Convention. This trend may increase if Southern Baptists can shuck their racist image.

The separation after the Civil War did provide blacks with one place where they could be truly free from the white man's bondage. From this freedom and deeply felt worship experience came the modern civil rights movement.

And what of Plains? The churches there remain separate and segregated. Blacks live on the south side of the tracks, mostly in small, cheaply constructed houses. Most whites reside on the north side in more commodious residences. Blacks cross the tracks mainly to work as maids and gardeners for their white neighbors. The races even patronize separate businesses for the most part. Only the schools are integrated.

Perhaps the most knowledgeable and respected black in Plains is white-haired Booker Schley, sixty-eight, chairman of the deacons of the black Lebanon Baptist Church, who lives in an old four-room house east of the church's newly erected brick sanctuary. He bears the name of a former governor of Georgia who he thinks may have owned his Schley ancestor. His grandfather on his mother's side was Macklin Biggins, the first pastor of the blacks after separation. His maternal great-grandfather, he believes, was a slave to a white family in the old church.

Schley delights in showing visitors the Lebanon cemetery. On one such excursion he walked among the marble tombstones of the white pioneers of Plains. "Somewhere in here my great-grandfather is buried," he said wistfully. "Before freedom, the slaves were buried with their white families. But they seldom marked their graves.

"Come over into the woods and I'll show you where my ancestors were buried after freedom." The stones are rough and hand-hewn in this section, hand-lettered and hard to read. "This is my grandfather's grave. The preacher. This is where my father and my mother are buried. The stones aren't as fancy, but at least I can find them. I guess my wife and I will be buried here if we can afford to buy the lots from the white man who owns the land."

Plains has been segregated as long as Booker Schley can remember. "The undertaker who used to be here even had two ambulances, one for blacks, one for whites. Oh, he did have just one embalming table. Said he couldn't see any sense in gettin' another.

"I know some of our young folks are gettin' better schoolin' and better jobs. And they don't have a hard time voting now. But for me only two things have changed. I go in white folks' front door now instead of the back. And they don't call me 'Boy' anymore."

Booker Schley is an unabashed Jimmy Carter fan. He was invited to the inauguration but "it was too far for an old man like me to go. We all voted for Jimmy. Don't know of any blacks who didn't. I worked with him in the fields. If you needed somebody to shovel or unload a truck, he was always there. Always respected his mama and daddy, too. And was nice to us. I think he'll give poor people more of a chance."

Then as his guest turned to leave, he reminded, "Don't you go bad-mouthin' Plains. We've had better race relations here than most southern towns. Why, there's never been a lynchin'. Not one. I know that for a fact."

7

«« »»

Keeping Women
in Their "Place"

IF BLACKS are the discriminated minority in the kingdom of Southern Baptists, women are the discriminated majority. By preference of the men who run things, they are to be seen modestly dressed in church and not heard. With a few exceptions, that's the way it has been since the denomination's founding in 1845.

Take Nina Pratt Carter, the president's grandmother, with whom he spent much time as a boy growing up in Plains. "Miss" Nina, as she was known, was a delicate woman with beautiful features. "A real pretty woman who cared about herself," her old cook and housemaid, Rosie Lee Scott, remembers.

She came from Due West, South Carolina, in 1885 to marry William Archibald Carter. This "Billy" Carter was the namesake of the president's irrepressible brother. Young Billy, according to his uncle Alton, "is a lot like his grandpa in that he's always talking about the hypocrites in the church and never attends."

The first Billy Carter was a loyal family man, but something of a rowdy—perhaps because his grandfather Wiley had killed a man and his father Walker had been murdered in 1874 in a drunken row over a homemade merry-go-round, although Alton Carter disputes the latter. "I've always heard that Grandpa died of diphtheria one day and Grandma the next," he says. Whatever the case, this Billy Carter was orphaned at fifteen.

Billy and Nina lived in a rip-roaring community called Rowena, about fifty miles south of Plains. "It was fitly named," recalls Charles Davis, who operates the only remaining store in the town. "There was lots of drinking and fighting, and a number of killings back then."

Billy Carter had three sawmills, a gin, and a store in Rowena. "He was a tough one, I've heard," adds Davis, whose great-uncle, Will Taliaferro, was Billy Carter's business competitor. "One time the flue stopped up in one of his mills. It'd take a day or two to cool it down. He didn't want to stay shut down that long, so he asked the niggers to go in and clean it up. They wouldn't go, so he had them wrap him in wet burlap bags and he went in that red-hot boiler and cleaned it out. He was right back sawing logs the same day."

Grandpa Billy was listed on the church roll at Arlington Baptist Church about four miles away. Nina was the churchgoer, but by the custom of that day her name didn't appear. Only single women were listed. Married women were regarded as belonging to their husbands. Alton, their oldest son, remembers there was a hardshell church in Rowena, "but Mama preferred the progressive church."

The "progressive" Southern Baptist church in Arlington had a Sunday school and a women's missionary society. But in other ways it was like the hardshell congregation. Women members couldn't speak or pray in public worship, nor teach men in Sunday school. The text for this was chapter 14 of Paul's first letter to the Corinthians, verses 34 and 35: "Let your women keep silence in the churches: for it is not permitted unto them to speak; but they are commanded to be under obedience, as also saith the law. And if they will learn any thing, let them ask their husbands at home: for it is a shame for women to speak in the church."

The evangelical feminist movement, spawned among abolitionists in the North, never swayed Southern Baptists, particularly not Calvinists who saw women's place as fixed as the election of a chosen few to salvation. Only the Freewill Baptists, whose theology was reflected in their name, ordained women to the ministry. Southern Baptist women were expected to be keepers at home, servants to their husbands, and when they appeared in public, to keep their necklines high, elbows covered, and dresses long.

The contributions of women to Baptist growth were not considered. A woman, Catherine Scott, had persuaded Roger Williams to make a public profession of his Baptist views and be baptized. But even in free Rhode Island, only the male heads of families were put on church membership rolls. Women often stood with their preacher husbands in resisting arrest. For example, when Georgia's Daniel Marshall was hauled into court at Augusta, his wife accompanied him and preached a sermon so persuasive that both the constable and magistrate were converted. The *Encyclopedia of Southern Baptists* mentions Marshall's baptism of the constable, but ignores his wife's sermon.

About all women could do was pray among themselves and collect money for missionaries. A woman made the first missionary contribution, $50, to the Triennial Convention in Philadelphia. However, a year later, a widow, Charlotte White, requested appointment as a foreign missionary, even offering to pay her own way, and was turned down. She was allowed to go only after agreeing to "attach herself to the family of Brother Hough."

Before and after the 1845 schism between northern and southern Baptists, numerous "cent" and "mite" societies of Baptist women met to pray and pool their money for missions. Stories of missionary sacrifices were told and retold. A favorite heroine was Ann Hasseltine Judson of Burma, whose husband Adoniram was arrested as a spy, tortured, and imprisoned. Sick from fever and barely able to stand, Ann smuggled in food and the precious Burmese translation of the Bible on which he had been working. She badgered Burmese authorities almost daily until he was released. Then, shortly after bearing him a child, she died. Ann Judson's devotion moved thousands of southern women to tears.

Some churchmen saw the prayer meetings as a prelude to a women's organization. Richmond deacons asked their pastor to "nip in the bud" the women's activities in their church. The preacher begged off. "I never heard of praying doing any harm," he said. "Let the sisters pray on."

This fear heightened in the South after northern Baptist women set up the Women's Baptist Foreign Mission Society in Boston in 1871. They raised their own funds and appointed their own missionaries without any authorization from men. Southern women weren't this far along, but they were holding special meetings in every state. One group in 1867 dared ask the Almighty to persuade the SBC Foreign Mission Board to appoint unmarried women missionaries. Five years later the first two, Edmonia Moon of Virginia and Lula Whilden of South Carolina, went to China.

Pastors' wives began having prayer meetings at the annual Southern Baptist Convention assembly. They weren't allowed to participate in the business sessions and there was little else to do.

The preachers got edgy. At the 1885 convention in Augusta a contingent of males crashed the women's meeting. Sallie Rochester Ford, a well-known novelist and wife of the Baptist editor in Kentucky, was presiding. She wanted a central women's organization to represent all Southern Baptist women and was not going to be intimidated. "I move that henceforth the meeting shall be for women only," she declared, adding that "the committee [might] invite [men] speakers if they so desired."

The men were uptight that year because of two women messengers (delegates) from Arkansas. One was the wife of a prominent pastor; the other, the spouse of the speaker of the Arkansas House of Representatives. When the alarmed parliamentarian could find nothing in the denomination's constitution barring women, the convention was thrown into an uproar.

The husbands defended their wives. The pastor, M. D. Early, asked, "The question before this Convention is, 'Shall the Baptist ladies of this country, who have sent more money into the vaults of this Convention than the men, be excluded from a part in its deliberation?' "

The male assembly decided they should. Upon the recommendation of a five-man committee appointed to deal with the disturbers, the men adopted an amendment to their constitution substituting the word *brethren* for *members*.

They then conceded that there could be central committees of women in each state *approved* and *supervised* by men. Funds raised by the committees must go to denominational agencies administered by men, they added.

The women weren't appeased. Three years later they met in the Broad Street Methodist Church in Richmond while the SBC men were holding business conference in a Baptist church. Their leader was Martha F. McIntosh, a missionary widow who had felt the sting of discrimination. After taking up her husband's work in China, she had been called before a board of men to answer charges of preaching. "I suppose I do preach," she admitted. "Well, have you been ordained?" one asked soberly. "No, but I was foreordained," she replied. That ended her missionary career.

Delegates from ten states said they wanted to go ahead with a central organization. "Think not of prejudice," en-

couraged Mrs. L. B. Telford of Florida. "When God is for
us, who can be against us?" But Virginia said they needed
the approval of their men and three other states were not
ready.

After long discussion a constitution for an executive
committee of the women's mission societies was accepted.
It called for a separate organization of women for "stimu-
lating the missionary spirit and the grace of giving among
the women and children of the churches, and aiding in
collecting funds for missionary purposes, to be disbursed
by the Boards of the Southern Baptist Convention. . . ."
They would trust their money to the male-dominated
boards, but their organization would be an "independent"
auxiliary of the denomination. Martha McIntosh was
elected their first president.

They met every year thereafter while the men convened
in business conference to hear reports and discuss the affairs of the denomination. Male representatives of the mission boards worked the financial reports of the women into
their own and presented the figures to the official convention. Finally, in 1913, the Woman's Missionary Union,
as it had been renamed, was allowed to share the platform
with men.

In 1890 there were WMUs in 669 of the denomination's
then 16,091 churches. Plains Baptist women organized with
nine members in 1892 at the urging of Leola C. Parker, a
public school teacher.

The women of tiny Plains were more aggressive and
better educated than their sisters in most other Southern
Baptist churches. There are three possible reasons for this:
One, only two men were left in the church during the Civil
War, leaving women to exercise leadership. Two, there was
the presence of the Universalist Church in Plains, a rarity
in the South, which allowed women more freedom and
promoted female education more than Baptists did. Some of

this had to rub off on the Baptist women. Three, the Plains church had in recent years had a string of unusually outstanding pastors for a small congregation, including a prominent surgeon, an editor, and a judge.

The pastor at the founding of the Plains Baptist Women's Missionary Society was A. C. Wellons, an architect and builder who constructed many of the charming nineteenth-century homes still standing in Plains. Wellons then took the pastorate of the Arlington Baptist Church in 1895, which Nina Carter and her children were attending. He was there in March 1897, when a violent tornado slammed into the Arlington schoolhouse killing ten children. One was his daughter.

Alton Carter was then only eight, but he remembers the storm vividly. "It was just like a bad dream. One of the boys was blowed clear out the window. Another had his head mashed like a sack of corn by the chimney that fell. My sister Ethel wasn't hurt, but a two-by-four fell on me and broke my arm and leg. Somebody went and got my daddy and he came and chopped the wood off."

A greater tragedy for the Carters came seven years later. This is how Alton Carter recalls it: "This feller Will Taliaferro was renting from us, and my daddy put him out because he was gambling and drinking on the place. When he moved to another store he took an old thread case that Daddy had made into a desk with him. Daddy sent me over after it, but he wouldn't give it back. 'I'll go see him myself,' Daddy said. Well, I heard them fightin' and ran over that a'way. I was within twenty feet when the feller started shootin'. Hit my daddy right in the head. I ran up quick but there was nothin' I could do."

At the time Nina Carter had three other children besides Alton and a fifth on the way. "Uncle Calvin Carter came from Americus to administrate the estate," Alton recalls. "He moved us to Plains, which he said was a good place and close enough for him to look after us. They had three mistrials for the feller who killed Daddy and then let him loose."

(Court records in Blakeley, Georgia, show only two trials, the first a mistrial and the second ending in a not-guilty verdict. A relative of the accused Taliaferro claims Billy Carter was "cutting out Will Taliaferro's guts" when someone else entered and shot Carter. An ironic footnote: Jeff Carter, son of the president, married Annette Davis, a descendant by marriage from Taliaferro, in the Arlington Baptist Church in 1975.)

After the Carters came to Plains, fifteen-year-old Alton attended school only four months before quitting to work in Oliver McDonald's store in the building where Alton's son Hugh has his antique store today. The estate proceeds were invested in real estate, providing the seed for the vast Carter holdings around Plains today.

Young Alton was regarded as the head of the family, with Uncle Calvin as adviser. "Mama didn't have all that much business sense," Alton recalls. "Her place was at home and church."

Nina Carter took her Baptist faith seriously, transferring her "letter" of membership from Arlington to Plains Baptist soon after her arrival. She became active in the Plains WMU as did her daughters and daughters-in-law after her. Since she wasn't educated to teach school or nurse, there was little else she could do outside the home.

When Nina Carter was bringing up her three daughters in Plains (Jeanette was born four months after her father's murder), suffragettes were campaigning for the vote. Southern Baptist preachers opposed their crusade as stubbornly as they had fought abolition of slavery. Editor B. J. W. Graham of Georgia Baptists' *Christian Index* warned that "the conduct of men at voting precincts . . . would be repulsive to refined womanhood." A Texas Baptist leader said men were only trying to protect women from corrupt politics that were "out of harmony" with the "sweet, modest, home-loving female nature." L. S. Darling, a Kentucky pastor, accused suffragettes of "pointing womankind to the path that leads to harlotry and to hell." Some Baptist men did favor suffrage because they felt women would be more likely to vote for prohibition.

Not until 1918, the year woman's suffrage was finally approved, were women seated as voting messengers to the Southern Baptist Convention. That year a woman spoke to the annual assembly for the first time. Mrs. W. A. Taliaferro (no relation to the man accused of killing Billy Carter) talked about enrolling adults in Sunday school, hardly a controversial subject.

In 1929 Kentucky Baptists tried to put women back in their "place." Dr. J. W. Porter presented the request from his state that women not be permitted to address the annual Southern Baptist assembly at Memphis. M. E. Dodd, pastor of First Baptist Church, Shreveport, Louisiana, retorted from Paul's letter to the Galatians: " 'In Christ Jesus there is neither male nor female. We are one in Christ!' " There was applause. The motion was voted down. The Kentuckian stomped out in disgust. Then Mrs. W. J. Cox, seventh president of the WMU, gave her report.

Religious education was another long struggle. Baptists had started a number of women's academies and colleges to protect their "fairer sex." A few schools were coeducational, but the official Southern Baptist Theological Seminary at Louisville was a sacred male preserve. In the late nineteenth century a few women had been allowed to take notes in classes as long as they did not speak up. In 1902 trustees advanced a bit further by ruling that women could enroll and take exams, but would not receive credit.

Zealous for trained women missionaries, the WMU started its own missionary training school in 1907 adjacent to the seminary campus. There was a great hullabaloo among the brethren that the women were bent on training women preachers. WMU leaders denied any such heretical idea. The male clergy finally accepted the school on the basis that men professors from the seminary would provide orthodox teaching and the women who didn't become single missionaries would make good preachers' wives. In 1952, after the seminary agreed to admit women students for full credit, the name was changed to Carver School of Missions and Social Work and men began enrolling. Five later Southern Baptist seminaries (Southwestern in Fort Worth, New Orleans in New Orleans, Golden Gate in San Francisco, Southeastern in Wake Forest, N.C., and Midwestern in Kansas City) have accepted qualified women from their beginnings.

The much maligned WMU gained more acceptance from the Southern Baptist male hierarchy in the 1930s. The men had to grudgingly admit that women had saved the denomination from bankruptcy.

Southern Baptists had gotten into trouble in the twenties after payments of pledges fell short in a crash program for missions, colleges and seminaries, and hospitals. With the Depression fast approaching, the denomination was $18 million in debt.

Responding to the emergency, the WMU office in Birmingham mailed out 30,000 "alabaster offering boxes." Executive Director Kathleen Mallory begged women to sacrifice Liberty Bonds, dresses, Sunday eggs—anything to help pay the debt. Baptist colleges and hospitals might have to close, she warned. Missionaries might have to be called home. The WMU women paid more than their assigned quota.

Close on the heels of the pledge shortages came the biggest theft of church funds in American history. In September 1928, Clinton Carnes, treasurer of the Home Mission

Board in Atlanta, disappeared. Investigators looked in his safe and found he had been keeping a double set of books. A hurried accounting showed he had embezzled $953,000 from secret loans made to the denomination under his name. Carnes had been a Baptist deacon, a pillar in Atlanta civic affairs, and a realtor and mortgage banker from whom other Baptist officials had borrowed money to buy homes. Greatly embarrassed, they admitted having trusted him fully. His wife had also been kept in the dark. When told the news, she collapsed in a horrified faint.

There was more embarrassment when it became known that he had been imprisoned for mail fraud in Atlanta before becoming employed by the board—and that among his bad investments were the careers of movie starlets. At that time Southern Baptist preachers saw Hollywood as an instrument of the devil and frequently preached against the "harlots" of the film capital.

After a long pursuit Carnes was arrested in Wisconsin and brought back to Atlanta for trial. He served a term in prison, then fled in disgrace to Mexico, where he died. But the money was gone and the mission board had to pay his debts.

Again the WMU came to the rescue, helping promote a Baptist Honor Day across the South to pay missionary salaries and keep orphanages and other missionary institutions from being sold at auction.

By 1933 the denomination was still $3 million in the red. The women gave one officer the title WMU Promoter for a Debtless Denomination. They raised one-third of the amount, other church organizations solicited the balance, and the denomination was at last debt free.

"Banks were settling with other church bodies for as little as a third on the dollar," recalls Louie D. Newton, then pastor of the prestigious Druid Hills Baptist Church in Atlanta. "We paid them a hundred cents to the dollar with interest. I think that's one reason we've grown to be the biggest. We paid our debts."

Southern Baptists also came out of the Depression with a marvelous Cooperative Program for fair-share financing of denominational work. Churches promote membership tithing and send a portion of their local collections to their state Baptist convention office. Part of the money is kept in the state for Baptist colleges, children's homes, and other enterprises. The remainder is sent on to the headquarters of the Southern Baptist Executive Committee in Nashville and is divided among the two mission boards, the six seminaries, the Radio and Television Commission, and other operations that relate to Southern Baptists in all states.

Translated into dollar amounts: In 1977 the Southern Baptist Convention reported receiving about $55 million from the state conventions. Almost half of this Cooperative Program money went to the Foreign Mission Board; one-fifth was sent to the Home Mission Board. Two special offerings sponsored by the WMU women brought in additional millions for missions. The Lottie Moon Christmas Offering for Foreign Missions tallied $26.2 million. The Annie Armstrong Easter Offering for Home Missions took in $9.6 million. Totaled: Southern Baptists gave to their mission boards over $70 million in 1977. Most of this was collected by the women.

With a 1.4 million enrollment, the WMU women constantly promote tithing and missionary support. Their biggest event is the Lottie Moon Christmas Offering, the largest short-term, freewill collection of money in the world. Lottie Moon was a Virginia society beauty who went to China as a missionary and starved to death after sharing her last personal funds with suffering Chinese friends. The Easter offering honors Annie Armstrong, a WMU leader from Baltimore who tirelessly raised funds for missionary work and initiated self-help ministries to poor black women.

Much criticized by Baptist men and sheltered women, she once sighed, "I wonder if we will have to wait until we get to heaven before we can do anything that there will not be some good person to see flaws in it."

Annie Armstrong and Lottie Moon are household names in Southern Baptist churches today. One Southern Baptist pastor was overheard singing in the shower one December Sunday morning, "Shine on, shine on, Lottie Moon, for me and my church. . . ." The irrepressible W. A. Criswell, pastor of First Baptist Church, Dallas (18,869 members and the largest in the SBC), is reported to have given this tongue-in-cheek advice to a preacher friend: "Be a streaker for missions. Give your fanny to Annie and your body to Lottie."

The WMU women ignore such crudities and go marching on.

Collecting money for missions is just one leg of the triad of WMU work. They also conduct a cradle-to-grave missions education program for their sex, from preschool Mission Friends to Women's Missionary Society circles for adults. In between there are Girls in Action for grade-schoolers, Acteens for high school girls, Young Women's Auxiliary for collegiates, and Baptist Young Women for young matrons and singles. The youth groups are a blend of Girl Scouts, Old South coming-out rituals, Bible study, and missionary programs. The Acteens, for example, take a series of "Forward Steps" leading to coronation ceremonies.

For many years the WMU directed Royal Ambassadors' clubs for boys. As an RA at the Plains Baptist Church, young Jimmy Carter repeated the motto "I am an Ambassador for Christ" taken from Paul's second letter to the Corinthians. In RAs boys rise through a six-tiered ranking from Page to Ambassador Plenipotentiary by completing projects in sports, handicrafts, scientific research, Bible and mission study, and missionary field programs. In 1957 the Baptist Brotherhood took over the boys' missionary education.

The SBC Brotherhood organization was belatedly founded in 1907 to educate men in missions. It was unthinkable that women should teach men.

The third leg of WMU work is community missions. The first projects began in 1908 in Maryland. Baptist women visited the sick, taught illiterate women and children, took food to impoverished families, and held prayer meetings in nursing homes. Such activities are multiplied thousands of times by Southern Baptist WMU women today.

In 1912 a settlement house patterned after Jane Addams's Hull House in Chicago was opened in Louisville, next to the WMU Training School. Here young women received on-the-job training for similar Baptist houses in other cities. In 1914 the settlement houses were renamed goodwill centers with the motto "Peace on earth, goodwill among men." Today there are over sixty such centers in urban areas. The centers are funded through the Home Mission Board, with voluntary workers from local churches assisting professional staff.

The Baptist women in Plains have done all the usual WMU things—promoting the Easter and Christmas mission offerings, leading the boys' and girls' organizations, holding circle meetings, participating in service projects such as collecting household goods for burned-out families—but always within the confining social system of the Old South.

Nina Carter accepted the traditions, but her daughter-in-law Lillian balked. Lillian came from the nearby community of Richland to study nursing at the hospital that had been started by the "Three Wise Men," doctors Thad, Sam, and Bowman Wise, sons of the pioneer medic of Plains. Her erudite Methodist politician father, Jim Jack Gordy, had encouraged his daughters to develop their own views about the world. After Lillian met and married Earl Carter (she was twenty-six, he thirty), she joined her husband's church but never conformed to his beliefs about blacks. In segregated, Jim Crow Plains, she became by her own admission "an avid integrationist."

She attended Baptist worship services more regularly than Earl, who often left her and the children at church and walked on into town to talk with the "boys." But she thought the women's Sunday School parties and WMU circle meetings were a waste of time. The other women didn't appreciate her opinions about the blacks. Some thought she was too uppity and brash. She eventually dropped out of the Baptist women's social circles altogether.

In Plains today black women think more endearingly of her than do the white matriarchs. A typical story comes from Mrs. Fanny Hill. "She saved my boy George's life when he was nine months old. He had some kind of dysentery. The doctor said he had done all he could. Lillian came to my house in her nurse's uniform and said one of her boys had had the same sickness. I was desperate and told her to go ahead and try her remedy. George was well in no time. He's now a lieutenant colonel in the army in Germany."

Mrs. Hill's father, William Johnson, was a bishop in the Colored Methodist Episcopal Church. He was responsible for thousands of black Methodist congregations in Alabama, Texas, and as far away as California. But he kept his residency in Archery, the little community two miles west of Plains where Earl and Lillian Carter had a "company" store for the 250 blacks who worked their land. Here the bishop had a school for black children.

Bishop Johnson had the largest private library around Plains. "He was the smartest man I knew as a boy," Jimmy Carter recalls. "He had running water, electricity, and a radio before anybody else." The bishop generated his own electricity and gave Earl Carter the idea for rural electrification that helped launch the president's father into prominence in Sumter County.

Lillian Carter thought the bishop was smart and didn't mind telling anyone so. When Earl wasn't around, she would invite him or any other black in through her front door, a practice Earl pretended never happened. This charming story is told by the bishop's son, Reverend William D. Johnson, Jr., now a Methodist editor in Atlanta: "Daddy pulled up to the Carters one day in his black Cadillac. Jimmy bounced out to see the car. He was about ten or eleven then. He walked all around it, then sidled up to Daddy and asked, 'Are you the bishop of all the colored folks in Texas?' Daddy said, 'Just the colored Methodists, son.' Jimmy was still impressed. He hiked one foot up on the fender and declared, 'Well, if you can be the bishop of all the colored Methodists in Texas, I guess I can be the president of the United States.' "

Much has been written about the crowds at Earl Carter's funeral when he died from cancer in 1953. But the throng at Bishop Johnson's funeral in 1936 was much larger. After Earl died, Lillian's world "seemed to come apart," according to her daughter Ruth. She didn't fit in with the other windows in Plains and took a job as housemother for a fraternity at Auburn University about seventy miles away. Perhaps to show her rebellion at Baptist morality, she drank beer with the boys. Then after six years she took over a nursing home in Blakeley, Georgia, the town where Will Taliaferro had been tried for her father-in-law's killing.

When she came back to Plains in 1961 she still couldn't adjust to woman's role in the Baptist-dominated town. She took up with her daughter Ruth, who had also become weary of women's work in the Baptist church and had become an evangelist. At one of Ruth's meetings she found a sick woman who needed to be at the airport by a certain time. When Ruth and the other women prayed too long, Lillian interrupted tartly and asked if there was anyone "not so religious that they will help me get this woman to the airport."

In 1965, the year before her son's humiliating loss to Lester Maddox, Lillian accompanied Ruth to hear a Methodist evangelist, Tommy Tyson, in Tennessee. At the end of the sermon he gave an altar call for "anyone willing to give up everything for Christ." Lillian went down.

Aggravation awaited her back in Plains when the Baptist church voted to exclude blacks from services. Lillian was angry, but didn't quit the church right away as her other daughter Gloria did. Shortly thereafter she saw a recruiting commercial for the Peace Corps during the "Johnny Carson Show," and went into the kitchen and wrote her application that night. Next morning she mentioned this to Jimmy and Billy at their office. After the shock wore off, Jimmy said, "I believe if Rosalynn and I had no ties we would like to do that. If that's what you want I'm all for it." But they kept it quiet because Jimmy was planning to run for governor again and many Georgians didn't approve of the Peace Corps.

The story of her two years in India, working with lepers and giving vasectomies to fathers who couldn't feed the families they already had, is now well known. She came back in 1970 to make speeches about India and to experience continuing frustration in her church.

In 1973 the segregationist deacons whom she had long opposed forced the resignation of Reverend Fred Collins, a young pastor she dearly loved. She was getting to like the new pastor, Bruce Edwards, when the same people began pressing him. When the church met to vote on admitting blacks and firing Edwards on November 14, 1976, she was ready to tell the obdurate deacons off. Her son, the president, must have known what she intended to do. "Don't open your mouth, Mama," he counseled. She didn't quite obey. When some began haranguing the pastor, she bolted from the pew and ran and sat down between Edwards and his wife Sandra. Drawing an arm about the young minister, she snapped, "It's a shame how they're persecuting you."

Rosalynn Carter conformed more to the role a Baptist woman is expected to follow in Plains. She faithfully attended the missionary circle meetings and accepted speaking assignments on programs. But she had children active in the WMU youth organizations and a husband involved in brotherhood work for the church and the area Friendship Baptist Association. As associational brotherhood president, he persuaded churches to send freight carloads of corn annually to one of the Georgia Baptist children's homes for feeding livestock. He also instigated the building of a youth camp for the association.

After becoming governor, Jimmy Carter was elected a trustee of the SBC Brotherhood Commission, which promotes mission work for men in all the churches. Rosalynn continued in the WMU, though she was less active in Atlanta than in Plains.

The separation of the sexes in Southern Baptist missionary education and programs continues, although the brotherhood and WMU have begun a joint promotion of "Love Thy Neighbor" family mission action opportunities. Enrollment in both organizations is now leveling off, perhaps indicating more togetherness in church activities. A few Baptist leaders are even conceding that age- and sex-graded church groups may contribute to the fragmentation of families.

But among Southern Baptists generally, a woman's place is still in the separate WMU, teaching children and other women in Sunday school classes, singing, doing secretarial work, and in churches unable to afford custodial service, cleaning the buildings. Only a minority of SBC Sunday schools even offer couples' classes.

The women's rights movement has hardly dented Southern Baptist churches and the institutions they support. Consider:

—In all its 132 years the SBC has never had a woman to hold any top position in the denomination, excepting the independent WMU.

—Of the 891 persons serving on trustee boards of SBC agencies (mission boards, seminaries, and the like), only 5½ percent are women. Nine policy-making groups are without any female representation.

—None of the SBC women's colleges have female presidents. Only 20 percent of their trustees are women.

—Only 11 percent of faculties at the six SBC seminaries (enrollment over 8,000; one-sixth of all theological students in the United States) are women, all in departments of religious education, counseling, missions, and so on. There is not one recognized Southern Baptist woman theological professor teaching in an SBC seminary. Female student enrollment in seminaries has declined from a high of 17.1 percent in 1950 to the present 11 percent—in contrast to the trend in other major church bodies.

—On the local church level, only one ordained woman minister serves a congregation. She is employed by the Home Mission Board to pastor a small inner-city flock in Philadelphia. Her home church in Kentucky, which ordained her, has been expelled from the area association of churches for the action. Another white woman has been "called" to co-pastor with her husband a 150-member racially integrated church in Louisville. She is expected to be ordained shortly. The remaining 35,071 Southern Baptist churches are led by males.

—Women do fill about 10 percent of auxiliary staff positions in local churches; principally they are directors of religious education, music, and youth activities. But studies show they receive less pay and fewer fringe benefits, such as secretarial help, than men holding similar positions. Many churches prefer to hire women simply because they can get them to work for lower pay than men.

—Women do better in the foreign mission field, where slightly over half of the 2,715-member force are women. However, women occupy only 7 percent of the administrative/management jobs in foreign missionary work. Their jobs tend to be nontheological—in nursing, teaching, medical technology, social work, secretarial, and mass media. Men are most often seminary professors, evangelists, doctors, engineers, and business administrators. The Home Mission Board does not provide a breakdown by sex. It has also set another precedent in SBC life by referring in publications to women by their last names, as is now done in most secular journals. Even the WMU lists its married trustees and officers by the husbands' names.

Theoretically, ordination of women should be easier in the SBC since the churches are autonomous. Practically, however, it is more difficult because most (perhaps 99-plus percent) of the churches are glued to southern tradition and literal application of biblical prohibitions. This is just as true in the "mission fields" of the northern United States as in the South. Most pastors of the "mission" churches come from the South, as do most of their members.

No more than a dozen Southern Baptist women have been ordained. The first occurred in North Carolina in 1964, when the Watts Street Baptist Church of Durham ordained Miss Addie Davis. The controversy died after she accepted an American Baptist (formerly Northern Baptist) pastorate in Readsboro, Vermont.

The second led to an ecclesiastical donnybrook. With

Southern Baptist college and seminary degrees, Miss Shirley Carter (no relation of the president) was ordained for a chaplaincy in an institution in South Carolina. After marrying a former Catholic priest, W. Pringle Lee, she was reported to have been pregnant before the wedding. The church quickly rescinded her ordination. She charged prejudice, claiming that many male preachers had been found guilty of adultery and had not lost their credentials.

Many more women, perhaps several hundred, have been ordained as deaconesses or deacons, a lay position. But even though there is clear precedent in the New Testament and in Baptist churches before the nineteenth century for this, the practice is still widely opposed.

Jimmy Carter's evangelist sister Ruth Stapleton doesn't care to be ordained. "It is not a criterion for ministry," she says. "I have no need to serve Communion or act as a priest. My membership is in the Baptist church, but I have declined offers to be ordained." Ruth Stapelton's ministry is mainly to ecumenical groups. She is not in the Southern Baptist system. Nor is her faith-healing theology palatable to most Southern Baptists.

The new president of the Southern Baptist Convention, Jimmy Allen, pastor of the 9,000-member First Baptist Church of San Antonio, doesn't think women's ordination is "all that important. In our church we lay hands on (ordain) both men and women for appointed tasks. Baptists began as laymen. We ought to get back to that."

Allen is more highly regarded by rights-seeking Baptist women than W. A. Criswell, whom they see as one of the most extreme male chauvinists in the SBC. (In 1872 Criswell's Dallas church was "saved" by women members collecting $500 for a building foundation!) Allen has publicly called for more women in Southern Baptist decision-making posts.

But many Baptist women already in or preparing for full-time church vocations want ordination now. They want to share in privileges that ordination brings from society and government, one of which is tax exemption for housing allowances.

Ordination of women is most favored by male Southern Baptist seminary professors. Dean Earnest Loessner of Southern Seminary's School of Religious Education in Louisville believes it should be for anyone earning a living by the Gospel. W. Morgan Patterson, professor of church history at Golden Gate Seminary in San Francisco, sees women's ordination as an application of the traditional Baptist concept of the equality of all persons before God. Dr. Harry L. McBeth, his counterpart at Southwestern Seminary in Fort Worth, is impressed by the "convincing case" women are making for their ministry. But he is not optimistic because he finds "no convincing evidence that Southern Baptists have ever influenced their culture, or been in advance of the culture, on the question of 'women's rights.'"

The most outspoken SBC theologian for change has been William Hull, former dean of the School of Theology at Southern Seminary, now pastor of First Baptist Church of Shreveport, Louisiana.

Hull attributes Southern Baptist male chauvinism to a biblical literalism that interprets each Scripture passage on the same level of importance and fails to see the movement of God in history toward the ideal of sexual equality. Southern Baptists don't disagree so much over what the Bible says, he maintains in an article for the seminary journal *Review and Expositor*, but "on the most valid procedure for interpreting the available evidence."

Hull finds three "distinct" levels in the relationship of male and female presented in the Bible:

1. The "Old Age" of ancient Judaism where polygamy and concubinage was the norm, where a man's wife was "lumped together" with his house, cattle, and other property, and where a single woman was to be subject to her father and a married woman subservient to her husband.

2. The "Messianic Age" in which God became incarnate in Jesus to potentiate God's original intention in creation before the Fall: "God created man in his own image, in the image of God created he him; male and female created he them" (Gen. 1:27). The woman "helpmeet" of Genesis, Hull says, is a "companion," a "kind of mirror image of man's humanity," an "opposite number . . . . Just as a piece of paper must, by nature, have two sides, so humanity, by its created nature, must have two sexes. Neither the male nor the female alone, but only the two of them together as 'one flesh,' constitute and complete what it means generically to be human."

   Jesus, he continues, made faith "the basis of one's standing before God," thus putting men and women on an equal footing before God. Faith in the Savior leads male and female into the freedom of the Kingdom of God where the creation ideal can be realized.

3. The "Age to Come in which even our redeemed sexuality will be abolished and our unity-in-reciprocity will be fulfilled not by oneness with the opposite sex but by a perfect oneness with God-in-Christ."

Biblical history, Hull stresses, is linear. God dealt with situations as he found them. For today, he suggests, it is a question of where Southern Baptists and others want to position themselves on God's calendar.

Harry N. Hollis, Jr., an SBC specialist in family life, agrees with "the idea that all human beings can be free came with Jesus Christ." He added at a conference in New Mexico on societal problems Southern Baptists face today: "This idea will not go away. It cannot be killed by women who want to stay in their male-imposed places so they will not have to face the risk of freedom. Male arrogance cannot kill it. Female indifference cannot kill it. It is Christ's idea and it is here to stay."

If so, most Southern Baptists haven't gotten the message. At the 1974 SBC convention in Dallas, the denomination's Christian Life Commission moved that agency boards have at least one-fifth representation by women. A Houston pastor's wife, Jessie Sappington, led the opposition, reminding that Paul said, "Women are to keep silent in the church." With preachers shouting "Amen!" the motion was decisively defeated.

At the same convention, Georgia's Louie D. Newton, a patriarch of the denomination, was asked at a meeting of SBC historians how he saw the role of women in Southern Baptist life. The old Georgian replied testily, "No change. No change at all. Same role as always."

For all the hopeful rhetoric from those wanting women to emerge from men's shadow, that's about the way it is among Southern Baptists. For most women desiring to serve in the church, their place is still the Women's Missionary Union.

Where does Jimmy Carter stand in all this? He has "trouble interpreting Paul literally that women are to keep silent in the church." He has vowed not to discriminate on the basis of gender in office and has appointed two women cabinet members and two more as top aides. He and his wife Rosalynn have campaigned for the Equal Rights Amendment. He is classified a liberal on women's rights. But as long as he remains a Southern Baptist, he will be viewed with suspicion by feminists. They know that most men leading the giant denomination are dedicated to keeping women "in their place."

8

«« »»

All about Sin, Sex, and Racism

GOOD SOUTHERN Baptists seldom talk about sex in public, much less joke about it. Yet here one of their own, candidate Carter, had made this most intimate relationship the butt of jokes across the land. And in *Playboy* magazine! One jest suggested that the national motto should now be changed to "Oh, God, We Lust." Remembering Goldwater posters from 1964 brought another line: "In his heart, he knows your wife." The cartoon classic showed a group of winking deacons eyeing a *Playboy* centerfold. "Why, I just know Brother Jimmy's got a sermon in here somewhere," one is saying.

The *Playboy* interview gave new life to the right-wing conservatives among Southern Baptists. A loose coalition had been hunting for liberal "bear" since the 1975 SBC assembly in Miami when Dallas's W. A. Criswell and about 200 other pastors of large churches met privately to consider how to get more "Christians" in government. Jimmy Carter wasn't one they had in mind. They didn't like his record as governor, his choice of Mondale as running mate and association with other "big spenders," and his campaign promises. But until the *Playboy* interview, Carter's churchmanship had dampened any efforts to excite much Baptist emotion against the Georgian.

Their moment came on a balmy October Sunday in Dallas. President Gerald Ford had attended the Texas-Oklahoma college football game on Saturday and was staying over for services at First Baptist Church, the largest congregation in the denomination. Billy Graham is among the 18,000 members. H. L. Hunt belonged until he passed on to his mansion in the sky.

In his presermon remarks, Pastor W. A. Criswell said he had been in Washington with a group of religious broadcasters the week before for a conference with the president. "I was mightily impressed by the warm spiritual atmosphere in the White House. Before leaving I invited the president to attend our church when he came to Dallas. And here he is."

Then in an aside that brought jubilation to Republicans everywhere, Criswell alluded to the "other candidate's" *Playboy* interview. He termed the magazine "pornographic" and "salacious," and praised Ford for turning down a *Playboy* offer.

Reporters waited expectantly until Criswell finished his sermon on tithing. When the preacher and the president broke through the crowd at the outside door, one shouted, "Does this mean you're endorsing Mr. Ford?"

Criswell smiled and turned to Ford. "I am for you! I hope you win in November."

Ford, carrying a Bible Criswell had given him, beamed. "Thank you very much. I am gratified by your support."

That Criswell didn't represent all Southern Baptists was soon apparent. Jimmy Allen, pastor of First Baptist Church in San Antonio, declared he was now for Carter all the way. From South Carolina came a petition signed by the president of Baptist Wake Forest University, U.S. Senator

Robert B. Morgan, and other prominent business and professional men:

> Dr. Criswell's intervention is not new. He attacked those of us who labored in the struggle for human rights. He attacked the religion of John F. Kennedy. He has not been noted for attacking crime in the White House.
>
> Dr. Criswell now attacks Carter for witnessing to his faith in a magazine interview. We commend the governor. In a hostile medium, Jimmy Carter gave strong and courageous expression to the biblical view of marital fidelity.

Carter's discussion of a broad range of issues in *Playboy* was ignored. Southern Baptist readers centered on the last paragraph, where Carter confessed to having "looked on a lot of women with lust" and paraphrased Jesus as saying, "Don't consider yourself better than someone else because one guy screws a whole bunch of women while the other guy is loyal to his wife. The guy who's loyal to his wife ought not to be condescending or proud because of the relative degree of sinfulness."

Many SBC theologians and denominational leaders validated Carter's theology as expressed in the interview. "Everyone who is honest knows that most men have some degree of guilt," said James L. Sullivan, then president of the denomination. Deacon Jerry Clower, the SBC's most famous comedian, later put it more pungently: "Any red-blooded American male who says he ain't lusted after a woman he's seen is just plain out lying. When a woman puts a craving on me, it makes me want to run home right then to Mama. That's what Jimmy Carter was trying to say, but he ain't as countrified as I am."

Criticism focused on the magazine and the euphemism

for intercourse. Larry Jerden, associate editor of the Brotherhood Commission's *World Mission Journal*, termed *Playboy* "sinful," "worldly," and "used of the Devil." But Carter, Jerden wrote, had "accomplished something few other 'missionaries' could ever do—he was able to present the good news of the Gospel to an audience that needs it perhaps more than any other...."

There was practically unanimous assent that Carter had used the wrong words, although SBC President James L. Sullivan quoted "some" Southern Baptists as saying, "'if Mr. Carter hadn't used that language, the *Playboy* audience wouldn't have known what he was talking about.'"

Carter is not the first politician to feel the sting of his fellow Southern Baptists for using naughty language. Harry Truman had an honorary doctorate withdrawn at the last minute by Baylor University because of alumni complaints that his salty language dishonored the Southern Baptist school. Although Truman never trimmed his talk, he did gain respect from his denomination. In 1963 the SBC was meeting in Kansas City on Truman's birthday. A delegation was sent to ask if he would come and receive greetings. "I never thought I'd see this day," he said in a choked voice. When he arrived the Baptist delegates broke out in applause and sang, "Happy birthday, dear Harry."

Georgia Baptists haven't been so forgiving of Mercer University Professor F. Robert Otto. On the night of April 11, 1968, Otto was crossing the Macon campus of the school built by Abe Simon's liquor and gambling money when he overheard a student use a standard four-letter word for intercourse to show his disgust for the establishment. Otto understood why this student and others at Mercer were upset. The local Tattnall Square Baptist Church had rejected a Nigerian student's request to attend worship services, and then fired the pastoral staff when they stood in opposition. The Nigerian had been brought to Mercer by Baptist missionaries whom the church supported through the Southern Baptist mission program. The Mercer students, reacting angrily, had then hung a sign on the church's outside bulletin board: MINISTERS WANTED. NEED NOT BE CHRISTIAN. As a professor of Christianity and dean of the chapel, Otto had himself protested the racist actions. But he felt students were defeating their own cause by using profanity.

The next morning, April 12, Otto quoted the student's angry blast, four-letter word included, in his chapel sermon. He cited it as "thoughtless, foul talk," which should not be in the vocabulary of Christians.

A recording of Otto's sermon was played before the Macon Baptist Pastors' Conference. Several of the preachers had long had a "contract" out for Otto for alleged liberalism and stirring up racial trouble. The word used in chapel was just the springboard they needed. They quickly rammed through a resolution asking Mercer trustees to have Otto removed from his chapel post and to consider firing him from the faculty.

The trustees passed the hot potato to Dr. Rufus Harris, president of Mercer. Harris defended Otto, saying the use of "one such phrase in a whole sermon" couldn't make the Gospel "impotent." Otto's own pastor praised the professor, noting that he faithfully attended services three times a week and came to a 6:30 A.M. Saturday men's prayer meeting as well.

Finally Otto appeared to answer charges before the Macon Pastors' Conference. He expressed regret for using the four-letter word, but defended his theological views vigorously. The meeting became heated, with some preachers shouting to make themselves heard. An old divine had been sitting quietly at the front of the room, listening, frowning, shaking his head in consternation. Suddenly he jumped up and stalked to the back door. Turning around, he yelled, "Baptist preachers are like cow manure. Spread them out and they do a lot of good. Lump them together and they stink." He slammed the door and left. For a few seconds there was embarrassed silence. Then someone announced "I move we adjourn."

Editor Jack Harwell in Atlanta tried to put the incident in perspective.

> It does seem strange that we will get so upset about the utterance of a vulgar word—a word which is more common in modern vocabulary than any of us are willing to admit—and blandly ignore dozens of other gross sins all about us, such as racial prejudice, missionary indifference, economic injustice, war across the world, sexual license, and spiritual mediocrity.

But the die was cast on Otto's influence among Southern Baptist churches in Georgia. Before the incident he had preached almost every Sunday. In the nine years since, except for his own church, he hasn't spoken to another Baptist congregation. He once thought of transferring to another Baptist college, but a good friend on the faculty told him, "This administration wouldn't touch you with a ten-foot pole."

Southern Baptists also hold strong feelings about alcohol. Ask Billy Carter, who says, "I lost the mayor's race in Plains because I drink beer on Sundays and because I'm a Carter."

Or Jimmy Carter, who had more trouble with his fellow Georgia Baptists over prohibition issues than anything else while governor.

Particularly the Reverend Dr. Louis Devotie Newton. At a ramrod-straight eighty-five, Newton is the nearest twentieth-century comparison to Jesse Mercer that Georgia Baptists have. He taught at Mercer University, edited *The Christian Index*, and pastored the prestigious Druid Hills Baptist Church in Atlanta for forty years. He also served as president of the Southern Baptist Convention and as vice-president of the Baptist World Alliance. No elder statesman still living deserves the title Mr. Southern Baptist more than he.

For many years Newton wrote a daily column for the *Atlanta Constitution*, where the late editor Ralph McGill was his close friend. McGill's only son attended Sunday school at Druid Hills, and the editor himself occasionally dropped in for church. In his column Newton never feared to lambaste anyone for moral deviations. He scalded President and Mrs. Harding for introducing dancing into the White House. He accused the Ku Klux Klan of profiteering on the sale of robes. He slammed Sinclair Lewis for writing "the most humiliating illustration of the American novel of this generation"—*Elmer Gantry*. He lashed out at candidate Al Smith as "not fit for the presidency."

He tangled with every governor that came along, mostly on legislation relating to the sale of alcoholic beverages. That Georgia has more legally dry counties than any other state in the nation can largely be credited to the continuing crusades of Louie Newton.

Carter rankled Newton and other Georgia drys when he moved into the governor's mansion by endorsing and working for a bill giving eighteen-year-olds the right to drink. Next he refused to veto a bill allowing municipalities in dry counties to hold local option elections. The crowning insult came in November 1973, when he was quoted by the *Constitution* as saying he would prefer to see every county in Georgia wet.

Newton picked up Methodist bishop Arthur Moore, an old comrade-in-arms in the prohibition fight, and headed downtown. He laid the newspaper on Carter's desk and pointed at the incriminating story. "Governor, are you correctly quoted there?" he asked.

"No, I didn't say that. I said that some dry counties have become so politically corrupt that it might be better if they were wet."

"All right," Newton said. "There's the telephone. Call the *Constitution* and demand a correction."

By Newton's remembrance, "The governor was the picture of embarrassment. He wouldn't say a word."

Baptist state conventions generally hold their annual meetings in November. Both Georgia and South Carolina Baptists met the same week. Deacon Carter was due to speak to South Carolina Baptists. He flew off, leaving Newton to tell the Georgia Baptist Convention that the newspaper quote was not in keeping with Carter's "personal commitment to us." Newton asked that the public affairs committee call on the governor for an "explanation, so that there be no misunderstanding" about his position on prohibition in Georgia.

Carter read the story in the newspapers when he got home. He hurriedly dashed off a message to the Georgia Baptist Convention, declaring, "I have no intention of changing liquor laws to change dry areas to wet. However, in every community that professes to be dry, liquor is sold with the full knowledge of community leaders. My point of view is that it is much more serious to condone the illegal sale of liquor in dry counties than it is to sell liquor legally in wet counties . . . ."

He dispatched his chauffeur to deliver the letter to the Baptists, who were holding their last session at the Wieuca Road Baptist Church in Atlanta. Because they were in the midst of a worship service, the clarification was not read. Carter was reportedly infuriated.

Carter knew that Jack Harwell as editor of *The Christian Index* was on the public affairs committee. He called and asked Harwell to bring a tape recorder. "For once I want to make sure I'm not misquoted," he said.

When the committee arrived, Carter made them comfortable around a coffee table. One of the preacher members (Harwell was the only layman) began lecturing about the evils of alcohol and how important it was that "our Baptist governor make a positive stand" against the wet forces. Carter broke in to say that misuse of alcohol was only a symptom of a greater curse, sin. The preacher apparently didn't hear or understand, for he kept lecturing. Carter reminded him again—louder. Another preacher broke in. Harwell tried to get in a word for Carter. Finally Carter stood up. "I can't believe what's happening here," he said in a raised voice. "Here are you preachers trying to convince two laymen that alcohol is our number one problem when really it's sin. I haven't been to seminary, but I've listened to preaching all my life and I know a little bit about the Bible. I know that sin is the basic problem and misuse of alcohol is just one manifestation of sin."

"Well, Governor," one of the preachers countered, "you've never been a pastor and had to deal with the ravages of alcohol."

"Don't tell me I don't know anything about alcohol. I've dealt with alcoholics all my life. Don't tell me what the Bible teaches." The now famous blue vein on his neck was visibly throbbing.

His patience was gone. "This has degenerated into a theological argument. We're not getting anywhere and I've got more important things to do. Now, if you'll excuse me, please."

One member of the committee recalls that Louie Newton was the main spokesman for the group. Newton claims he wasn't present. But Georgia's crusty Mr. Southern Baptist clearly remembers how he voted in the 1976 presidential election. "I went for Ford. He was the best man." And

Deacon Carter? "He's a good man, but not the strong person we need in the White House. We found out in Georgia that when the water hit the wheel, he wouldn't stand with us against the liquor interests. Something else. When he was running for president, he attended a conference in New York with one of the big liquor tycoons. In my column I quoted the reference in the *New York Times* and said: 'How unfortunate that any candidate for the presidency of the United States would be even a little under obligation to liquor money.' No, Sir, I didn't vote for him. If you ask me, his wife Rosalynn is made out of stronger stuff."

Jimmy Carter's prohibition clashes while governor were not publicized in other southern states. But it was well known that he was no abstainer. A well-circulated picture of him and Rosalynn toasting their thirtieth wedding anniversary on July 7, 1976, with champagne irritated Baptists all over the South. Because of that picture one high SBC official still turns red whenever Carter's name is mentioned.

Southern Baptists are just as strongly against all forms of legalized gambling. In 1976 Georgia Baptists, for example, lobbied their state legislature to defeat a constitutional change that would legalize bingo gambling for nonprofit groups. Louie Newton was in the thick of this successful fight. The Baptist lobby in Georgia was also a major force in holding off a track-parimutuel wagering bill that gambling interests had been trying to get through the legislature for years. Still another Baptist effort led to the defeat of bills that would have allowed Sunday hunting and billiard parlors to remain open on the Christian "Sabbath."

The alcohol, gambling, and blue law hassles between Southern Baptists and their elected representatives may seem contradictory to the traditional Baptist stand on church-state separation. Jimmy Carter says "in general" he is against blue laws. "But I have favored prohibition against the sale of alcoholic beverages on Sunday, and I don't know if there is any logical way to rationalize that."

Southern Baptist morality is rooted in the stern life-style of early America. Says Dr. Duke McCall, president of Southern Seminary in Louisville: "We have a more puritan ethic in our official pronouncements, if not in our personal practices, than many other religious bodies. We regularly make our collective statements about alcoholic beverages, pornography, and dancing. Whatever these sound like to us, they sound like voices out of the past to modern Americans. We are different."

The records of old Baptist and Methodist churches as well are filled with evidences of this ethic. There was hardly a business conference in any church where someone was not chastised or even expunged from the church roll for drinking, gambling, or dancing.

The Baptist and Methodist churches in Plains are typical. In the early twentieth century nearby Magnolia Springs was the frolicking spot for straying church members. "There was a dance pavilion and roller skating rink out there," Alton Carter remembers. "That's where the young people of my generation went to have fun."

A number of Alton Carter's contemporaries were "disciplined" for dancing—"hugging set to music"—at Magnolia Springs. His sister Ethel and her husband Jack Slappy were among them. "Jack was kicked out of the Methodist church. But he later went back and apologized and was restored. Ethel was disciplined by the Baptist church. I don't recollect whether she ever asked for forgiveness or not."

Another transgressor was J. W. "Cap'n" Murray. "When the Methodists kicked him out, he came over to our church," the Carter patriarch chuckles. "Made one of the best members we ever had." Cap'n Murray is Rosalynn Carter's grandfather. How was it then that Rosalynn was

raised a Methodist? "Her momma married a Methodist and
they went to that church. Then Rosalynn married my
nephew Jimmy and changed over to the Baptists."

The Williams family, business competitors to the Carters,
might also still be Methodists if the Plains Methodist
Church had not expelled Oscar Williams for dancing. Like
his friend Cap'n Murray, he came over to the Baptist church
and brought up his family in that congregation. His two
sons, Albert and Frank Williams, are Baptist deacons there
today.

The old dancing taboo is not enforced today and seldom
preached against. But it is the rare Southern Baptist church
that will even sponsor a square dance.

Drinking is still unacceptable, although any pastor will
concede that some of his members probably drink. Never
in his presence, of course. Preachers often make sarcastic
jokes about other denominations who accept alcohol use—
such as "where you find four Episcopalians, you usually
find a 'fifth.'" Only the most "modern" Southern Baptist
ministers will admit to sipping table wine or imbibing an
occasional martini.

Other taboos vary from state to state. For example, coed
bathing is okay in coastal areas, but condemned by some
churches in places where there are few facilities. And
smoking is a "sin" in states where tobacco isn't grown, but
a pleasurable tension breaker in North Carolina, where the
economy is dependent on the weed. North Carolina Baptists' Wake Forest University holds a multimillion-dollar
endowment from the R. J. Reynolds tobacco fortune. The
income from it is reported to be a half million dollars a
year. It was at Wake Forest where *Hustler* publisher Larry
Flynt spoke in 1977 at the invitation of a student group,
setting off a furor among churches in the state.

Southern Baptists have always been selective about applying the Bible to morals because they are a grass-roots

people organized into independent churches. They also preach a highly individualistic gospel, proclaiming that changed persons can change society. Preaching against social evils (except alcoholic beverages, gambling, marijuana, hard drugs, and pornography) is generally taken as meddling in social customs—especially preaching against racial segregation and discrimination.

One agency is consigned to help "create . . . the kind of moral social climate in which the Southern Baptist witness for Christ will be most effective. . . ." This is the Christian Life Commission, the most controversial agency among Southern Baptists and the whipping boy of die-hard segregationists.

It was born in 1913 as the Temperance and Social Service Commission to join other dry forces in the battle for national prohibition. Along the way it provided tracts and made reports against "obscene" literature, racetrack gambling, divorce, Sabbath violations, and organized crime— all evils against which Southern Baptists could unite.

Bigotry and discrimination against Catholic and Jewish immigrants and blacks were ignored. Criticism of the Ku Klux Klan, which terrorized the South in the 1920s, 1930s, and into the 1940s, was avoided.

The Klan boasted of having thousands of southern preachers, lay church leaders, and politicians in its membership. In 1923, the year Earl and Lillian Carter were married, it was reported that the Klan had 227 members in the U.S. House of Representatives, twenty-seven men in the Senate, and five members in Harding's cabinet, most from the South. If only half true, this is astounding.

The following year on October 1, the day of Jimmy Carter's birth, newspapers reported that the governor of Georgia, C. M. Walker, had given an opening address at the national convocation of the Klan. In a publicity release, the Klan quoted the governor as making "forceful arguments against the hierarchy of the Catholic church and the threatened destruction of America by encroachment of Jewish, Celtic, and Mediterranean races."

Southern Baptist "social gospelers" tried in the thirties to add a research bureau to investigate causes of labor grievances and racial injustices. The leader of this effort, E. McNeill Poteat, Jr., a missionary returned from China, charged the denomination with failing to relate biblical concepts to contemporary society.

The "Poteat Pimple Bureau" and the "South-wide Smelling Committee," as it was called, was set upon with a vengeance. It was all right to provide information to the churches, as the Temperance and Social Service Commission had done, critics said. But a "fact-findin' detective agency" staffed by high-salaried experts meddling in business and politics was something else. Jesus and the Apostles hadn't tried to clean up the slums of Jerusalem. They had proclaimed salvation to individuals, not a social gospel. Opponents added that cleaning up the world was futile anyway, since the final judgment wasn't far off.

This same conflict was raging within denominations in the North, except for one important difference. There the social gospelers had departed from basic evangelical doctrines, such as the divine inspiration of Scripture and the deity of Christ. This resulted in a split between modernists and fundamentalists and the spawning of new denominations. The Northern Baptist Convention (now American Baptist Churches), born from the 1845 schism with the South, lost thousands of members to the new conservative Baptist movement and the General Association of Regular Baptists.

Southern Baptist losses had come earlier to the landmark revolt against denominational boards. But this time there were few departures because liberal theology wasn't a big issue in the South, and because there were enough votes to cool the ardor of Poteat and his social gospel friends.

Southern Baptists rocked along in the cradle of southern culture until 1954 when the Supreme Court ruling that all public school segregation is "inherently unequal" jolted them awake. Ironically, the decision was an interpretation of the Fourteenth Amendment, which had been adopted as an extension of the First Amendment, the first of the Bill of Rights that Virginia Baptists had been influential in securing.

Seven years before, a little-noticed "charter of principles" had been nudged through SBC channels by the Social Service Commission. The charter obliged Baptists to love their neighbors and recognize the inherent worth of the individual and the right to social justice in a democracy. It called for church members to overcome prejudices, protest injustices, demand equality under law, pay fair wages, and even join in interracial activities. It was high sounding and well meaning, but since nothing had been done to disturb the southern way of life, the rank and file paid no attention.

Perceptive Southern Baptist leaders could see the handwriting on the wall. Fortunately, the 1954 convention was held in St. Louis, far removed from areas most strongly opposed to integration. The Christian Life Commission (formerly the Social Service Commission) introduced a resolution declaring that the Court's decision was "in harmony with the constitutional guarantee of equal freedom to all citizens, and with the Christian principles of equal justice and love for all men." It passed against a minority of loud opposition.

The onus was now on the giant Sunday School Board, which provided teaching material for the churches. The challenge was to change racial attitudes and practices that had been inbred for generations. Moving too fast might ignite a revolt, with the autonomous churches switching to other publishers that would not disturb their conscience on race. Moving too slow would be a bertayal of Christian faith.

While planners in other denominations were preparing to sledgehammer their constitutencies into doing right, SBC Sunday School Board executives consulted secretly with sociologists from the Massachusetts Institute of Technology and the University of Iowa. James L. Sullivan, then head of the Sunday School Board, recalls: "They told us a revolution couldn't be effected by coercion, but only by educational process. This would take at least seven years. We decided to take their advice and make a general approach: God created all mankind. God had a purpose for every life. As Christians we could do no less than help each person discover their divine purpose and to reach their highest level of potential. We didn't deal directly with race, because we wanted to hang on to our people. We couldn't publicize our purposes. The segregationists would have blocked us."

As Sullivan remembers, the Sunday School Board walked a tightrope between the Klan, the John Birch Society, and the White Citizens Council on one hand and civil rights activists on the other. "Each side was waiting for an opportunity to attack us."

An opportunity for segregationists came in 1964 when a Sunday School Board publication recommended James Baldwin's *The Fire Next Time* as a book to help understand black problems. "It was a mistake," Sullivan says. "The editor who was supposed to check that issue had just resigned and it got through."

The fire fell. A jackleg organization called the Circuit Riders took pages filled with profanities from the Baldwin book, photostated the Sunday School Board cover, and distributed bound copies so as to make readers believe it had been printed in Nashville. Hundreds of churches canceled literature orders.

During this time the giant publishing agency could do nothing right. As a further example, the Sunday School Board produced a new Sunday evening teaching periodical named *Quest*. Thousands of copies were printed in anticipation of approval at the upcoming New Orleans convention. When the periodical was presented for a vote, a preacher howled that Quest was the name of an intimate deodorant for women. "We aren't questing for anything. We've found the truth," he shouted. Waves of laughter rolled across the auditorium as Sunday School Board officials turned red. *Quest* was rejected by a thunder of no votes.

Other agencies were also trying to educate the constituency. The Woman's Missionary Union and the Home Mission Board spoke plainer than the Sunday School Board, spelling out injustices to blacks and urging white Baptists to work actively for change. They were deluged with angry letters and threats from churches to cut off financial support. Boldest of all was the small "Un-Christian" Life Commission, as opponents now dubbed it. Almost every year at the annual convention there was a determined effort to abolish the CLC or reduce its appropriation.

Congressman Brooks Hays of Arkansas, a racial moderate, was chairman of the CLC's board of trustees when Orville Faubus became governor. Faubus, a Southern Baptist and an avowed hold-the-line segregationist, looked around for a suitable church to join in Little Rock and reportedly settled on Immanuel Baptist. According to the story that later leaked, he summoned the pastor, W. O. Vaught, Jr., to his office and stated his intention. Vaught replied, in effect, that the governor should choose a church more compatible with his racial views.

The Little Rock crisis erupted before the world in 1957

when Faubus defied a federal court order and called out
the National Guard to prevent integration of Central High
School. He was opposed by Congressman Hays and all but
one of the Southern Baptist pastors in Little Rock.

Hays had tried to mediate between Faubus and Eisenhower, but the governor had gone too far. The president
sent in federal troops to enforce the integration and Faubus
backed away.

It was a hollow victory for Hays, who had been elected
president of the Southern Baptist Convention earlier in the
summer. In his campaign for reelection to Congress, he was
defeated by a write-in vote for a rabid segregationist. And
Faubus, in a public opinion poll, was listed among the ten
"most admired" men in America.

The agony of Southern Baptist leaders trying to correct
their denomination's morality on civil rights continued.
After 1960 the focal point of resistance centered on Foy
Valentine, the new executive director of the CLC. A drawling Texan, Valentine could sting with his moral applications of the Gospel. A sampling: "We must not be like the
role-playing, stiff old Lutheran minister in John Updike's
Rabbit Run, of whom it was said that 'even in his under-
shirt he somehow wore vestments.'" "I know some church
members who have changed their minds about hell and
tithing, but not about racism." And he often quoted his
theological professor, W. T. Conner, at Southwestern
Seminary: "The proof of the Holy Spirit's presence is not
how high you jump, but how straight you walk when you
hit the ground."

Every year during the traumatic sixties, Valentine made
the segregationists see red when he reported for the Christian Life Commission. He seldom got all he asked, but he
got the CLC on the record.

Valentine and other outspoken SBC agency leaders were
protected in their jobs by sympathetic trustees. Pastors

calling for equal rights for blacks did so at great risk. Scores were driven from their pulpits to seek employment elsewhere. One, the Reverend Paul Turner, was severely beaten by a white mob after he escorted twelve black students into a high school in Clinton, Tennessee.

Among the courageous pastors who survived was G. Avery Lee, minister of the First Baptist Church in Ruston, Louisiana. Lee preached a sermon titled "God Has Made [all races] of One Blood." The state's lieutenant governor, then a member of the church, declared, "If he gets away with that sermon he's here for life." Two years later Lee repeated the sermon. The church was then constructing a new building. The local bank called in the deacons and threatened to cancel the construction loan unless they buttoned their pastor's lips on race. The deacons refused, saying, "We may not like what he preaches, but we don't think the bank or anyone else should tell him what to say."

But for every pastor who spoke clearly against racial discrimination from the pulpit, scores remained silent or acquiesced to racist church leaders.

Hundreds of churches, such as Plains Baptist, quietly passed rules instructing ushers not to seat "Negroes and any other Civil Rights agitators," or reaffirmed old bylaws excluding blacks. The Plains action came in August 1965, when the nightly news was showing battles and burnings in Los Angeles (Watts) and other American cities. A hundred Georgia state troopers occupied nearby Americus where blacks were demonstrating for voter registration and a young white Baptist had been shot and killed. The strife had spilled over into Plains, with civil rights workers becoming the target of bricks and bottles from angry citizens.

On Sunday afternoon, August 1, the Plains deacons heard that "agitators" had tried to crash churches in Americus that morning. Fearing their church might be next, they met that night and agreed to ask the church to "instruct" ushers not to seat them for worship services. According to the minutes, Pastor Robert Harris was present, but Deacon Jimmy Carter, then a state senator, was not. There is no record that the pastor objected. In his defense, his widow, Dr. Ethel Harris, asks: "If you walked into a room and smelled gas, would you light a match?"

The church vote came two weeks later with the pastor absent. Jimmy and Rosalynn Carter had been in Atlanta attending a wedding and had hurried back when they heard that the deacons planned to introduce the resolution excluding blacks. Carter was not known in Plains as an extremist on race questions, but it was common knowledge that he had refused to join the local White Citizens Council and that his business had also been boycotted for a time by segregationist farmers.

Carter spoke and asked the church to reject his fellow deacons' proposal and permit entry of any blacks who seemed to sincerely want to worship. His plea failed and they voted 54-6 (Jimmy and Rosalynn Carter, sons Chip and Jeff, Lillian Carter, and Homer Harris, a hard-of-hearing farmer) to approve the deacons' request. Afterward, "several dozen" nonvoters told Carter they felt the church should be open to all people, but had not wanted to speak in the business conference.

The turning point for Southern Baptists in the civil rights struggle came after Martin Luther King was assassinated on April 4, 1968. Moderates suddenly became bold; gradualists shifted to a higher gear. In Atlanta white and black Baptist pastors began meeting in joint conferences for the first time ever.

Baptist editors penned stern editorials. Georgia's Jack Harwell, for example, pulled copy from the issue of *The Christian Index* ready for the press. " 'The Southern way of life' for too many decades has meant a way of life that denies full citizenship to all people," he wrote. "It's time to

make 'the Southern way of life' stand for a Christian respect
for people of all races." Editors at the Home Mission Board
allowed aroused seminary students to pay for a full-page
pictorial tribute to King in *Home Missions* magazine. These
and similar actions by other Baptist editors brought a tor-
rent of mail and phone calls alternating between praise and
condemnation. *The Christian Index* alone dropped 10,000
in circulation, partly because of his editorial, Harwell
thinks, and partly as a result of a recently announced price
increase.

A sampling of letters received by *Home Missions* magazine in reaction to the memorial picture of Martin Luther
King indicates how one segment of the Southern Baptist
grass roots felt at this time:

> . . . You print the picture of Martin Luther King
> on the back cover. That is flaunting a red flag at a
> bull.   Arabia, Louisiana

> . . . The fruits of this man [King] were those of
> violence and disorder. I would not be surprised
> now to see a full page advertisement paid for by
> Falstaff Brewing Company in *Home Missions*.
>   Harvest, Alabama

> Please cancel my subscription. . . . It just makes
> me sick at my stomach. . . .
>   Lenoir City, Tennessee

> . . . It's bad enough that leaders of our nation have
> bowed down to this Communist leader, resulting
> in complete chaos and disregard for law as a re-
> sult of his 'nonviolent'—extremely violent—move-
> ment, but to have our Southern Baptist colleges
> and leaders promote and allow it to infiltrate our
> literature is unforgiveable. . . .
>   Birmingham, Alabama

> . . . What a disgrace to our Christian way of life!!!
> God have mercy upon us Baptists. What is wrong
> with our leaders?   Whatley, Alabama
>
> Our concern has grown over the past months with
> regards to the leftist-socialistic leaning of *Home
> Missions* magazine. After receiving the June issue
> we have really had it. . . . Cancel our subscrip-
> tion.   Maitland, Florida

Ignoring the backlash, seventy-one Southern Baptist
leaders presented a crisis statement to the annual convention in Houston. They confessed a share of the blame for
"the shame of lawlessness, the agony of injustice, and the
spirit of strife" in the nation. They committed themselves
to "strive to obtain and secure for every person equality of
human and civil rights" and to "accept every Christian as
a brother . . . and welcome to faith and worship every person irrespective of race or class." They begged "fellow
Southern Baptists" to "dare to accept the full demands of
the love and lordship of Christ in human relationships and
urgent ministry."

Adopted by the Houston convention, it was one of the
strongest declarations ever made by a religious body on
race. Then, astonishingly, the unpredictable Southern Baptists elected W. A. Criswell as their new president. More
surprise followed when Criswell, renowned for his criticisms of the civil rights movement, announced that he
had repented. "Never had I been so blind," he told the denomination's executive committee. He asked SBC pastors
and churches: "Can't we agree to love all mankind, to call
no man common or unclean?" Then he returned to Dallas
and asked his church to reverse its long-standing segregationist policy and become a "Church of the Open Door."

If the church did not change, he hinted, it might become the target of "designed destruction." The congregation voted his wish.

The crisis statement and the public repentance of Criswell set segregationists back permanently. A new attitude was shaping up among Southern Baptists. A new South was aborning, even though pockets of hard-core resistance in places such as Sumter County, Georgia, would remain.

The much-maligned Christian Life Commission emerged from the civil rights trauma as "the conscience of Southern Baptists." It could now speak to Southern Baptists on broader aspects of morality, but not without controversy.

The CLC began holding annual national seminars, inviting a mix of Southern Baptists and speakers representing other views to participate. The one for 1970 was scheduled for Atlanta and titled "Toward Authentic Morality for Modern Man."

The program was like nothing Southern Baptists had ever seen. Varying views on the "*Playboy* philosophy" were to be presented by Anson Mount, public affairs manager for *Playboy*, and ethics professor William M. Pinson, Jr., from Southwestern Seminary. And "Situation Ethics" was to be debated by Joseph Fletcher, who had coined the term, and Henlee Barnette, an ethics professor from Southern Seminary. To make the seminar even more controversial, black legislator Julian Bond was to talk on "The Constructive Uses of Black Power."

CLC opponents who had been forced to eat integration crow joined other critics to condemn the seminar. Valentine and his staff, they said, were giving atheists and fornicators a Baptist platform and paying them to speak with Baptist money. "Lie with dogs and you'll get covered with fleas," said one critic, quoting an old aphorism.

The CLC responded that only SBC leaders had been

invited; that their registration fees were paying for the speakers. They went ahead with the seminar.

The meaty give-and-take exchange of philosophies put Southern Baptists up front in newspapers where before they had been relegated to religion pages. The speakers came well prepared.

Mount, for example, said that the *"Playboy* philosophy" was a response to a "very real anti-pleasure, anti-play streak of puritanism in today's society." It was based on a "profound concern for the rights of the individual in a free society," not a society "completely devoid of restrictions," but one in which the individual and his interests are paramount. Organized religion, Mount charged, was guilty of being antisexual, not *Playboy.* "It is religion . . . that has looked upon woman as a depersonalized object or possession and has continuously associated her with its antagonism toward sex."

His opponent, Dr. Pinson, denied that religion was the anti-sex culprit and quoted a former president of the American Psychiatric Association, Francis J. Braceland, as saying that premartial sexual relations resulting from exposure to the so-called new morality had greatly increased the number of young people in mental hospitals. *Playboy's* problem, Pinson declared, was that it wasn't sexy enough. "It misses the full power and beauty of sex by majoring on the physical aspect of sexual relations. . . . It talks more about what is permissible than about what is preferable. It lacks a clear statement of what the ideal in sex should be. *Playboy* dismisses any suggestion that sex is important enough, powerful enough, and wonderful enough to need careful discipline. Others may go hopping down the bunny trail," the professor concluded, "but I'll follow Him who said, 'I am the way, the truth, and the life.'"

As it happened, another Baptist professor, Dr. Frank

Stagg, drew the most criticism for a speech on militarism. "Authentic morality," Stagg said, "could only be expressed" when the United States withdrew from Vietnam and dropped out of the arms race. The CLC and Stagg's seminary in Louisville were bombarded with angry telegrams.

The controversial Baptist agency took the flak in stride and continued planning programs that featured a broad range of views on crucial social issues. The 1975 seminar, for example, probed integrity in politics, health care, world hunger, family relationships, race relations, the mass media, and even in the organizational life of Southern Baptists. Cecil E. Sherman, pastor of First Baptist Church, Asheville, North Carolina, lambasted SBC agencies for failing to disclose salaries of their top personnel. "Baptists have a right to know what their leaders make," he said. (This was made mandatory in 1977, but only after spirited opposition. Top salaries, with fringe benefits, run up to $60,000 a year —no mere missionary pay.)

The CLC's 1976 seminar on citizenship was held in Washington and drew some of the biggest names in government. Senators Humphrey, Kennedy, McGovern, Baker, Tower, and Hatfield spoke, as did congressional representatives Barbara Jordan, Andrew Young, Les Aspin, and John B. Anderson. Such a distinguished roster pointed to the growing influence of Southern Baptists on decisionmakers in the nation.

A raft of thorny moral matters confronted Southern Baptists in 1977. At their June convention in Kansas City they took on an "action campaign" against violence and moral laxity on television. "If we don't control television, it will control us," warned CLC Executive Director Foy Valentine.

They denounced "abortion on demand and all governmental policies and actions which permit this." Only a parliamentary wrangle probably kept them from asking for a constitutional amendment banning abortion except for rape or incest or when a mother's life is endangered.

They turned their big guns on gays. "I appreciate compassion on sinners, but we've been too easy," thundered a Louisiana preacher. "God says the homosexuals will end in hell."

"God was against homosexuality in Israel and destroyed Sodom for it," declared a California pastor. "If we don't take a stand against it now, better look for the fire."

Then they voted to oppose the "radical scheme" of gays "to secure legal, social, and religious acceptance by portraying homosexuality as normal behavior," and commended Baptist Sunday school teacher Anita Bryant's "courageous stand" in her successful crusade for repeal of the gay rights ordinance in Miami.

Does this mean that the descendants of the people who fought hardest for human rights in colonial America are now out to police the nation? Hardly. Southern Baptists see their moral crusades as part of their missionary cause. As Foy Valentine puts it: "Christianity validates the primacy of persons, to be sure, but it also affirms the validity of principles. Today's world could use some more of the unambivalent principles of the Ten Commandments and the Sermon on the Mount."

Jimmy Carter meant the same thing when he "hope[d] all of you [government workers] living in sin will get married."

9

«« »»

Helping People

THE YEAR Jimmy Carter was appointed to the naval academy and said good-bye to Plains, 1942, a Georgia preacher came home from Southern Baptist Seminary in Louisville with a Ph.D. He was Clarence Jordan, the seventh son of ten children, a banker's son from Talbot County, where Carter's ancestor James had once owned a plantation. Jordan (pronounced Jerden), a lean, drawling, folksy man of the soil, was destined to become the most hated man in the Baptist stronghold, Sumter County—all because he tried to practice the New Testament as he understood it and help poor blacks. He was considered a radical, an unwelcome prophet, a man whose applications of Scripture could not be tolerated in the cocoon of southern culture that Southern Baptists had wrapped around themselves.

Jordan had earned a degree in agriculture before going to the seminary. His doctorate was in New Testament Greek, and his professors felt he had the makings of a scholar. But a stint as a city missionary in Louisville had made him aware of the plight of poor blacks migrating to urban ghettos from sharecropper cabins in the Deep South. And his study of the New Testament in the original language had convinced him that the ideal of Jesus ran contrary to the traditions of his fathers. Now he was back to put into practice what he had learned, come the White Citizens Council or the Ku Klux Klan.

His dream was a model farm where blacks could learn skills in agriculture, for county agents at that time in Georgia never got around to helping "niggers." His plan further called for Christian "partners," black and white, sharing equally, to operate the farm as a demonstration of their faith. With a down payment from a merchant friend, he purchased 440 acres along Dawson Road, about four miles from Plains and eight from Americus, the Sumter County seat. Then he, his wife Florence, and a missionary couple recently returned from Burma moved into an old four-room house on the property. Jordan named the place *Koinonia*, a Greek word used in the New Testament to describe a spirit of sharing.

The Klan came first, just a couple of red-necked farmers who had heard the couples "had been taking meals with niggers. We don't allow the sun to set on anybody who eats with niggers," they warned. Jordan was an easygoing fellow who didn't believe in provoking violence. He grinned and introduced himself as a Southern Baptist preacher, a native Georgian, just back from the seminary. "I've heard of people who had power over the sun," he ventured, "but I've never met any until now. I'm pleased to meet you." The Klansmen laughed. Jordan offered another wry comment. And so it went, talking and laughing, until the sun went down and they left without ever mentioning their business again.

Jordan and the others went about cleaning up the farm, getting it ready for planting, dropping around to see neighbors, black and white, talking corn and peanut yields, and inviting them to return the visit. Before long other "partners" joined, mostly friends Jordan had met in the seminary, and black farmers were coming regularly for on-the-job lessons. Then their wives started coming for sewing and cooking lessons from Florence and other women at the farm.

The farm prospered. Jordan developed the first mobile peanut harvester in the county, even before the Carters in Plains got one. Koinonia also built up a herd of milk cows as sort of a bovine library. A poor family could check one out, return the animal when dry, and get another one.

After the first call from the Klan, the whites of Sumter didn't seem to pay much attention to what was going on. The Koinonia families seldom went out; they couldn't afford to. They did join and participate in the activities of the nearby all-white Rehoboth Baptist Church. Since they didn't bring any black friends, nobody got upset for a while. During this time Jordan was invited to preach in white Baptist churches around the county. He said some pretty radical things, such as, "Religion that don't help people ain't worth a plug nickel." When his south Georgia audiences finally caught on that what he had in mind was helping blacks get their share of the Lord's benefits, tongues began to wag.

The opinions of Jordan and others from Koinonia un-settled the Rehoboth church. Because Jordan was a preacher trained in one of their seminaries, and Florence and the others were "so nice," they didn't quite know what to do until a dusky young stranger came with the Koinonia group one Sunday morning in 1950. He was an agricultural student from India, up from Florida State University to look at the farm. The deacons took him for a "disguised nigger" and paid Jordan a visit. After considerable discussion they realized that Jordan was a worse heretic than they had thought. He didn't believe Christians should take up arms, not even in war. And he felt the well-to-do ought to share with the less fortunate. He didn't recommend that everybody put their money in a common pot and all share alike as they did at Koinonia, but it was something worth thinking about, he said.

The troubled deacons finally recommended that the Jordans and their friends be put out of the Rehoboth church for "disrupting the Christian spirit and unity" and other lesser offenses. The church so voted. When the Koinonia partners continued to attend, saying "We love you no matter what," the deacons ordered them to stay away.

The real persecution started in 1955 after Jordan tried to help two blacks enroll in the Georgia State College of Business in Atlanta. There were ugly phone calls in the night. Merchants in Americus launched a boycott, refusing to sell seed or to buy produce from Koinonia. When the partners opened a roadside market, gunmen roared by and shot it up. When they reopened, the market was bombed.

The Jordans' fourteen-year-old son was threatened at Plains High School. They sent him to live with friends and attend school in South Dakota, where he would be safe. Then Sumter County authorities canceled the integrated children's camp Koinonia had scheduled for the summer. One complaint was that at past camps they had let children see pigs being born. On that one, Jordan told a court hearing he couldn't see how sows giving birth could be immoral, unless God was immoral since he had planned it that way. "Anyway, our hogs are kinda stupid," he added. "We can't train them to give birth when the kids aren't around."

The violence continued. Three hundred Koinonia fruit trees were chopped down. Sugar was put in the gas tank of a car belonging to Jack Singletary, a white supporter from Plains. Singletary had parked his car outside an Americus hospital and was visiting his son who was dying of leukemia. There were more bombings, a machine gun attack, then a chilling visit by a motorcade of seventy carloads of Klansmen.

Jordan appealed to county and state authorities, Senator

Herman Talmadge, then to the federal government and got no relief. The U. S. attorney general referred the request back to Georgia. The Georgia attorney general replied only that his office had been investigataing Koinonia for "subversive activities." Finally the Koinonians were summoned before the Sumter grand jury in 1957 for investigation of Communist affiliation. Jordan tried to explain the difference between Jesus and Marx, but the farmers on the jury didn't appear to understand. None of those perpetrating violence against the Christian group was arrested. Instead, the Koinonians were lectured for provoking the attacks.

Clarence Jordan was a peace-loving man. He was known to fight back on only two occasions. Once when a mule kicked him, he kicked back. The second lapse came after a Sumter County white went to Talbot County and told Jordan's dying father that his son was stirring up trouble in Sumter. When Jordan learned what he had done, he hurried to the man's office. "If you ever do that again," he warned, "I'll have to ask Jesus to excuse me for fifteen minutes while I beat hell out of you."

Nothing changed until the Birdsey Flour and Feed Store in Americus broke the boycott. The store was bombed and that upset the editor of the *Americus Times-Recorder*. He couldn't "believe that such a thing could happen in Americus, a city of peace-loving, church-going, cultured people. . . . Regardless of how we feel toward Koinonia," he editorialized, "this violence, from whatever source it comes, must be stopped."

The chamber of commerce sent a committee to Koinonia to ask the group to leave Georgia "before somebody gets killed or lynched." The Koinonia partners refused and launched a direct-mail shelled pecan business. "Help us get the nuts out of Georgia," they advertised. There was more violence, even beatings. Three Koinonians were jailed. When white children of Koinonia partners were refused enrollment at the Americus High School, the group went to court. In the hearing, Jordan was asked if he believed racial integration was morally right. "Our Christian practice," he replied, "is to accept anyone as a brother who is a son of God, whether white or black or what." A lawyer school board member was won over. He apologized to Koinonia and tried to be a reconciler during the ensuing civil rights struggle. His law practice was boycotted and he was forced to move away.

The violence finally subsided in the sixties. Koinonia established a Fund for Humanity, bought more land, and built small, modest brick homes for poor black families who paid the fund back at $25 a month. Jordan also began translating his "Cotton-Patch" New Testament, using Deep South names and idioms that anyone could understand. In the Gospel "according to Clarence," Nazareth was Valdosta (Georgia) and Jerusalem was Atlanta; Pontius Pilate was governor of Georgia and Herod was governor of Alabama. In the parable of the Good Samaritan, a white Sunday school teacher asked Jesus, "Who is my neighbor?"

> Then Jesus laid into him and said, "A man was going from Atlanta to Albany and some gangsters held him up. When they had robbed him of his wallet and brand-new suit, they beat him up and drove off in his car, leaving him unconscious on the shoulder of the highway.
>
> "Now it just so happened that a white preacher was going down that same highway. When he saw the fellow, he stepped on the gas and went scooting by.
>
> "Shortly afterward a white Gospel songleader came down the road, and when he saw what had happened, he too stepped on the gas.
>
> "Then a black man traveling that way came

upon the fellow, and what he saw moved him to
tears. He stopped and bound up his wounds as
best he could, drew some water from his water-
jug to wipe away the blood and then laid him on
the back seat. He drove on into Albany and took
him to the hospital and said to the nurse, 'You all
take good care of this white man I found on the
highway. Here's the only two dollars I got, but
you all keep account of what he owes, and if he
can't pay it, I'll settle up with you when I make a
a pay-day.'

"Now if you had been the man held up by
the gangsters, which of these three—the white
preacher, the white songleader, or the black man
—would you consider to have been your neighbor?"

The teacher of the adult Bible class said,
"Why, of course, the nig—I mean, er . . . well, er
. . . the one who treated him kindly."

Jesus said, "Well, then, you get going and start
living like that."

Jordan had now become a hero to many outside the
South. In his speeches around the country, he often told
about a church in Georgia that spent $25,000 to install a
large circulating fountain on its lawn when hundreds of
neighboring homes didn't have running water. "I was
thirsty, and ye built me a fountain," he mocked. He also
reasoned that churches should spend at least as much housing their brothers, whom they had seen, as building a house
for God, whom they had never seen.

In May 1969, Jordan was invited to speak to the American
(Northern) Baptist Convention in Seattle. "The job of the
Church," he declared, "is to be the womb through which
God can bring his children into this world. Now the early
Church was willing to become pregnant. But . . . the trouble

with (the Church) today is that she either has passed the menopause or she is on the pill. . . . Or perhaps even worse, the Church has gone awhoring."

At fifty-seven, he was visibly slowing. That fall he collapsed at the farm from an apparent heart attack and died. The Sumter County coroner's office refused to send a doctor to pronounce him dead. Nor did any Southern Baptist church in the area offer facilities for his funeral. They buried him in an old cedar crate on the farm with only about seventy-five relatives, friends, and black neighbors standing by. No white politicians were there, not even Jimmy Carter, who was running for governor again. To have come and paid tribute to the uncle of his young friend Hamilton Jordan—now one of his top presidential aides— would have been political suicide. Recalling Carter's avoidance of Koinonia, Florence Jordan says gently, "He never visited here, but his silence was no more than anyone else's."

During his seventeen years at Koinonia, Clarence Jordan never repudiated his denomination. Southern Baptists, except for a few admirers at the Home Mission Board, the Christian Life Commission, and Southern Seminary, ignored him, although his "Cotton-Patch" translation was sold in Baptist bookstores. The great powers of the denomination shunned him as an extremist, as they did the Ku Klux Klan. His death was hardly noted.

But the basic ideas of Jordan—that Christians were to be reconcilers and servants in society and that people were more important than structures and traditions—were being mulled over in the seminaries and some of the denominational agencies, particularly at the Home Mission Board. How much influence Jordan had in this ferment is hard to gauge, for these thoughtful Southern Baptists were reading books on church renewal and social ills by authors from outside the denomination. And they were listening to pastors who were pursuing new forms of ministry outside the pale.

One of the most influential pastors was Gordon Cosby, a classmate of Jordan's at Louisville. Cosby came out of the army chaplaincy with a new perspective on what a church should be. In 1954 he established the independent Church of the Savior in Washington, D. C., with perhaps the toughest requirements for membership of any church in the nation: a year or more of preliminary study, a discipline of daily prayer and Scripture reading, faithful attendance at worship, giving at least a tithe of income, and active participation in a mission service group. The latter could involve medical work, teaching literacy, cleaning up dilapidated houses, even helping congressmen find God's will in decisionmaking.

Cosby's plan was to identify a need, then invite a group of members to cluster around and devise a plan for action. Christians, he said, were not to be moralists or builders of a materialistic kingdom, but servants to the struggling and the oppressed. As Cosby's wife Mary, who had been raised in a Baptist pastor's home in Mascon, Georgia, put it later to a SBC Christian Life Commission seminar on integrity: "When an outcast of the earth can meet any member of the church of the Lord Jesus Christ and know when he meets him, 'This man is for me,' then the church has found integrity."

Cosby and Jordan were birds of the same feather. But Cosby was more acceptable to Southern Baptists, perhaps because he did not challenge the racism of the Deep South as Jordan had.

Cosby became close friends with Findley Edge, professor of religious education at Southern Seminary in Louisville. One of the most creative thinkers among SBC teachers, Edge was captivated by Cosby's methods for ministry. "I have become so imbued with his thinking," Edge later wrote, "that I am unable to tell what is mine and what is his."

The Edge-Cosby synthesis held that Southern Baptist churches were ineffective in touching the nerve endings of hurting persons, especially in the cities, for two reasons: (1) The clergy were trying to do all the work. Edge and Cosby saw the primary clergy role as training and equipping the laity for ministry. (2) Church work was relegated to Sundays and Wednesday nights in the church buildings. The buildings needed to be utilized seven days a week, they said. Church workers should get into the community and help people.

Edge began holding church renewal conferences at the seminary in Louisville, inviting concerned SBC pastors, seminary students, and laymen to hear and discuss new ideas with Cosby, Keith Miller, Elton Trueblood, and other challenging voices from outside the denomination. It was Edge's belief that the SBC had become too dull and ingrown, too self-serving, too smug and self-contained. To see that he was correct, one only had to attend SBC conventions and conferences and hear the loyal sons of the denomination praising one another and subtly pressuring pastors to keep their churches in conformity with the denominational programs. And one could attend practically any SBC church and observe tired holdover rituals from pioneer days. Freshness and creativity in SBC churches was rare in the late fifties and early sixties.

The civil rights revolution was breaking and pulpits were silent. The Jesus movement was exploding, and most Southern Baptists were unable to understand why the young people weren't content with the "you-sit-still-and-I'll-instill" lessons and sermons from church leaders. Family life was disintegrating and pulpit moralists were thundering against divorce. Alcoholism was spreading and drug addiction was on the rise, and the preachers were raging against the liquor traffic and the drug peddlers. To many young seminarians it seemed that the institutional SBC church was irrelevant and obstructionist to efforts of compassion and mercy.

Some young divines left the denomination and joined more socially active church bodies. Some sought fulfillment in VISTA and the Peace Corps, and some took pastorates and began flailing at the windmills of tradition, only to be thrown out of their pulpits by angry laity. Some merely griped a lot, then settled down to try and make the system work.

Edge and other worried professors tried to keep the frustrated young men in the field. Agency leaders sought to reshape and redirect policies. Here and there new light began to shine as churches groped to adjust their programs to meet community needs.

The Oakhurst Baptist Church of Decatur, Georgia, a nearby suburb of Atlanta, was one of those churches. The Oakhurst neighborhood had changed swiftly from majority white to majority black. White members who had moved away were joining further-out churches more convenient to their homes. The church had new buildings and a half-million-dollar indebtedness, and was sinking fast.

The usual options for a church in this situation were to sell the property and relocate or insulate from the newcomers and try to hold the status quo. Oakhurst's new minister, Canadian-born John Nichol, and key laity felt neither solution was Christian. They decided to remain and serve the community, white and black.

They sought guidance materials for coping with the population transition from denominational agencies. None were available, but the Home Mission Board said it would make a two-year study of what to do in such situations.

Oakhurst couldn't wait. Leaders attended one of Findley Edge's renewal conferences at the seminary in Louisville. They invited Clarence Jordan up for a "revival." (Jordan returned their honorarium of $200 to help their black janitor buy a house.) Then, in a series of dramatic steps, they sold part of the property, took on a social worker whose salary was paid by the mission board, began aggressively canvassing the black newcomers and inviting them to services, and launched a series of helping ministries designed to show that the church cared for the total community.

For example, they turned the parking lot into a skating rink on Saturdays and held skating parties for neighborhood children. They showed free movies on Saturday night. They opened a coffeehouse for older youths in the sanctuary basement, which had never been used before. They invited neighborhood mothers to a Wednesday club for social chit-chat, study, and classes in cooking, sewing, budgeting, and family planning. They began tutoring disadvantaged children in the church library. They equipped a mobile library to take books directly to homes. They started a boys' club, art classes, and a baby clinic using church facilities.

Such expansion caused trauma and many old members left. But Sunday school attendance stabilized at around 400, compared to 800 before blacks began moving into the neighborhood.

The headquarters of the Home Mission Board was only a few miles away. Several staff members, including Walker Knight, editor of the board's leadership magazine *Home Missions*, were members at Oakhurst and kept board officials informed of what was taking place.

The executive director of the giant mission agency was then Arthur Rutledge, a Texan. No standpatter, Rutledge was determined that the board react positively to the cataclysmic upheavals in American society.

Not that Southern Baptists hadn't been involved in social

ministries. The denomination owned and operated fifty-three colleges and universities, seven academies, thirty-three hospitals, twenty retirement homes, and twenty-seven children's homes. These represented vast institutional investments. The hospitals alone had assests of over half a billion dollars. The children's homes, which cared for about 3,750 children, were worth $60 million.

Additionally, the Home Mission Board had goodwill centers scattered across the South, plus several emergency missions for derelicts and unwed mothers.

Rutledge knew these institutions were reaching only a small percentage of people needing help. Something had to be done to break the stained glass barrier, to get church members out of their comfortable pews and practicing what the church preached.

Rutledge gave editor Knight the go-ahead to begin sensitizing readers of the leadership magazine to family ills, sexual perversion, unemployment, poverty, racial discrimination, juvenile deliquency, and other acute social maladies. The new format was answered with howls of indignation from pastors and deacons in the Deep South that the Home Mission Board was straying from the revivalistic old-time Gospel. "Give us less controversy and more Gospel," was a frequent plea. Rutledge backed Knight to the hilt.

At the same time, the mission board was stepping up chaplain appointments to prisons, hospitals, and industries and recruiting a new breed of missionaries called directors of social ministries. A shift of role and goals for missionaries was also instituted. A missionary was to be primarily a catalyst and get local Baptists to work. The overall plan was to decentralize and depaternalize operations and lead local churches into a whole-person ministry of serving all the people in their communities.

A spot-check of Southern Baptist home missionaries and

rank-and-file members who are making things happen indicates the present significance of these new directions to
the denomination and the country.

Take "Super Rev" Wayne Hulon, one of a growing number of industrial chaplains who are commissioned by the
Home Mission Board and paid by private companies to
serve as counselors and ombudsmen for their employees.
Hulon, a twenty-four-year-old, Seminary-trained bachelor,
is director of pastoral services for an Atlanta trucking company that has over a thousand drivers.

Some of the tough, double-clutching truckers weren't
sure they liked their new chaplain at first. One hauled off
and punched Hulon. The preacher, who had lost a pro-
football contract because of injuries in an auto accident,
instinctively punched back. They later became friends
when Hulon visited the man's wife in the hospital.

In his counseling Hulon handles everything from drug
overdose to slam-bang marital spats. "I try to correlate
good mental health and good theology," he says. "It brings
life all together."

Company personnel are stationed at terminals in several
southern cities. This means Hulon has to fly a lot to stay in
touch with personnel and to answer emergencies. He tries
to be at the bedside when a company employee or a family
member dies. Terminal manager Jack Lynch in Miami recalls his wife's fatal bout with cancer. "I don't think either
of us would have been able to cope with the problem if it
hadn't been for Wayne."

Sam Simpson, a native Jamaican, is a different type. His
official title is pastor-director of church extension, with
salary paid jointly by the Home Mission Board and the
New York Baptist Convention. His co-workers call him the
Baptist Bishop of the Bronx.

In thirteen years Simpson has started four Southern
Baptist churches for blacks and Spanish-speaking people

in the New York City borough. In between, he's been active in community projects.

For example, he became concerned about abandoned housing and joined ministers of other faiths in forming the Twin Parks Association. They bought buildings from the city for a token $1, secured repair loans, and leased apartments to tenant associations. The buildings went from 60 to 95 percent occupancy and rent collections from 20 to 97 percent.

Simpson is trusted both by neighborhood street gangs and police. One night he was studying late when he heard footfalls and youthful voices outside. Peering through the glass-encased foyer of the church, he spotted about twenty black youths armed with chains, sticks, bottles, rocks and other weapons. After they had passed he ran to his car, circled the block, and stopped about fifty feet ahead of the leaders. "Leroy, Jerry—this is Reverend Simpson," he shouted. "What's goin' on?" They admitted that they were headed for a rumble with an Italian gang.

Suddenly three police cars converged, lights flashing. A lieutenant jumped from one car ready to lock up the bunch. "Wait, officer," Simpson requested. "Let's get both groups together at the church and talk this out." The police and the blacks consented, provided the preacher would round up the Italians.

Both gangs showed up. After a lengthy airing of mutual complaints, Simpson got each group to select four leaders to meet with him and the police officer in another room. There, crucial decisions were hammered out.

Each gang would honor the territory of the other and stay out unless invited. They would keep in communication and try to avoid fights. Finally, they would organize basketball teams and play each other. The preacher and the policeman would get permission for the boys to use a nearby school playground for afternoon and night games.

During summers, Simpson runs a study and recreation program for hundreds of Bronx kids with the aid of volunteers from Baptist churches outside the city. The curriculum includes Bible study, singing, crafts, and remedial math and reading for five- to twelve-year-olds. The summer climaxes with a fun day on streets closed off by police for the occasion. The kids play softball, volleyball, and other street games, then enjoy a late afternoon puppet show.

Sam Simpson goes home exhausted, but satisfied.

John Hopkins in Kansas City, Kansas, finds his missionary work just as exhausting and satisfying. Hopkins had a first career with the Criminal Investigation Division of the U. S. Army before enrolling at Midwestern Baptist Theological Seminary. Partway through seminary, he signed on with the Home Mission Board. His handle is Christian social ministries consultant for the Kansas-Nebraska Baptist Convention.

The no-nonsense ex-investigator quickly made friends with juvenile court workers in Kansas City. He and his wife Shirley and other Baptist volunteers revamped the badly outdated court file system. Then, working with court officials, they set up a system in which volunteers could establish personal relationships with young offenders and their families. Through an arrangement approved by the Kansas governor, the Law Enforcement Assistance Agency provided $3 for every $1 contributed by the Home Mission Board for the project.

Terry Showalter, director of court services, says Hopkins and his Baptist volunteers have accomplished what other volunteer groups failed to do, because "they have something deep inside besides interest."

One of the volunteers is Wanda Collins, a blonde mother of four. After an interview and training, she was asked to go to a detention home and pick up twelve-year-old Robin. "She doesn't belong there," the court worker said. "Take her home with you."

The mother found the girl wearing an expensive fur coat and high-heeled boots and clutching a cardboard box with her few belongings: a doll, a toy mouse, a toothbrush, and a postcard. She had fled from an uncle in California who had molested her. Her parents were alcoholics.

Robin's weekend visit with the Collins family stretched into weeks. They asked to be her foster parents, and at a court hearing her real parents gave their consent.

Hopkins counsels many adult prisoners himself. One of his successful clients is Richard Melton, twenty-nine, who admits to a "rap sheet" running twenty pages. When Melton was released, Hopkins became his parole sponsor, arranging for new clothes, paying the deposit on a house trailer, helping him find a job, then cosigning a $400 note so he could buy a car. Recalls the ex-con, "He didn't come waving a Bible at me. He was the first man ever to come at me fair and simple and say, 'Let me help.' "

But Hopkins's main job is to set up departments of Christian social ministries in each of the twelve associations of Southern Baptist churches in Kansas and Nebraska.

His effort to get churches involved is succeeding—slowly. His own church provides facilities for a senior citizens' lunch program that also gives monthly blood pressure checks. Other Baptist churches in Kansas have held a retreat for the aging where legal, social, economic, and spiritual needs were discussed.

Hopkins has a reputation of being hard on preachers. "I'm not angry with pastors," he says. "I do think they need to develop relationships with social agencies and become change agents in their communities."

The Home Mission Board's new thrusts for helping people

where they hurt has meant adjustments in traditional ways of starting Southern Baptist churches in "pioneer" areas outside the South.

Before World War II, Southern Baptists and American (Northern) Baptists had an understanding to stay out of each other's territories. In the 1950s Southern Baptists decided this agreement should no longer hold. Thousands of Southerners had followed industry to the North and didn't feel at home in the more formal northern churches. There was also a feeling that Northern Baptists had copped out on their responsibilities by honoring "comity" agreements with other denominations to stay out of many new towns.

The first Southern Baptist preachers went hunting for their own kind. A newly arrived parson from the South would drive slowly through a new housing tract looking for southern license plates. When he'd spot a down-home tag, he'd knock on the door and invite the residents to attend services in a rented building. When he got about fifty members, he would organize a church, often taking the name First Southern Baptist Church of the locality. Then with a loan from the Home Mission Board, they would buy land and build.

Thousands of up-North and out-West Southern Baptist churches were started this way. Most were no different from churches in the South. Indeed, they were often more wedded to southern traditions than churches in Charleston or Birmingham.

These early southern culture congregations drew in pockets of homesick migrants who could indulge their nostalgia and worship God as their ancestors had. They made little effort to reach the native populations or to make visitors feel welcome. One "native" recalls going to the First Southern Baptist Church of Joliet, Illinois, with her southern husband. Members recognized his familiar speech patterns and asked if he had brought his wife. "Yes, ma'am," he drawled, "she's right over there." "Oh," came the reply, "we didn't connect her with you. She talks like a foreigner."

In the early sixties Southern Baptist planners began emphasizing community churches and playing down the southern reference, although the initials SBC were deemed okay in the church title for identification. Also, buildings were rented or constructed that could be used seven days a week and programs begun to meet both the spiritual and social needs of neighborhood populations.

During this time Southern Baptists began expanding into areas where southern nuclei were small or even nonexistent. Church extension missionaries found it harder to gather new members, but once a congregation was established, it was easier to innovate in ministry. There wasn't a power structure of traditionalists around to object "That isn't the way we did it back home."

New England was one of the last regions entered. Dire predictions that the SBC would be shunned as alien didn't come true. By 1977, after little more than a decade, there were fifty-nine SBC churches from the southern shores of Connecticut to the coast and woodlands of Maine. A new member in Maine, noting that the first Baptist church in the South had been organized by a congregation fleeing persecution from her state, remarked, "You're not foreigners. You've just come home."

The Worcester (Massachusetts) Baptist Church is one example. It was started in a decaying inner-city neighborhood abandoned by some other Protestant denominations. It is led by church extension missionary Mark McAllister, the pastor, and social worker Carl Holden. The salaries of both men are paid by the Home Mission Board. Holden is charged with coordinating social ministries for all Southern Baptist churches in greater Worcester, but he centers his work in the inner city.

The Worcester Baptist congregation sponsors a youth

coffeehouse, a commodity foods delivery program, nutritional lunches for senior citizens, literacy classes, and renovation of decaying homes. "And we're just scratching the surface," McAllister declares. "We need to do something for the mentally handicapped and the children."

Says the Home Mission Board's Missions Ministries Division director Wendell Belew about the focus on inner-city neighborhoods: "Our objective is people, not economics. We try to go where people are, however much the cost."

The forgotten people in downtown Worcester are grateful. Eighty-six-year-old Ann Keith, a blind woman living in an apartment across from the Baptist church, talks about the "great change" in her life. "Carl [Holden] has given me the desire to live and be a part of something." Carrie Gates, an elderly widow living nearby who was recently baptized in the church, concurs. "I prayed to God to take me. Now I don't look backward anymore; always forward. That church over there, that's my place."

The expanding social ministries of Southern Baptists have amazed leaders of other faiths who once considered the SBC as the most backward and reactionary of all major American denominations. The rapid expansion of Southern Baptists is equally impressive. In 1977 only 670 of the 3,049 counties in the United States were without a Southern Baptist congregation.

The aggressive Southern Baptists intend to keep expanding. As William M. Pinson, now president of Golden Gate Theological Seminary in San Francisco, declared at the 1977 SBC Kansas City Convention: "We must be concerned for the total needs of people—spiritual, physical, mental, emotional, personal, and social. There is no place in the world that is off limits for the people of God as they carry out their mission."

The idea of "total person ministry" has been slowest

catching on in traditional Southern Baptist areas, where congregational life centers on organizational meetings. In this syndrome, success is measured by Sunday school attendance, numbers of baptisms during the year, gifts to the SBC Cooperative Program of missions, and new buildings erected. Members minister to "our kind" and strive to "keep sweet."

Churches that have broadened their outreach are usually located in cities where they have had to respond creatively and energetically to a multiethnic population or close doors. One of the most notable is First Baptist Church of San Antonio, pastored by Dr. Jimmy Allen, who was elected president of the Southern Baptist Convention in 1977.

Allen describes his 9,000-member church as a "little United Nations with blacks and browns and Orientals and Caucasians." He baptizes from 300 to 600 new converts of a dozen nationalities each year. A Chinese congregation uses the same building. Four Spanish congregations are related to the main church. And there are Vietnamese and Spanish pastors on Allen's staff.

At least a third of the regular attenders staff thirty-one helping ministries of the church. These include:

—A friendship program for international women. Around fifty internationals have Sunday dinner at the church each week. Bible study groups in various languages are held in homes around the city.

—A home for transients with work therapy. The church has purchased an old hotel in the neighborhood to house street people and help them plan a new life.

—A counseling program for teens with problems or already in jail. Sociology students from a local university receive on-the-job training.

—A restaurant called the Fourth Street Inn. Fifty-five volunteers serve meals to business people and keep alert for counseling opportunities. Individuals in deep trouble are referred to the church's extensive professional counseling service.

—A Loving Listeners telephone contact program for shut-ins. Persons in difficulty can call an advertised church telephone number and receive help.

—A free meal service at the church for anyone who shows up hungry and is unable to afford a meal. There is no requirement to hear a sermon first, but counseling is available for those who request it.

—An Adult Basic Learning Enrichment class. Around fifty people a week are learning to read and/or prepare for high school equivalency tests.

Although located in one of the poorest cities in America, this congregation gives almost $200,000 each year to outside missionary work and sends out "action teams" of volunteers to distant places. In 1978 thirty-seven adults from the church will go to Honduras for evangelism, medical-dental work, and church building construction.

The biggest volunteer program among Southern Baptists is in the Rio Grande valley along the Texas-Mexican border, where 3 million people live, many in dire poverty. The program began in 1967 when Hurricane Beulah devastated the Brownsville-Matamoros, Mexico, area. Upstate churches sent teams of volunteers—construction workers, doctors, dentists, and nurses—to help. They brought home vivid descriptions of poverty, high illiteracy, and abysmal health conditions along the border. That fall the Texas Woman's Missionary Union raised $600,000 for relief help in the valley.

Every year since, around 2,500 Texas Baptist volunteers have poured into the sultry valley. Their goal is expressed by Susi Carver, from San Antonio, back for her second summer. "We want to show them Jesus is not just a name—he's got something to give them."

What Jesus "gives" the valley residents through the Baptist volunteers is literacy classes, health clinics, agricultural expertise, help with house repairs, and a string of vacation Bible schools that enrolls thousands of children.

Only one person in twenty-five was a Baptist when the volunteers started coming. That ratio is increasing. But the volunteers have done more than win converts. They have inspired the native Baptists to start helping their neighbors in practical ways that they never associated with religion before. Some examples:

—The First Baptist Church of Brownsville operates a medical-dental clinic and an orphanage for Mexican children. The clinic, on the orphanage grounds, often has 350 patients a week.

—Loraine Shores, a pastor's wife, manages a self-help industry for poor women called Mighty River Handcrafts. While teaching sewing to four Mexican women, Mrs. Shores learned why they were forced to take their children out of school each year and follow the crops as migrant workers. Starting with scraps and faith, she began a handcraft "factory" in her own living room. The first month's income for seven women workers was $37.50. Mighty River Handcrafts today produces $4,000 a month for 100 women. Only after receiving a $20,000 contract from the SBC Sunday School Board in Nashville for teaching puppetry did Mrs. Shores began taking a small salary for herself.

All of this and much more indicates that President Carter's giant denomination is beginning to flex its muscles of compassion, in the United States and in the eighty-four countries where its missionaries serve abroad. But perceptive leaders realize Southern Baptists have a long way to go to overcome the prejudice, apathy, and callous insensitivity many church members still hold toward social ministries. James L. Sullivan, the former president of the Sunday School Board and president of the SBC until June 1977, believes his church stands like Abraham at a crossroads receiving a "call from God to move. God is calling, even ordering," Sullivan told the 1977 convention in Kansas City. "The hour to move out and upward is upon us. . . . This is not the time for the routine and the ordinary. The challenge must be met with faith and daring.

"Our denomination is in the era of its greatest strength and testing," Sullivan continued. "For the first time we have the resources, manpower, the know-how, the national coverage geographically and the nation's eye. . . . God has brought us to this hour."

10

«« »»

Jimmy Carter's Preachers

"WE ARE a strange species not easily classified," says William L. Self, minister of the fast-growing Wieuca Road Baptist Church in Atlanta. "We are as diverse as the talented W. A. Criswell and the insightful John Claypool, as Duke McCall and Randall Lolley, as Foy Valentine and Adrian Rogers." All Southern Baptist preachers. All, excepting Criswell, were little known to Americans at large, but household names in the largest fraternity of Protestant divines in the world.

They are indeed diverse. "Brother Bob" Harrington, self-styled "Chaplain of Bourbon Street," is "a nut for Jesus, but screwed on the right bolt." Robert G. Lee, ninety-one and the last of the old-time orators, places no faith in "dainty pastries of intellectual subtleties." W. A. Criswell affirms that the "inspired [Bible] cannot contain any scientific mistakes because God knew every truth and fact of science from the beginning." Carlyle Marney thinks "church can happen in the lab, on a walk, or on a surgeon's Sunday morning rounds. . . . A man is in church anywhere he is being made whole."

In the theological spectrum, they are left, right, but mostly in the evangelical center. In life-style they are 99 percent square, but a few can be found who enjoy an occasional drink and don't see anything wrong with looking at nudes in *Playboy*. In marital relationships they are almost all husbands and seldom divorced, though the incidence of parsonage splits is rising. In income they are doing much better than that poor soul of whom his deacons prayed, "Lord, you keep him humble, and we'll keep him poor." Average pay from an average size church of 300-399 members runs about $12,000, which includes payments for housing and other fringes. Salaries in larger churches run up to $40,000, with an affluent half dozen said to be making $60,000, about what some Baptist organization heads receive.

They come in all dispositions from happy backslappers to owls of doom, from steeple climbers to heresy hunters, from county-seat squires to boardroom brokers. They can be found in all locations, from the dry flats of southwest Texas, to the canyons of Wall Street, from the Florida Keys to the Alaska slopes. As one reminded, "You'd better get used to us. We're in every state in the Union and in almost every foreign country. If you're promoted to heaven, you'll find many of us there. And if you are demoted to hell, you'll likely have some of us for company." Now they're coming and going from Deacon Carter's new residence. One telephoned the president of his seminary alma mater in New Orleans "just so you can say you got a call from the White House."

The sheer numbers of them are staggering. About 30,000 pastor churches, some serving more than one congregation, which account for the over 35,000 available pastoral positions. Nine hundred are full-time evangelists such as Bob Harrington; Hyman Appleman, a Jewish lawyer; Anis Shorrosh, a seminary-educated Palestinian refugee; and colorful Sam Cathy, who is "a Southern Baptist from my radiator cap to my taillights." Another 2,000 are denominational editors, executives, traveling field men, and bureaucrats. Another 19,000 are listed in the official directory as retired or in secular occupations. Republican Congressman John H. Buchanan of Birmingham is in the latter grouping. Since Jimmy Carter's election, rumors have surfaced that Buchanan is thinking of becoming a Democrat. The best-known former SBC preacher in secular life, Bill Moyers, the CBS commentator, is no longer carried in the official directory.

And this doesn't include some 15,000 more who are classified as associate pastors and ministers of youth, education, and music.

Nor is the well expected to run dry. Eight thousand are enrolled in SBC seminaries, one of every six ministerial students in the United States.

At the power center of the world's biggest religious democracy are the pastors of the largest churches (3,247 in the SBC have more than 1,000 members). These are the personalities who serve on the most prestigious agency boards and parade across the platform at the annual national meeting. Never in recent memory has the pastor of a small church been elected president of the convention. The little preachers don't seem to mind, however. They can be elected to offices in state conventions and associational offices, and as they rise in stature among the brethren and are recommended to larger churches, they will receive larger responsibilities.

Denominational affairs aside, it is in the local churches where the preachers count most. Power, as well as money ($1.6 billion in 1976), flows upward from there.

The local pastor may not be the "neighborhood pope" of H. L. Mencken's cynicism, but if he is the pastor of a First Baptist Church in the Deep South, he is likely the first citizen of the town. The most influential men, including the school superintendent and mayor, may be his deacons.

Hundreds, sometimes thousands, look to him for spiritual and moral leadership and are influenced by him in varying degrees.

Jimmy Carter's former pastors are a good cross section of Southern Baptist preachers from the 1920s on. They will also have to be considered by future historians in the development of his character and beliefs.

The first preacher he saw in the pulpit was Jesse Eugene Hall, a scholarly graduate from the Louisville seminary who read his New Testament straight from the Greek. Hall served the Plains church from 1923 to 1927 and again from 1941 to 1951 when Carter was away in school and the navy.

Hall died in 1968. His daughter, Mrs. Grace Chappell, recalls that he "was kind of liberal for folks in the twenties. Baptists were arguing over how long it took God to create the earth. Daddy said the Lord could have done it in six days, but that the Hebrew word for 'day' in Genesis didn't necessarily mean a twenty-four-hour period. Another thing about Daddy. He was interested in black people long before this racial trouble started. He gave the Negro preachers his old sermons and books.

"When he went to Plains the church was just half time. He preached one Sunday at Richland and the next at Plains. When the economy got real bad, he asked them to reduce his salary. But we got along. One member brought us syrup from his cane mill. Another gave us corn meal from his grist mill. We had chickens and a vegetable garden behind the pastorium. And Daddy also had a rose garden right in back of the Plains church."

Jesse F. Ray, who followed Hall and pastored at Plains from 1928 to 1931, is living in retirement in Florida. His memories of young Jimmy are scarce. He remembers Earl and Lillian Carter as "the finest people in the county. Just tops and the kind who couldn't do enough for their preacher. Once when times were real hard Earl sent us a nice fat pig, dressed and ready to 'enter' the ministry. And Earl's brother Alton was one of the best deacons I ever had."

Ray says Plains was "the best town morally of all the places I pastored. While I was there I checked on how many white people had been arrested the past five years. Only nine, and only three of these for serious crimes.

"I have to give Miss Julia Coleman, that great school-teacher, more credit for that than any preacher or deacon Plains ever had. She was the embodiment of modesty, refinement, culture, education, faith, hope, and love in their highest qualities. Her power was spiritual, intellectual, and moral, mixed with WISDOM in the right proportions."

The next minister at Plains baptized Jimmy Carter. He came from the renowned Callaway family, which claims over thirty Baptist preachers. Royall Callaway, seventy-eight and retired in South Carolina, stirs his memory for a recollection of the baptizing. "You say it was in 1935, eh? I must have baptized him at the close of our summer revival. And here he is the president. I never thought anybody in Plains would be president."

His wife Ruby has a better recall. "That cute little boy! I can still see him selling peanuts in front of his Uncle Alton's store. Don't you remember, honey, how you'd always buy a nickel bag from him?"

The preacher doesn't and his wife continues. "Last year Jimmy came to Charleston for a campaign appearance. They wanted everybody special to sit in the front row. We just stood back and when Jimmy came in he recognized us immediately. I couldn't resist telling people, 'He was a little boy in our church when my husband was pastor in Plains.'"

Old-timers at Plains say that Royall Callaway was a pre-millennialist who preached that the Jews were going to return to Palestine and that Christ would soon return and "rapture" his church out of the evil world. Ruby Callaway, whom he married while at Plains, had been the private secretary of Dr. Bob Jones, Sr., then the leading trumpet of Southern Fundamentalism. The Jones camp thundered against evolution, theological modernism, movements for social reform, movies, and bobbed hair, bossy wives, and women preachers.

Tommie Jones (no relation to Bob Jones) was pastor at Plains when Carter resigned from the navy to take over his dying father's business. A Louisville graduate, young Jones had supervised the building of a youth camp for the Baptist Woman's Missionary Union of Georgia. While at Plains he borrowed $250 from banker Alton Carter to marry the director of Christian education at First Baptist Church, Gainesville, Georgia. His wife Louise was also a seminary graduate.

Jones was an outdoorsman and community activist at Plains. He supervised the building of a youth camp for the Friendship Baptist Association. He joined the Lions and became scoutmaster of the troop they sponsored. One of his scouts was fifteen-year-old Billy Carter.

Jimmy Carter had taught Sunday school at Annapolis and held services for his submarine crewmates at sea. When he landed back in Plains he volunteered to help the preacher with the scouts. Jones, in turn, assigned him a Sunday school class of nine- to twelve-year-old boys and asked his assistance in building the youth camp. "Jimmy knew where to get the workers we needed for clearing the land," the former pastor says. "He was the best assistant I ever had."

While at Plains, Tommie Jones persuaded the church to take two giant steps, to project and adopt a unified budget and to employ him as a full-time pastor. Many members rebelled, saying, "We've always got along. Why change now? The unified budget isn't in the Bible." They also wanted to continue swapping visits with the Methodists who were serving half time also. But the determined young pastor won the battle, even though some continued to seethe over the changes.

The catalytic Tommie Jones was only at Plains for four years, from 1951 to 1955, before moving on. The next pastor, Robert Harris, remained twelve years. Jimmy Carter heard him preach practically every Sunday morning and night. Harris, a diabetic since childhood, was, as Southern Baptist preachers go, a meticulous organizer, a perceptive world watcher, a social reformer, and a strong environmentalist. More typically, he was extremely cautious on race questions.

Harris and his two preacher brothers were all graduates of Mercer and Southern Seminary in Louisville. They all pastored successively—Harris was in the middle—their home church, old Ebenezer in Wilkes County, organized in 1787.

In 1954 he and his schoolteacher wife Ethel were at Fort Gaines, Georgia, about sixty miles southwest of Plains, when they arranged for a white Baptist coed to lead a vacation Bible school for the local black Baptist church. The Georgia Baptist Convention had been providing this service to black congregations for several years.

At the end of the first week Harris got a call from the county sheriff. "Get that white lady out of that nigger church or I won't be responsible for her safety," he warned. Harris complied.

His elder brother Waldo thinks the incident eventually led to his leaving Fort Gaines and going to Plains in 1957. Waldo also believes it explains why his brother did not directly speak out on race during his dozen years at Plains while the civil rights crusades were exploding around him.

Robert and Ethel Harris were probably the most multigifted couple ever to serve the Plains church. Robert was a talented artist who frequently illustrated his sermons with beautiful pastels. Ethel was a specialist in early child-hood education, and later earned her doctorate in this field. "She revolutionized our preschool department," says Sunday school teacher Marian Harris, now director of family and children's services for Sumter County and chairperson of the Sumter Mental Health Association. "She changed our nursery from baby-sitting to a teaching experience. She specified the exact equipment and furniture we needed. 'Brother Bob' was a master carpenter and he made the furniture which we still use."

Harris had been a bookeeper for Standard Oil before studying for the ministry. He kept records on every church organization and devised charts for members to use in measuring their spiritual growth. A chart for lay evangelism was designed so a person could check off his activities each day:

1. Prayed for courage
   and power to witness: — — — — — — —
2. Extended an invitation
   to attend our church: — — — — — — —
3. Tried to locate an
   unenlisted person: — — — — — — —
4. Made an effort to
   cultivate a prospect: — — — — — — —
5. Gave out an appropri-
   ate tract or Gospel: — — — — — — —
6. Made a visit to give a
   personal witness: — — — — — — —
7. Spoke a word of
   Christian testimony
   "along the way":   — — — — — — —
8. Wrote a witness letter
   to an unsaved person: — — — — — — —

	S	M	T	W	TH	F	S
9. Took advantage of "special occasions" to show Christian concern:	—	—	—	—	—	—	—
10. Conducted myself "as becometh saints":	—	—	—	—	—	—	—

It was during Harris's ministry that Carter was ordained a deacon. Each year deacons were elected by the church by the simple method of asking members to list choices for filling vacancies. Those receiving the most votes then knelt for the laying on of hands by an invited presbytery of ordained men from other churches.

Jimmy Carter's name had been presented before, but not until 1962 did he place high enough for election. He was ordained in a candlelight ceremony along with P. J. Wise; Albert Williams, his business competitor; and J. D. Clements.

Carter likely would have received the honor sooner had he not disagreed with the pastor and several members on alcohol. Carter maintained that alcoholism was more a disease than a matter of low willpower. He saw nothing sinful about taking an occasional drink, a practice he had started in the navy. And he opposed his pastor's successful fight to keep Sumter County dry. "Jimmy knew better than Brother Bob just how bad the bootleggers were in the county," recalls one of the old members.

Harris strongly encouraged his parishioners to become involved in public life. He even promoted the Peace Corps, an organization many Baptist preachers disapproved of. He sermonized that members

  1. Must place God's men in office

2. Must pray God's wisdom for them
3. Must help them to eradicate evils in our country
4. Must reduce the crime rate and thereby reduce taxes
5. Must raise the moral standard and thereby get more for each tax dollar

How much Harris influenced Carter to enter public life is impossible to judge. That Carter was waist-deep in outside affairs by 1962 is well documented. He had been elected state president of the Certified Seed Organization, district governor of Lions International, chairman of the Sumter Planning Association. He had also served on the regional library board, the Sumter Hospital Authority, and the county school board. As school board chairman he angered some people in Plains by supporting the voter referendum that would have consolidated the county schools and moved the elementary school out of Plains. The referendum lost by eighty-eight votes.

Carter began seriously considering entering state politics the year he was ordained a deacon. He was mulling the idea over when the pastor brought a revival preacher over for dinner.

In his autobiography Carter says the visiting pastor "strongly advised me not to become involved in such a discredited profession. We had a rather heated argument, and he finally asked, 'If you want to be of service to other people, why don't you go into the ministry or into some honorable social service work?' "

Carter did not name the preacher in his book. He was Allen Comish, a close friend of Harris and one of the best-known Baptist ministers in Georgia. At the time of his visit to Plains he was pastor of Waldrop Memorial Baptist Church in Columbus, Georgia.

Comish, now at Mercer University, provides the background for the conversation: "After the meal we sat in his living room and talked. The matter of politics came up because Jimmy knew I had been involved in a rough mixed-drinks referendum in Columbus. He had seen me on television.

"It wasn't a structured discussion at all. He said he was thinking of running for the state Senate, but I don't remember that he asked for my opinion. I certainly didn't advise him against it. I had a couple of men in my church already serving in the legislature. What I did was lay out a political life from my viewpoint as pastor and as one who had grown up in a politically active family.

"My father was a pastor in Louisiana and a close friend of Huey Long's. I had a brother who was a judge and another brother who sometimes presided over the legislature when Huey was governor. When I was a teenager I used to go in the chamber on a pass and watch the wheeling and dealing. Huey Long, you know, would come right on the floor and go from desk to desk drumming up votes for his legislation.

"How much of that I told Jimmy, I don't remember. I must have said, 'You won't find a political life easy. You'll lose friends. You'll be subjected to personal attacks. You'll be pressured by special interests. You'll have to compromise a little and get a coalition to get your bills passed. Not many bills become law today on merit alone.'

"I don't think he responded in any yes-or-no fashion. Being Jimmy Carter, I know he would have thanked me, though. As I said, it really wasn't a structured conversation at all. Just informal after-dinner talk."

Carter did run for the state Senate and learned how dirty a political campaign can get. To win the election he had to go to court against alleged vote stealing in Georgetown, Georgia.

Another Baptist preacher adds more light on that. Comer

Williamson, who grew up with George Wallace in Alabama, was then pastor of the Baptist church in Georgetown. "We had a very bad situation there. Prostitution. Gambling. Killings. People got obligated to one political boss for their jobs and felt they couldn't oppose him. I took a very strong stand agaist political corruption and for honest citizens to clean the mess up. When enough people got upset, the situation changed.

"I've told Jimmy I was responsible for him getting in the Senate. I was just kidding, of course. He won the case, but he didn't clean up Georgetown. The local people did that."

Carter was a member of the Georgia Senate in 1965 when the Plains church voted to bar "Negroes and other civil rights agitators" from services. He would naturally have been disappointed that his pastor was on vacation that Sunday.

By this time Robert Harris's health had deteriorated to the point that he was having to go often to Duke University for special treatments. Ethel Harris was pressing ahead on her doctorate with the thought that she would soon have to earn the family living. The church was understanding and paid for supply preachers to fill the pulpit during the pastor's absences.

When Carter ran for governor in 1966 his ailing pastor backed him solidly, sending a letter of recommendation to every Baptist preacher in Georgia. Allen Comish also wrote letters to pastors and laymen promoting the candidacy of the Plains deacon.

After losing the election Carter came back to Plains to find his pastor worse. He had to go back to Duke for more tests. Then he lost the sight of one eye and had to spend several days in a hospital. The Plains church continued to pay fill-in preachers.

The man whom some Plains members call "the best pastor we ever had" hung on stubbornly. On February 12, 1967, he took a bold step in the Plains church and proclaimed "Race Relations Sunday." The occasion had been noted by thousands of Southern Baptist congregations for years, even though most just went through the motions, but this was a first for Plains.

The sick pastor's sermon that day was from Acts, chapter 10, about Peter's visit to the Gentile military officer Cornelius, and titled "The Kingdom Without Clan." His text was verse 34, where Peter declared, "Of a truth I perceive that God is no respecter of persons." Harris said in his written introduction: "Peter begins to understand that God's kingdom reaches beyond the Jewish clan and that he is to become a significant part in it. It is a turning point in his life, a new plateau of perception." He concluded, "Whatever prevents us from witnessing to any other person is a hindrance to the kingdom of God."

Three months later he presented his resignation. One story circulated that a committee of deacons had asked him to resign because his health had reached the point where he could no longer pastor the church. He was handed such a request. A less plausible tale intimated that Jimmy Carter wanted him out because of their differences over prohibition. The letter requesting his resignation was said to have come from a typewriter at Carter's office. He had been very close to the Carters. "Miss" Lillian had loaned him her car for a recent trip to North Carolina. And young Chip Carter had said more than once that he intended to become a preacher "like Brother Bob."

The most believable conclusion is that he was asked to leave both because of his health and his observance of Race Relations Sunday.

Still refusing to retire, he took the position of "Minister of Visitation" with Allen Comish in Columbus. He survived six years longer, continuing to go back and forth to Duke, where he died in 1973.

Jimmy Carter was elected to the next pulpit committee. The third prospect they heard was John Simmons, a stocky, enthusiastic navy veteran, a graduate of Mercer and Southeastern Baptist Seminary, with black wavy hair. "He stuttered a little," committee member Ted Brown recalls, "but we liked his sermon content and invited him to try out in Plains."

Attendance had flagged during the last months of Robert Harris's ministry. Simmons brought it back up. He didn't harp on alcohol, as some thought the previous pastor had done too much. He pushed soul-saving evangelism. He preached from the Book of Revelation about Armageddon, hell, and judgment, topics Harris had seldom touched.

The Men's Brotherhood flourished. Men from the church made the two mission trips to the North in which Jimmy Carter was involved. Carter also chaired a Billy Graham film crusade in Americus. He was the only layman they could get in the Friendship Baptist Association who would preside over an integrated audience.

After Carter moved to the governor's mansion in Atlanta, the steam Simmons had built up began to slacken. Attendance fell back. "Revitalization of visitation and devotion to the Lord's work is desperately needed," proclaimed Simmons in the church bulletin. He pleaded, cajoled, warned. But in a town the size of Plains there were just so many souls to be won, and the church members weren't enthusiastic about making another run for the hardened sinners still outside the fold.

Simmons resigned in 1972 after five years of ministry at Plains. The story ran that he was asked to leave by certain deacons who had learned from the termination of Robert Harris how to get rid of a preacher they didn't want around any longer. Simmons got another church in Georgia easily, then later moved to Brushton, New York, where he now pastors a church that sponsors four mission chapels.

In Atlanta the Carters had joined the Baptist church nearest their residence. At Northside Baptist Church, located in one of the poshest sections of town, they had one of the brighest young pulpit whips in the state.

Forrest Lanier had already distinguished himself at First Baptist Church, Savannah. He had a theological degree from Southern Seminary, an honorary doctorate from Mercer, and had done postgraduate study at the University of Heidelberg, Germany. Well versed in world affairs, and having been raised in rural south Georgia, he could hold his own in any circle.

At Savannah he had won an open-door policy without having to resign, no small feat for a Southern Baptist pastor in the sixties. "They told me they had a middle-of-the-road policy on race. I said the middle of the road is yellow and I'm not going to be there. They voted to receive blacks as members and haven't had a black come since."

When the Carters moved into the mansion, Lanier came calling. "But I don't kid myself," he says. "They joined Northside because it was the nearest church." He also concedes that "on a scale of one to ten, I didn't influence him more than two. I spoke to the issues. He knew where I stood. At some points we disagreed."

The major disagreement between the preacher and the governor was over the million-dollar building program at Northside. Carter felt it was too extravagant for a congregation of 400. "Let's build for the Lord, not for our own comfort," he reportedly said. He liked a fellow deacon's proposal to put up a high-rise building for senior citizens and use the first floor for church activities. "That's hiding Jesus in the basement," countered Lanier. "I want a sanctuary that will honor God, not just a memorial to myself." The majority supported the preacher and the Carters went along in hopes that the affluent congregation would expand its missionary work. At the ground breaking, little Amy Carter tossed up the first shovel of dirt.

Carter had a hometown friend, Dr. George Mims, practicing medicine in Marietta, a suburb north of Atlanta. Dr. Mims had recently taken a missionary trip to Honduras. With the governor's encouragement, he came to Northside and showed slides. This resulted in the pastor leading a team of twenty-five young people and a half dozen doctors and dentists to the Central American country for two weeks of medical missions in June 1971. Northside Church provided $5,000 for travel expenses and Atlanta medical supply houses donated drugs.

Rosalynn Carter was the spark plug behind "Operation Touch—1972," which operated out of a small building in a black Atlanta ghetto. About thirty-five Northside youths supervised a recreation program and assisted medics giving eye examinations and dental and anemia tests to children. Those needing special care were sent to Baptist doctors and dentists from the church who donated their services.

Later that same year the pastor took another team back to Honduras. He has continued leading missionary trips every year since.

Among all the Baptist parsons who have preached to Jimmy Carter, none has likely been closer to him than Nelson Price, pastor of Roswell Street Baptist Church in Marietta, which has the largest Sunday school attendance (1,900) of any SBC church in the state. Once a college basketball star in Louisiana, the six-foot-five Price delivered the prayer at Carter's gubernatorial inaugural and later gave the sermon for the private preinaugural family worship service at First Baptist Church, Washington, before Carter was sworn in as president.

Price came to Marietta in 1964. "The church was sick,"

he says. "They had $30,000 in unpaid bills and a declining membership. They were poorly organized, lacked leadership, and weren't reaching new people."

Price remembered an old seminary professor, Dr. Clayton Waddell, saying, "A minister's move to a new church ought to be the most important event in that community for the next fifty years." And an explanation from his college coach that "if you want a team to play on your court, you've got to play on theirs." Before moving to Georgia, Price wrote every school principal, bank president, service club officer, labor leader, and prominent merchant in populous Cobb County. "I'm excited about coming to your community and I want to help make it better," he said. Then he set up four consecutive Sunday nights for get-acquainted invitational teas with different segments of the community.

He eliminated the possibility of a power struggle with the deacons by convincing them they should be pastoral visitors and ministers, rather than act as an official board of business managers for the church. He arranged for a finance committee to oversee money affairs and a board of trustees to manage church property.

He personally went after the toughest sinners in the community. One was a transvestite, another a canny old bachelor whom preachers had chased for decades without success. He netted them both. The old man was hardest. The first time Price came to visit, he ran out the back door. The next time Price knocked on the front door, then sprinted around the back to catch him and ask for a drink of water. That opened the way to a conversation about the "living water" that Jesus offered to the Samaritan woman at the well. They soon became good friends and the old man went to the church he had vowed never to attend and was baptized.

Price installed a new pulpit shaped like a cross. He began every sermon with the two words "Jesus Christ." He announced intriguing titles, such as "Get Up Off Your Apathy," "Choose Your Master or Mistress," and "I Didn't Promise You a Rose Garden."

He planned church programming as "the Baptist answer to Baskin-Robbins." One of the most popular innovations featured a procession of flags. First, the American flag was carried down one aisle while choir and congregation sang "God Bless America." Then the Christian flag was taken down another aisle while they sang "Praise God from Whom All Blessings Flow." Least approved of was a squad of miniskirted teenage girl usherettes escorting visitors to pews. Most touching was a sin-confessing ceremony called "As the Urn Burns." Participants dropped their written sins into a heat-resistant container to be consumed as a symbol of God's forgiveness.

To promote still higher attendance he held student appreciation nights and invited a bevy of high school homecoming queens to sit on the platform. He challenged then Governor Lester Maddox to a bicycle race in the church parking lot. (Maddox's son is a member of the church.) The preacher won. He did magic shows at the county fair. He capitalized on current events with catchy slogans on "the world's largest marquee" in front of the church. During the space travel madness, he messaged:

APOLLO 16 ASTRONAUTS: IF YOU BUMP
INTO OUR SPONSOR, GIVE HIM OUR LOVE.

When Evel Knievel made his Snake River jump, the pastor had a motorcycle mounted on top of the marquee with the prayer below:

DELIVER US FROM EVEL.

In an airwave wasteland of screaming preachers and tinny quartets, Price created two audience-grabbing radio shows: a daily five-minute "Dear Abby" type answer program and a Sunday evening live talk show with celebrity guests and open-line phones for discussion of the most controversial topics of the moment. As if this weren't enough, he wrote a Sunday editorial for twenty area newspapers.

The supertalented preacher met Jimmy Carter in the fall of 1967 at a Marietta Jaycee awards banquet where both were on the program. Afterward, they talked about their Christian faith, then Carter asked for directions back to the interstate highway. "Follow me, I'll take you there," Price offered.

At the entrance ramp Price parked on a grassy spot and Carter pulled up behind him. They talked some more, then Price, sensing a mutual affinity, proposed "a covenant to pray for one another regularly." Carter nodded. "Yes, I need your prayers. And I'll pray for you."

About six weeks later Price phoned Carter at Plains "just to let you know I'm keeping my promises." Carter replied that he was keeping his.

They continued the covenant. When Carter ran for governor the second time, Price came to Plains and addressed a fund-raising rally. When Carter came to Cobb County, the preacher promoted him to local civic and business leaders.

When Carter moved to Atlanta, Price invited him to worship in Marietta. Carter said he would join the nearest church, Northside, but might drop in at Roswell Street. He did a number of times, arriving without prior announcement and slipping in quietly.

One day Carter invited Price to attend the stock car competition at Raceway Track in Atlanta. Price agreed and the governor's helicopter picked him up Sunday afternoon from the church parking lot. He gave a short sermon to the crowd of around 100,000, then rode with the governor at 160 miles per hour in the pace car.

The Marietta preacher set up Carter's first "Governor's

Prayer Breakfast," inviting Mississippi businessman Owen Cooper, later to be president of the Southern Baptist Convention, to speak. At the breakfast Carter asked Price privately to be praying for the reorganization of state government that he was about to begin. Later he named Price to serve on his Board of Human Resources and to chair his Council of Human Relations.

Sometime in 1973—Price doesn't remember the month—Carter invited his preacher friend to "drop by the mansion. I've got something important to talk with you about." When Price arrived and they were alone, Carter confided his intention to run for president. Price remembers saying, "Dear fellow, I want to talk to you about this, but first let's get on our knees and talk to the Lord." When they finished praying, Price put his hand on Carter's shoulder and said, "Dear fellow, you'd better get your life ready because God has a ministry ahead for you." According to Price, Carter responded, "Well, this clinches it."

Every week during the campaign Price wrote the candidate an encouraging letter. He made speeches for him, but avoided political references in his sermons. Then he went to the Democratic National Convention and called on state delegations with Carter's Jewish adviser, Robert Lipshutz, "just to answer questions they might have," he says. But when the *Playboy* controversy broke, he kept quiet. "I had a million-and-a-half-dollar building campaign going," he confesses. "I guess I got cold feet."

It was after Carter won the Democratic nomination that square-jawed Bruce Edwards at Plains became a national figure. Edwards had succeeded the quiet, scholarly Fred Collins, who had had one of the shortest tenures in the history of the church.

Collins had come to Plains in 1972 just out of the SBC's largest and most conservative seminary, Southwestern in Fort Worth. His troubles began his first Sunday when he announced that he wouldn't be going to the door to shake hands after his sermon. "I don't want anyone to feel they have to compliment me. If you need me, I'll be here at the front." That didn't set well with some of the deacons. The next Sunday he moved the pulpit Bible to keep his sermon notes from sliding off. An upset deacon ran down the aisle to ask why. Collins tried to explain, but the deacon declared the sacred book had to remain in its resting place. Collins's next "faux pas" was changing the order of worship so as to have the announcements made at the beginning. This caused a real uproar. But Collins dug in and refused to quit. "It was a question of whether it would be the deacons' church or the people's church," he says.

The young couples and the Carters liked him—particularly Miss Lillian, who thought he was the best preacher she had ever heard. But the deacons won the power struggle and he resigned in the summer of 1974.

When Collins resigned, the Plains pulpit committee called Georgia Baptist Convention offices for recommendation of a successor. Georgia, like most other SBC state conventions, has an "information service" for church personnel. They were given a résumé on Bruce Edwards, a recent graduate of the New Orleans seminary. He had once been a guest preacher at Plains.

Edwards, then twenty-eight, was a solid Southern Baptist product. He had been raised in an SBC church in Jacksonville, Florida, where his father was a deacon, then attended college in Georgia, where he met his wife Sandra through Baptist Student Union activities.

Before going to the seminary in New Orleans, Edwards had pastored Bethel Baptist in eastern Sumter County. While there he had come to Plains and preached a weekend "youth revival." Jimmy Carter was just beginning his second campaign for governor and Edwards recalls that Hugh Carter told him, as he was getting out of the car,

"You'll be preaching today to the next governor of Georgia." When then pastor John Simmons called on Carter to give the opening prayer, Edwards peeped to see who he was.

His trial pastoral sermon was received well. Miss Lillian allowed he was "almost as good as Brother Fred," the highest compliment she could make.

He officially took the pulpit the second Sunday in January 1975. Jimmy and Rosalynn Carter were back from Atlanta, and this time cousin Hugh remarked, "Today you'll be preaching to the next president of the United States." That morning the Carters transferred their membership to Plains.

All went smoothly until he mentioned the Greek word *koinonia* in a Sunday morning sermon. A deacon rushed up to him afterward and thundered, "Never use that word again!"

"But, but, it's only a Greek word meaning fellowship," Edwards sputtered. "I was only trying to explain the text."

"It may be that to you," the deacon retorted, "but it means something else to us. Don't use it." Then Edwards remembered that the controversial Koinonia Farms was close by.

Except for that incident, all went well for the first year and a half. Sunday school attendance climbed above 200. The church raised his salary to $15,000, third highest among the thirty-seven churches in the Friendship Baptist Association.

In his second year he began working on a doctorate of ministries, a new seminary degree that would involve field projects, a day of classes in Atlanta every two weeks, and a dissertation. He and Sandra already had one son; now with Sandra unable to bear another, they adopted a Hawaiian-Caucasian baby through the state adoptions office.

Very little was made of this in Plains, although one church
nursery worker did initially refuse to change the baby's
diapers.

Criticism flared after Edwards gave a prayer at a Carter
campaign rally and made a couple of speeches for the candidate in other towns. "The Methodist pastor in Plains
stayed completely out of it," says Edwards, "and I could
understand that. But Jimmy Carter was a member and a
deacon in my church. I felt I had to speak up for his Christian commitment or people would wonder." The critics
among his members were Republicans and States' Rights
Democrats who felt it unfair for their pastor to be helping
the candidacy of the neighbor they wanted to keep in
Plains and out of the White House. They also complained
that Edwards was neglecting home visitation and making
people come to his office for counsel. Edwards contended
that he could counsel more people there.

Race never entered the picture until September 1976.
The church had sponsored an integrated Sunday school
class at the nursing home for years. Nothing had been said
about an occasional black reporter dropping in, but when
four black women tourists came for worship, jitters went
through the congregation. Nevertheless the women were
courteously seated.

The next big stir against Edwards came in October when
he defended Carter's *Playboy* interview in a letter copied
by the Democratic National Committee and mailed to
every Baptist preacher appearing in the SBC directory. He
said in part:

> . . . After reading the interview with *Playboy*, I
> am afraid that I must accept the responsibility for
> his accepting the interview. I have been his pas-
> tor for two years and have always taught all my

people to take advantage of every opportunity to
share our faith in Christ. The news media only
published a small portion ....

... Jimmy, of course, is not perfect. However, I
am convinced that he is a sincere Christian and I
do not believe that he is using religion to win
votes.

The letter was dated October 19. The following Sunday,
October 24, UPI reporter Helen Thomas asked Carter between Sunday school and worship, "Why are there no
blacks here?" "His face changed," Thomas remembers.
"He drew back shaking as if I had sort of punched him in
the nose. He said, 'I can't answer that,' then added, 'I guess
it's because they don't come. They don't come.' He was
sort of shaking."

Edwards, who had not heard the interchange between
reporter Thomas and Carter, preached that morning about
how Christians should not let barriers separate them, declaring there shouldn't be a "color line drawn in worship."
Thomas hurried to file her story, in which she quoted from
Edwards's sermon.

That afternoon Edwards flew to Tennessee, where he
addressed a public affairs seminar at the 2,500-member
Red Bank Baptist Church in Chattanooga. The pastor,
Fred Steelman, was also in the doctoral program, and had
asked him to "come and answer any questions our people
may have about Jimmy Carter."

The next morning black pastor Clennon King dropped
his bombshell letter at the Plains parsonage that said he
intended to apply for membership in the Plains church.

After reading the letter, Edwards did some checking on
King. He lived in Albany, forty miles away, where he
pastored a storefront interdenominational church. He was
known to be a Republican; he had once been associated

with a plan to persuade blacks to emigrate to Africa. He had a court and prison record for nonsupport of his children. Edwards felt certain he was out to embarrass Jimmy Carter.

Edwards took the letter to his deacons Tuesday night, one week before the election, and told them what he knew. The deacons, he suggested, could recommend that the church reject King on justification that he was not a proper candidate for membership. But this, he said, might make the church look bad before the world. He asked that they recommend repeal of the old 1965 ban and then endorse admission of King for membership.

Edwards had a reserve plan in case the deacons didn't buy this one. He would ask them to recommend revocation of the 1965 resolution and let King be considered on his own credibility. But before he could say anything else, the old ban was read and reaffirmed. Edwards protested that he couldn't go along with that, and several deacons replied in effect, "If you can't, then start looking for another church." After a long, awkward silence, a deacon moved that the next Sunday's services be canceled. Edwards went along, fearing violence and hoping that King might fade away after election day.

After the meeting, Edwards tried to call Carter to brief him on the explosive situation. When Carter returned the call and was told what had happened, he expressed only confidence that his pastor would do what was right and that he would be praying.

The next Sunday Carter was in Texas attending integrated services at the University Baptist Church, Fort Worth. In Plains Edwards met King and three black associates at the locked church door. Before a large crowd of reporters and photographers the pastor explained that the deacons had voted to cancel the services. "It is my belief that the church should be open to all people," he said.

The press quickly surrounded him, asking for more information. Edwards told them that the deacons had read the 1965 act as barring "niggers and other civil rights agitators." Hugh Carter, standing next to him, shouted, "No! No! It says Negroes—N-E-G-R-O-E-S." But the reporters ignored him. When the deacons learned of Edwards's quote, they hastily assembled for another meeting that evening.

Bruce and Sandra had gone to visit Sandra's parents that afternoon and returned to find cars around the church. The pastor went inside to find the deacons in the process of voting on his resignation. In the hassle that followed, some brought up that he had quoted them as saying "niggers" in reference to the old rule. He apologized but added that he had indeed heard some of them use the term "niggers" during the previous meeting. Nevertheless they voted 11-1 to demand his resignation; the dissenter was young county extension agent Tim Lawson.

"You don't have the authority to fire me," Edwards then declared. "I serve at the pleasure of the church." After more wrangling, an agreement was reached to call a church business conference for November 14 to vote on the questions of admitting blacks and the pastor's future. The deacons would find a supply preacher the next Sunday, then Edwards would return the following Sunday for the vote.

Edwards was practically sure he would have to leave Plains and told his friend Steelman so. Steelman arranged for a pulpit committee to hear him at a Tennessee church the next Sunday. Only the committee knew that he was Carter's pastor. He was simply introduced as "Brother Bruce."

At Plains a retired Methodist preacher, Earl Duke, filled the Baptist pulpit. Carter discreetly stayed away and attended Episcopal services on St. Simon's Island.

On Monday, the day before the election, the Republican

National Committee's "black desk" sent telegrams to 400 black ministers, questioning whether Carter could lead the country "if he cannot lead his own church." The obvious reference to Clennon King's desire for membership apparently created a backlash in black communities. A Harlem preacher, for example, telephoned Edwards that he was "taking buses and rounding up blacks on the street and in the bars to vote for your deacon." Edwards now thinks that Carter's close wins in some states may have resulted from the black backlash.

With the election over, the next media event became the November 14 church business conference. It was regarded as a test of both the president-elect and his denomination.

As the time neared Carter called old friends on both sides in a compromise effort to heal the wounds and break the race barrier. Every day during the final weeks hundreds of letters and calls came to the parsonage from Southern Baptists and others pledging prayer and support. Personnel from every Southern Baptist agency telephoned assurances. Saturday afternoon, thirty newly appointed SBC missionaries pushed through a throng of reporters on the parsonage lawn to hold a prayer meeting with the pastor and his wife.

That evening Edwards heard that Ashton Jones, the most feared white civil rights activist in Georgia, was at Koinonia Farms, planning to lead a march on the Plains church the next day. Jones had been the central figure in racial clashes on the steps of Atlanta's most fashionable churches in the mid-sixties and had served time in jail. Fearing a riot should Jones show up with a crowd of protesters, Edwards raced to Koinonia. "Give us this chance," he begged Jones. "If we don't get the church open tomorrow, then do what you feel you must."

The next morning the churchyard was transformed into

a media circus. "It's just like a little Scopes trial," chortled clerical columnist Lester Kinsolving. Out front was parked "Noah's Ark," a refurbished school bus with a plywood second story made to resemble the Genesis vessel. A black "Prophet Elijah" announced to reporters that his coming was "a sign of the last days." A woman proclaimed herself "True Messiah." Another woman circulated as "The Holy Spirit." Robed Klansmen, led by Imperial Wizard Bill Wilkinson from Louisiana ("I'm a good Southern Baptist"), exchanged verbal punches with Clennon King and other blacks. "We're going to take the offensive and recover the ground we've lost," the Wizard bragged.

The Sunday school lesson for the president-elect's class inside was entitled "The Reconciled Life"; the text, Rom. 12:21: "Be not overcome of evil, but overcome evil with good." Said teacher Clarence Dodson, "We have the opportunity to show the world the attitude which God's children should have."

At the bell the deacons cleared everyone from the church except members and Carter's black bodyguard. The motley crowd waited outside in a cold drizzle.

After almost three hours Carter emerged through a side door. "I'm completely satisfied with the votes," he declared. "I was proud of my church, God's church. We voted to keep our pastor, and more important to open the doors of our church to any person to worship. I think now our church will be unified."

Cousin Hugh Carter, the church clerk, appeared at the main door to announce the vote counts to the throng of reporters and photographers: A motion to fire the pastor had failed 100-96. Another motion to set up a "watch-care committee" consisting of the pastor and four deacons to "test the sincerity of all persons applying for membership and make recommendations to the church" had passed unanimously. A third motion to "open the church to all persons, regardless of race," had been adopted 121-66. This, the clerk said, nullified the 1965 rule.

Some members had taken notes during the closed-door meetings about what had been said. The president-elect had warned that "if you don't open the church there will be tens of hundreds of demonstrators here next Sunday." Jerome Etheredge, soon to go with his wife as missionaries to Togo, had made the "open-door" motion, pleading, "We can't do our work unless the world knows that this church is open to all people."

Apologies and prayers for forgiveness had been expressed. Hugh Carter and several other deacons confessed to having acted "hastily" in asking the pastor to resign. There was much hugging, kissing, and reconciliations, leading Ruth (Mrs. Hugh) Carter to exult, "We're ready for a revival."

Hardly. After the vote was taken for members of the screening committee, allegations were dropped that ballots for some persons had been cast improperly so as to ensure a majority of strong segregationists. Other stories spread through Plains that some of Edwards's supporters were involved in extramarital affairs, and that Carter had been born five months after Earl and Lillian were married. (They were married September 24, 1923; their oldest son was born October 1, 1924.)

The screening committee met and, as expected, rejected the application of King and two others from Los Angeles for membership. "People shouldn't just try to join a church because the president-elect belongs," Edwards said. Then he explained that King had been turned down for "failing to appear and to demonstrate cooperation in fulfilling the purposes of the church." The church, including President-elect Carter, voted unanimously to accept the recommendations of the committee.

Edwards's hope that he would be able to stay soared

during the next few weeks. His celebrity status kept climbing. Network talk shows vied for his appearance. On inauguration day he presided over a nationally televised "People's Prayer Service" at the Lincoln Memorial that featured a sermon by Martin Luther King, Sr.

Back in Plains he came crashing back to earth when a story appeared in a tabloid announcing "Carter's Pastor in *Playboy's* Stable." Edwards, the story reported, had signed a lucrative book contract with an agent for *Playboy*. Edwards tried to explain to his congregation that the agent was no longer employed by *Playboy*, that the book contract was with Simon & Schuster, that the advance was for a low five figures, and that as yet he had not received any money.

All to no avail. Refueled by the misleading article, the opposition began lining up votes—to show "that this is God's church, not Jimmy Carter's," some said.

On February 13, the Carters returned to Plains, ostensibly to help Edwards keep his job. But in a tactical move, the pastor's opponents delayed their motion for his resignation until the following Sunday, when the Carters were back in Washington.

Edwards's supporters were caught unprepared. Some did not know until the night of the nineteenth that the vote was coming the next day and that the opposition had been busy rounding up their troops.

The February 20 business meeting was more bitter than the one in November. Some of Edwards's detractors sat in the back and read newspapers and talked aloud when he spoke. Hugh Carter's plea that the vote be put off another week was greeted with derision.

After losing procedural votes, Edwards saw that his doom was sealed. He then presented his resignation.

One observer remarked about the obvious anti-Carter feeling: "They couldn't impeach the president, so they fired his pastor."

Edwards was now even more of a martyr to millions of Americans. Network talk shows had him back for another round of appearances. In each instance he was asked to explain why he had been forced out of the church. "It was my support of Jimmy Carter and the stand I took on race," he said.

On ABC-TV's "Directions" he was asked about a *New York Times* story that his adoption of a non-Caucasian child might have played a large role in his dismissal. (The *Times* reporter had quoted Billy Carter as saying that the baby was "99 percent of the preacher's trouble," a quote Billy later denied.) Edwards thought that angle had been "overplayed."

"I want to make it clear that I have not given up on Plains Baptist Church," he continued. "There are a lot of good people in Plains . . . people who have stood behind me . . . many times at the risk of great danger."

What kind of "danger" had his backers faced? Some he said had been threatened with loss of their jobs, and others had been harassed in other ways. He was referring to a petition presented to the Sumter County Board of Commissioners demanding the firing of county agent Tim Lawson, alleging he had been "too vocal in the affairs of Plains Baptist Church," the rock thrown through Hugh Carter's living room window, the suspected poisoning of another friend's dogs, and obscenities scrawled on the parsonage mailbox.

Black in Plains, Edwards and his wife declared their intention to remain in the parsonage until school was out. A move led by Tim Lawson and Hugh Carter to have him reinstated at Plains failed. Efforts to obtain another church were discouraging. A denominational leader declared, "He's dead in Georgia."

Jack Harwell, editor of the Georgia Baptists' newspaper *The Christian Index,* called Jimmy Allen at First Baptist Church, San Antonio. Allen set up a date for Edwards in his church and promised to have some pulpit committees from integrated churches there. Edwards went and spoke, but nothing came of it.

A church in Florida opened. The pulpit committee assured that the troubles in Plains would not be a factor in their decision. After they turned him down, Edwards "heard" they had received some telephone calls from Plains.

Finally he accepted a 125-member church in Hawaii, with his salary to be paid jointly by the small congregation, the Hawaii Baptist Convention, and the SBC Home Mission Board. He moved his family in July to become once more "just another Southern Baptist pastor."

11

«« »»

The Baptist
in the White House

FIVE BLOCKS north of the White House, near Scott Circle, the oldest Protestant congregation in the District of Columbia worships in an impressive Gothic edifice. This is the First Baptist Church of Washington, D.C., organized on March 7, 1802, in the old U.S. Treasury building to serve government workers. Of the six founding members, three were later excommunicated and two withdrew in dissent to form another congregation. The church now has about 950 members, some fifty of whom are black. The present building was erected in 1953 on the site of an older structure constructed in 1890.

The church is neither Southern nor Northern. Like most other churches in the District of Columbia Baptist Convention it is affiliated with both Baptist bodies. However, most of the present lay leadership is Southern Baptist, as is the pastor.

This is the Baptist "church of the presidents." Martin Van Buren, Franklin Pierce, and Lyndon Johnson sometimes attended. Warren Harding, the first Baptist president, came as often as he thought a politician should. Harry Truman was a regular. "I go because the preacher treats me as a member and not as the head of a circus," the plainspoken Missourian said. But Truman kept his membership back at his old home church.

The night before the Carter inauguration, a small group of Baptist clergy and laity gathered to pray for the man they had ardently supported.

The next morning the Carters, the Mondales, several cabinet nominees and their families, and other close friends came to the church for a private preinaugural worship service. Joan Mondale's Presbyterian clergyman father cited Mordecai's challenge to Queen Esther as a challenge to the new administration: "Who knows whether you are come to the kingdom for such a time as this?"

Nelson Price, Carter's Georgia "prayer partner," preached from the text "Whatsoever ye do, do it heartily, as to the Lord, and not unto men" (Col. 3:23). Speaking directly to the president-elect, who sat cradling Amy under one arm, he said: "Whatever you do, do it with all of your heart. Do it from the depth of your soul. Whatever you do, do it seeking not the accolades of people but the approval of the Lord. Choose the audience you seek to satisfy and let it be an audience of One, the true and living God. Henceforth, play it to Him. Don't run from the inevitable complaints and criticisms of the people, but run to attain the commendation of the Lord. For it is true of nations as of persons, he never asks us to do one thing that is not for our good.

"When one accepts the validity of our text there is no cause for despondency when people complain, for it is the approval of God which is sought, not theirs. Neither is there cause for grandiose flights of ego when lauded, for the intent is to please God, not garner the inflating praise of people. This . . . enables one to remain relaxed and to maintain emotional equilibrium."

Across town, Bruce Edwards was introducing Martin Luther King, Sr., at the nationally televised "People's

Prayer Service" before the Lincoln Memorial. "The sheep must be fed," the venerable black preacher orated. "That's why Martin Luther King, Jr., gave his life . . . that the least of these may not be forgotten. . . .That's why the president-elect is up here."

The big event at noon was, at the honoree's request, kept Baptist simple. He wore a plain business suit and paid no ceremonial bows to the prominent. He praised his defeated opponent for "all he has done to heal our nation"—an unprecedented act of tribute. Then he delivered one of the shortest and most thought-provoking presidential inaugural speeches in American history.

His first Scripture choice for his inaugural sermon had been II Chron. 7:14: "If my people, which are called by my name, shall humble themselves, and pray, and seek my face, and turn from their wicked ways; then will I hear from heaven, and will forgive their sin, and will heal their land." Aides had persuaded him he would be coming across too strong as an evangelist, and he switched to Mic. 6:8: "He hath showed thee, o man, what is good; and what doth the Lord require of thee, but to do justly, and to love mercy, and to walk humbly with thy God."

"I have no new dream to set forth today," he said, "but rather urge a fresh faith in the old dream.

"Ours was the first society openly to define itself in terms of both spirituality and of human liberty. It is that unique self-definition which has given us an exceptional appeal—but which also imposes on us a special obligation—to take on those moral duties which, when assumed, seem invariably to be in our own best interests."

He called for a "resurgent commitment to the basic principles of our nation, . . . human rights, . . . personal liberty, . . . a spirit of individual sacrifice for the common good," and helping to "shape a just and peaceful world that is truly humane."

He hoped "that when my time as your president has ended, people might say this about our nation:

"That we had remembered the words of Micah and renewed our search for humility, mercy, and justice;

"That we had torn down the barriers that separated those of different race and region and religion, and where there had been mistrust, built unity, with a respect for diversity;

"That we had found productive work for those able to perform it;

"That we had strengthened the American family, which is the basis of our society;

"That we had ensured respect for the law, and equal treatment under the law, for the weak and the powerful, the rich and the poor...."

Columnist James Reston termed the speech a revivalist's call to recover the spiritual and moral ideals and principles of the past, a challenge Washington hadn't heard since Woodrow Wilson. "What sets the new president aside from all his predecessors since Wilson," Reston noted, "is that his religion lies at the center of his life."

The following Sunday morning, the new president and his family surprised no one by going to Sunday school. Fred M. Gregg, Jr., an executive vice-president of the Equitable Life Insurance Company, would be President and Mrs. Carter's teacher. Gregg, a graying fifty, who taught top Southern Baptist agency executives at First Baptist Church, Nashville, before moving to Washington, recalls the event. "Back in November I had been asked to teach the couples' class until they got a regular teacher. I was very involved in my business and told the pastor I didn't have time. He talked me into teaching once more. That morning I entered through the back of the church and saw a little red-headed girl coming in the front door. Right behind her was Rosalynn and then the president. I knew they would be coming to my class. I began to shake. I felt as if my Adam's apple had dropped to my shoes. I said, 'Lord, of two hundred million Americans why did you put me here?' Finally I got my composure and walked down to welcome them to Sunday school and the church.

"The president smiled and said, 'I'm looking forward to hearing you teach.' I said, 'Why don't you teach, Mr. President?' 'Oh, I haven't studied the lesson for this morning,' he replied. I said, 'How about next Sunday?' 'Give me three or four Sundays and I'll be ready,' he replied."

In contrast to the bare basement where the men met in Plains, this class met in the church balcony with a tall stained glass window at their back. Also unlike the Plains class, women and blacks were welcome.

The lesson for January 23 was "Priorities in Life." Still nervous, Gregg sought to break the ice with a question. "Which Bible story precedes our lesson text for today?" he asked. The visitor replied instantly, "The Good Samaritan." Gregg relaxed. "Mr. President, you know this Bible real good. You help me out."

It was the least-kept secret in Washington that the presidential family would be at First Baptist Church that Sunday. The sanctuary was jammed with more people than the pastor, Dr. Charles Trentham, had seen since his arrival in 1974.

Trentham, fifty-seven, with white wavy locks and a wide, friendly smile, is rated as an outstanding scholar and preacher among Southern Baptists. He taught theology at Southwestern Seminary, then was dean of the School of Religion at the University of Tennessee for twelve years while pastor of First Baptist Church, Knoxville, one of the largest Baptist congregations in Tennessee.

At Knoxville he won the integration battle, then had his marriage break up.

Starting anew, he married Nancy Ballou, a talented solo-

ist in his Knoxville choir and accepted the pastorate of First
Baptist Church in Washington. His new position was a
step down.

Urban blight had spread around the Washington church,
driving members to seek homes in the suburbs. The year
he arrived, Watergate had left a pall over the church. He
began preaching to about 400 in a sanctuary that could
accommodate 1,400.

"I just had the feeling I would try to hold the fort for
a while," he says. "It was quite an adjustment for me,
preaching to fewer and fewer people."

Trentham did a little more than hold the fort. He got
the church to begin a counseling program for families and
a summer music workshop for inner-city children. They
also started a "Tuesday Cheer Up Club" to help discharged
mental patients from nearby St. Elizabeth's Hospital re-
adjust to community living. And the church teamed with
four nearby congregations to provide a free medical clinic,
a temporary residence for homeless women, and a "Break
for the City" program in which volunteers collected and
distributed food and clothing from a neighborhood store.

The Sunday the Carters came he looked the picture of
pastoral dignity standing behind the ornate pulpit. As he
customarily did, he wore a robe—something few SBC
preachers do.

"Suppose you had the responsibility of preaching the
first sermon the President of the United States would hear
after his inauguration?" he asked. "'Where would you begin? Well, I have chosen for my texts Gen. 1:1: 'In the beginning God . . . ,' and John 1:1: 'In the beginning was the
Word, and the Word was with God, and the Word was
God.'"

Nearing the close of his sermon, he suggested that
January was a month for beginning again for students returning to college and for government workers taking up

new jobs. When he gave the invitation for membership, the newest government worker in Washington, his wife, daughter Amy, son Chip and his wife Caron, and daughter-in-law Annette came forward.

"What an historic moment this is," the pastor announced with obvious emotion. "We welcome the president and his family." He read the names of those Carters transferring by letter. Then he turned to the youngest. "It is said, 'A little child shall lead them.' May I present the first citizen of Washington, Amy Carter, who comes confessing the Lord Jesus Christ as her Savior, and asking to be baptized."

After the benediction the congregation remained seated while the pastor escorted his new parishioners and their entourage outside. Standing together on the sidewalk, the new member from Georgia remarked, "I feel very close to you." "And I feel very close to you, Mr. President," the preacher assured.

The following Sunday Trentham prepared to baptize Amy and a sixteen-year-old black girl from the Cameroons. When he led Amy into the baptistry, a nervous Secret Service man demanded of an usher, "Now look here, what is he going to do to that child?"

The pastor's voice echoed through the sanctuary. "Upon the profession of your faith, I baptize you, Amy Carter, in the name of the Father, the Son, and the Holy Spirit." With one hand over her face and the other supporting her back, he gently lowered her under the water and raised her up again.

The boom in new members continued. Attorney General and Mrs. Griffin Bell transferred from the Second Ponce de Leon Baptist Church in Atlanta. "I've known Griffin Bell for a long time," Trentham said in introducing them. "He is a man who takes his Christian faith seriously."

Another new celebrity was Amy's nanny, a convicted murderess from Georgia who had been given a work release to care for Amy in the governor's mansion. She joined the White House staff as a salaried employee.

Carter, as he had at Plains and as he had promised Fred Gregg, taught Sunday school. "I'm always glad to help a busy man out," he told the insurance executive.

No other chief executive taught a Bible class while in office, although several taught before becoming president. James A. Garfield was a lay Disciples of Christ preacher. McKinley superintended the Sunday school at First Methodist Church in Canton, Ohio. Theodore Roosevelt taught a class at Christ Episcopal Church in Cambridge, Massachusetts, while a Harvard undergraduate. The priest there fired him after learning that he belonged to the Dutch Reformed Church.

In Washington, Carter followed the same teaching method pursued in Plains: read a passage of Scripture, comment, then invite reactions. And as at Plains, he spoke openly and unequivocally about his evangelical faith to a degree that no president ever had.

Ford, an Episcopalian, was known to be an evangelical, but rarely talked of his personal relationship with God. Nixon brought prominent evangelicals into the White House, but never dropped his mask. Johnson hobnobbed with Billy Graham and made occasional God talk, but didn't appear to be particularly devout. Eisenhower, the first president to join a church and be baptized while in office, couldn't bring himself to talk about Jesus in any personal, intimate way. Kennedy was hardly a Catholic saint.

Truman was a churchgoer from youth and said he had read the Bible through twice before he was twelve. He never attended Sunday school in Washington. From his personal papers, Truman appears to have been more of a Jeffersonian Unitarian than an orthodox Baptist. Like Jefferson, he thought Jesus "the greatest teacher of all time," but not unique in that he was the only way to God. "Any race, creed, or color can be God's favorites if they act the part," Truman said. His fellow Southern Baptists apparently never noticed this deviation from their doctrine. They lauded his devotion to Bess and castigated him for cussing. Harding proved to be a hypocrite who Baptists tried to forget.

Before Jimmy Carter, Lincoln was the president who spoke most often and most intimately about his religion. He frequently talked of "my Lord and Savior" and of praying to know God's will. His father was the lay leader of the Pigeon Creek Baptist Church in Indiana, and there is evidence that young Abe helped out as sexton.

Before becoming president, Carter discovered how risky the expression of religious views by a public figure can be. For example, on the evangelical "Seven Hundred Club" television talk show, he said that the modern state of Israel "is the foundation and fulfillment of Biblical prophecy." The taping was done before the election and shown in late November 1976. It was what he had been taught by most of his pastors. The statement pleased Jews and premillennial evangelicals. It displeased Arabs and also those evangelicals who see the church as the spiritual Israel of Bible prophecy.

A Sunday school lesson he taught in Washington brought almost the opposite effect. He was commenting on John 18:14 where the Jewish high priest Caiaphas told his fellow clergy that it was expedient for Jesus to die. "That was a turning point in Christ's life," the new president was reported as saying. "He had directly challenged in a fatal way the existing church, and there was no possible way for the Jewish leaders to avoid the challenge. So they decided to kill Jesus." Then he described the trial of Jesus as illegal. "The Jews had a rule that a trial had to be held in the daytime and in the open. Christ was tried at night in a home and only one witness was allowed to be called for the defense. . . . Caiaphas acted as both judge and prosecutor.

"Caiaphas," he continued, "represents an attitude that is part of all of us. There is a danger that the church of Christ can become anti-Christ. We can start to worship ourselves and give in to the temptation to set up our own standards. We can become proud and consider ourselves exceptions in God's eyes."

When printed, the comment about the Jewish leaders deciding to kill Jesus brought quick reaction. An ecumenically active Lutheran pastor in Washington, Reverend John F. Steinbruck, fired off a letter stating that many Christians and Jews were disturbed and wanted to know if the president held Jews responsible for the crucifixion of Christ.

Carter's reply was hand-delivered to the pastor, with copies provided for the press. He denounced as unjust and false the old anti-Semitic charge that the Jews killed Christ. "The Jewish people," he said, "were for many centuries falsely charged with the collective responsibility for the death of Jesus and were persecuted terribly for that unjust accusation which has been exploited as a basis and rationalization for anti-Semitism." He was "personally gratified" that his own denomination had condemned anti-Semitism as un-Christian and had pledged to root out any remnants of the hatred and replace it with "love for Jews, who along with all other men are equally beloved of God. To that I can only say 'Amen,' with all my heart." He noted that Jesus himself was a Jew and that those responsible for his crucifixion included "Judas, who was a Christian disciple; Caiaphas, who was a Jewish priest appointed by the Roman authorities; and Pilate, a Gentile who actually condemned Jesus to death."

The Lutheran pastor termed the presidential response "an historic repudiation of the 'Christ-killer' canard that has so long and so unjustly been the burden of the Jewish people." "Your action," he wrote Carter "will create a new basis for the embrace and reconciliation of the whole family of Abraham after 1,900 years of estrangement."

The Caiaphas flap was not the big difficulty that confronted Carter the week before Easter. There was the decision about where to spend the holidays.

Because the situation in Plains had gone from bad to worse, the president and his family finally decided to visit son Jack in northern Georgia. Carter was obviously avoiding his home church and the possibility of bringing more trouble to Plains.

The previous January he had assured his fellow church members that things would quiet down after the inauguration. The media, whom many home folks blamed for the town's problems, would go to Washington with him.

But a new breed of press had replaced the White House Press Corps. They were more interested in digging up town skeletons than in reporting news of national importance. These writers didn't wear their press badges out front, but blended in with the tourists, fishing for tidbits of gossip, then stringing together stories that inflamed already hurt feelings.

A tabloid ran an upsetting full-page piece about "The Bitter Feud Between Jimmy Carter's Wife and Mother," proclaiming, "It's the worst-kept secret in Plains that Miss Lillian won't be welcome in the White House." Ironically, the story appeared as Miss Lillian was beginning a long visit at the White House.

More damaging to the troubled church were stories claiming a long-standing feud between the Williams and the Carter families, who are business competitors in warehousing and processing peanuts. Albert Williams, in partnership with his brother Frank, was pictured as the town's arch racist and bitter enemy of Jimmy Carter. His segregationist feelings were well known, but some blacks said he was the man they would call on first for financial help.

About his former fellow deacon, the president, he said, "Jimmy and I disagree on a lot of things. I respect him and I think he respects me. But I'm not going to buckle under because he's in the White House." After the first vote to fire Pastor Bruce Edwards, Albert had resigned as deacon and church treasurer. Then President-elect Carter persuaded the congregation to table his resignation "until I have a little talk with Albert." He took an evening off from making cabinet appointments to visit his neighbor.

Actually members of the Williams family and the Carters have close personal ties. The then president-elect and his wife took New Year's Eve dinner with Frank and Virginia Williams. Virginia and Jimmy Carter are high school classmates. And Jan Williams, wife of Frank's son George, was Amy's teacher and handled her mail, then went along to care for her during the inauguration ceremonies and festivities.

Journalistic nit-picking and scandalmongering aside, there were frayed nerves and tempers in Plains from zoning battles between factions vying for the tourist dollars. The Baptist storekeepers, with one exception, had their businesses open on Sundays, something they had never done before the town became a tourist mecca. Only Ernest Turner, chairman of the deacons, kept his hardware business ("The Store That Hasn't Changed Since 1902") closed on the day of rest.

There were four tour services scrambling for business, and three newspapers where before there were none. All the newspapers were operated by out-of-towners.

Promoters arrived daily seeking a piece of the action. One television production company shot a $350,000 commercial in the town and paid the town council $150 for a permission fee.

The changes and pressures were mind-boggling to the local people who had led such quiet lives before. Traumatized by future shock, they could not fully realize the implications of one of their own becoming the most powerful man in the world.

The church was torn up and there was no sanctuary there. An elderly retired minister now supplied the pulpit, but his sermons roused little response. Still divided over politics, race, change, and the former pastor, neighbors hardly spoke across the pews. Some glared as if to say, "You are no longer welcome here."

The final straw for the group that had supported Bruce Edwards was the issue of an unsigned report by the church's "silent majority." Edwards, Deacon Hugh Carter, and other unidentified persons were blamed for making "irresponsible, disruptive, and misleading statements to the press contrary to the best interests of the Plains Baptist Church." The charges were basically a rehashing of old criticisms against the former pastor, concluding, "He [Edwards] was a victim of his own undoing by exposing church business to the public and by letting secular matters come ahead of his pastoral duties." Four deacons who had led the opposition to Edwards said the report was not intended to involve President Carter in the problems of the church. "We still love Jimmy Carter, and he cannot be responsible for this," they told Jeff Prugh of the *Los Angeles Times*. "We welcome him back and look forward to having him worship with us real soon."

The unsigned report, which had not been voted on by the church, was "like a slap in the face" to Hugh Carter, who had been working for months for a reconciliation. He had continued to lead the music and serve as a deacon and church clerk, even though his wife had given up on the church, saying she had "taken all the abuse I can stand." The others who had supported Edwards and an open church now agreed with him that there was no hope for a reconciliation.

They began services in May in the old vacant Lutheran sanctuary in nearby Botsford. A number of other church officers said they would serve out their terms in the old church and then make their decision at the end of the official church year in October. Some said they were remaining for the sake of the historic old Baptist building in which a president had received his spiritual training.

The new Baptist congregation called as their pastor Fred Collins, who had remained in the area since his forced resignation from the old church in 1974. They took the name Maranatha Baptist Church. *Maranatha* is a Greek word, meaning "the Lord comes." They announced plans to construct a sanctuary "open to everyone" on the main tourist highway leading into Plains.

It was well known that Fred Collins was Miss Lillian's "favorite." However, when the new church was being organized, she said, "I don't want to be in any split-up church. I've been going to the old one for fifty-two years, but I'm definitely not going to it the way it is. I'll have a long talk with Jimmy before I decide."

Her son in Washington had been kept informed of the news from home. He made no statement about which church he would attend when he came back to Plains. However, the Carter on his White House staff, Hugh Carter, Jr., called and asked to tender his church letter by proxy. "I want to be a charter member of the new church," he said.

When President and Mrs. Carter did make their next pilgrimage to Plains, they attended Sunday school at the Old Church, then motored into the country for worship with new Maranatha Church.

The president was reported to be deeply grieved over the split, remarking, "What a tragic thing to happen." But the division in his hometown that had separated some families did not cool his interest in Baptist life. He was already busy with a plan to greatly advance the outreach of his denomination.

His Sunday school teacher, Freg Gregg, recounts how it came about.

"One morning the president appealed for everyone in our class to consider their relationship with Jesus as active, not passive, to do something about it, to go deeper with God. He said he had learned that the Mormons had 26,000 lay missionaries giving full time for two years to the spreading of their faith. 'And they are much smaller than Southern Baptists,' he said. Then he challenged us to think about full-time service.

"I didn't catch on right away to what he had in mind. The following Sunday, he said, 'Gregg, I've got something on my heart that I need to talk with you about.' I asked, 'Do you want to talk now?' 'No, we need more time,' he replied. 'Can you come over to the house this afternoon?'

"Of course I could. I went up about two and was taken into his living quarters. He was in blue jeans and getting ready to write the talk he was to deliver the next night on the energy crisis.

"Just the two of us were there. He put everything else aside and presented his hope that Southern Baptists could do what the Mormons were doing so successfully, and recruit thousands of lay volunteers who would give their time and skills in missionary work. He asked me, 'Where should we go from here?'

"I said, 'Mr. President, I'll go to Nashville and talk to Porter Routh. You know that he's the top man down there, the staff director for the executive committee. I used to teach him in Sunday school.' He said, 'Get together with Routh and come back and tell me what I should do.'

"Well, I flew down to see Routh. I've never seen anyone

get quite so excited over an idea. We decided that I should take back a list of key leaders in our denomination, and suggest that the president have them up to the White House for a meeting. I told the president that and he said, 'Fine, we'll set up a luncheon.' "

Carter hosted the Southern Baptist brass in the Roosevelt Room, across the hall from the Oval Office. They included Routh and the heads of the Foreign and Home Mission Boards, the Sunday School Board, the Woman's Missionary Union, and Brotherhood Commission. The brotherhood executive, Glendon McCullough, had been at the White House a few days before when Carter had given a reception for trustees of the agency. Carter was a brotherhood trustee while governor and a personal friend of the director. Mc-Cullough was married at the governor's mansion with Carter serving as his best man.

Also present at the unprecedented meeting were Miss Annie Ward Byrd, a longtime youth editor at the Sunday School Board; Mississippi businessman Owen Cooper, president of the Southern Baptist Convention in 1973 and 1974, and a periodic guest at the Georgia governor's mansion; and the president's pastor and Sunday school teacher. For Southern Baptists, this was about the most influential group of denominational leaders that could be assembled on so short a notice.

The president sat between Charles Trentham and Fred Gregg and welcomed them in a voice so quiet that those furthest away had to strain to hear. He said he had missed some sleep the night before, explaining that Amy had come and "crawled in bed with us about four and behind her came her cat."

The SBC leaders listened to his appeal and then promised to do all possible to implement it at the upcoming convention in Kansas City. They asked if he would make a videotape presentation for the convention and he said he would.

What he said at the White House luncheon and on the tape can be summarized as follows:

—He had studied the denomination's goal to reach everyone in the world by the year 2000 and wondered why they should wait that long to get a massive mission program underway. He felt they should start now.

—He noted that the Mormons had 26,000 nonpaid volunteers serving while the SBC had only 172 volunteer laity doing missionary work.

—He pointed out that it was taking about 5,000 Southern Baptist church members to support one adult foreign missionary. The goal called for only a 2½ percent increase in personnel a year, while there was a documented need to increase the foreign missions force by 50 percent immediately. "Once we set such modest goals," he opined, "it is highly unlikely that we will greatly exceed them."

—He mentioned that membership gifts were less than 3 percent of total income, and that contributions to the Cooperative Program for supporting denominational causes had dropped from a high of 14 percent to less than 9 percent of church collections. This, he said, was small in consideration of the denomination's potential.

—He called for at least 5,000 volunteer missionaries. "I know three widows in Plains that could go," he said. "I could pay the expense of one. Another could pay her own way. I'm sure we can get somebody else to support the third." He recalled with pride how his mother had learned two dialects to go to India for the Peace Corps. He emphasized that the turning point in his own Christian life had come from his missionary trip in 1969 to Pennsylvania.

—He suggested that volunteers be sought from nineteen up, be given three months special training, then sent to serve in a needy place for one or two years without pay.

—He emphasized, "This is the best time we will ever have for a quantum step forward in our effort to be leaders in a much needed worldwide spiritual program."

The Kansas City assembly voted enthusiastically to back the Carter proposal. Leaders agreed to set up a data bank at the Home Mission Board in Atlanta and begin processing applications.

Then they elected as their new president a strong Carter backer, Dr. Jimmy Allen, pastor of First Baptist Church, San Antonio. Allen calls himself a "social application conservative," accepts the Bible as infallible, and is a strict church-state separationist. He had been one of the invited guests at the preinaugural prayer meeting.

The year before, Gerald Ford had been invited to speak to the Southern Baptist Convention at Norfolk—to represent the nation for the SBC's bicentennial observance, program planners said. Carter supporters in the SBC had pressed for their man's appearance, but the request was denied.

The Kansas City convention still belonged to Carter. While he was present only by videotape, his churchmanship and call for volunteer missionaries were the leading topics of conversation. The aura he had cast over his denomination was obvious. A record number of 213 newspapers, magazines, and broadcast stations were represented.

Some reporters speculated that Carter might have overstepped his bounds by issuing the missionary call. Asked Bill Willoughby of the *Washington Star-News*: "What would Southern Baptists have said if John Kennedy had called Catholic bishops to the White House and issued such a call?"

James F. Cole, editor of Louisiana's *Baptist Message*, conceded that his denomination would have howled. "But our criticism would not necessarily have been valid. Carter's

challenge didn't come as an executive order. That order
was issued nearly 2,000 years ago when the head of the
church [Jesus Christ] said, 'Go ye.' "

The Baptist press pundits fairly glowed over the influence emanating from the White House. Wrote Kentucky's
C. R. Daley: "The prayers of Southern Baptists for an open
door to world evangelization in this generation have been
amazingly answered. A Baptist deacon, unknown beyond
his own community a few years ago but now living in the
White House, has been used of God to give Southern Baptists their greatest visibility and opportunity in history.
If we do not capitalize on this opportunity, we do not de-
serve another."

Some of the glow faded three weeks later when Deacon
Carter appointed Miami attorney David M. Walters as his
envoy to the Vatican. It was reported and not denied that
he had cleared the appointment with Archbishop Joseph
Bernadin, president of the National Conference of Catholic
Bishops.

Truman had raised Baptist hackles for the same action.
It had not been expected of Carter.

Jimmy Allen declared it "unbelievable" that the president would appoint an official emissary to "an Italian
clergyman [Pope Paul VI] who has never enjoyed the privilege of living under the American system of church-state
relations." Foy Valentine, director of the Christian Life
Commission and another invited guest at the preinaugural
prayer service, said the appointment had been "an unnecessary mistake when made by other presidents in our recent
past, and it is an unnecessary mistake when made by
Carter."

"Let the Vatican communicate with the U.S. government
the same way other religious groups do," demanded Dr.
James E. Wood, director of the Washington-based Baptist
Joint Committee on Public Affairs.

For the president there was no backing down from what seemed a political nod to Catholics after giving the missionary call for his own denomination.

Where does he stand on other moral issues raised by religious groups?

On abortion, his stance is practically the same as that of Southern Baptists. During the campaign he repeatedly said, "I think it is wrong." But he refused to say he would call for a constitutional amendment, saying only, "We should do everything within the confines of the Supreme Court ruling to discourage it." After election he supported the Court's decision that states are not obliged to spend Medicaid funds for elective abortions. When pro-abortionists said this would mean discrimination against poor women, he replied, "There are many things in life that are not fair, that wealthy people can afford and poor people can't. But I don't believe that the federal government should take action to try to make these opportunities exactly equal, particularly when there is a moral factor involved." He added there were valid exceptions when the mother's life was in danger or when pregnancy resulted from incest or rape.

Southern Baptists at their Kansas City convention "confirmed" their "strong opposition to abortion on demand and all governmental policies and actions which permit this." A motion calling for the SBC to support a constitutional amendment outlawing abortion except in cases of rape or incest or where the mother's life is jeopardized was ruled out of order on the basis of a technicality.

On gay rights Carter is more ambiguous than Southern Baptists. He reportedly said on NBC-TV's "Tomorrow" show, March 18, 1976, that he favored an antidiscrimination law for gays. Later he pleaded in his *Playboy* interview, "The issue of homosexuality always makes me nervous. . . . To inject it into a public discussion on politics and how it conflicts with morality is a new experience for me. I've thought about it a lot, but I don't see how to handle it differently from the way I look on other sexual acts outside marriage."

But gay representatives have not been welcomed at the White House. One meeting was arranged with Margaret "Midge" Costanza, Carter's assistant for special-interest groups. However, she gave them no assurances and they have not been allowed back in since.

Southern Baptists at Kansas City "commended" but did not endorse (as some asked) Anita Bryant for her successful crusade in getting repealed the Dade County, Florida, ordinance prohibiting discrimination against homosexuals in housing and employment. Then, in a related official action, they reaffirmed a 1976 resolution that urged churches not to ordain or employ gays, and opposed the "radical scheme" of gays "to secure legal, social, and religious acceptance by portraying homosexuality as normal behavior." Jimmy Allen, the newly elected SBC president, was cold to gays teaching in public schools. "It is the right of a community to determine the kind of models it wants for its children," he said in a news conference.

Billy Graham, who spoke at Kansas City and also held a press conference, refused to be drawn into the controversy. He "admired the courage of my dear friend, Anita," he said, "but my thrust is against sin singular, not sins plural. I don't have time to go around mounting campaigns against every individual sin." When pressed about gay rights, he replied rather shortly, "I've said all I intend to on this subject."

On human rights, apart from the gay issue, Southern Baptists and their deacon in the White House stand shoulder to shoulder. They applaud his citation of violations in the Soviet Union and other Communist countries, though some would prefer he not be so bold about such misbehavior by more friendly governments. The strong feeling about Soviet practices comes from knowing that thousands of Baptists are languishing in Russian prisons. The most celebrated Baptist captive is the preacher Georgi Vins. His last letter smuggled out to the British Centre for the Study of Religion and Communism indicated he was in great physical pain. "But the Lord provided relief," he continued. "I feel much better again. I believe in the power of your prayers and the prayers of God's people."

In his conduct of foreign policy Carter is being called another Woodrow Wilson. A staunch Presbyterian elder and son of a minister, Wilson tended to decide right and wrong by Christian standards, not by material or strategic expediency. Many believe that his rigorous devotion to moral principle led to the collapse of the League of Nations.

Carter is called "the missionary" by State Department diplomats who prefer Kissinger's more pragmatic approach to dealings with other nations. Conservative columnist James Kilpatrick has warned the new president that in his zeal to convert the heathens, he should remember that "some of the heathens are out of reach." But Carter persists, and it is his adherence to principle that is undoubtedly puzzling the Kremlin. They cannot imagine a foreign policy based on something other than political expediency.

Carter's efforts to adapt social structures to further his Christian idealism are not applauded by all Southern Baptists. They agree it is Christian duty to help the less fortunate. They divide, for example, over whether such duty extends to reforming courts, voting new welfare subsidies, and providing more government programs for the less fortunate. In this respect, SBC social activitists say that many of their brothers and sisters are more southern than Baptist and more conservative than Christian.

Jimmy Carter was never the candidate of right-wing conservative evangelicals, who include some of the most prominent preachers of his denomination. Their first choice was Ronald Reagan, a Presbyterian who also professes to have been born again. Carter's sermons and Sunday school lessons bothered them.

For example, he told his Sunday school class at Plains the Sunday after receiving the Democratic nomination, "We ought to make our own social structure a better demonstration of what Christ is." In that same lesson he also observed that "a Baptist church in the South" is composed of "a social and economic elite. We're the prominent people in town. There's a tendency to feel that because we've been accepted by God . . . , we're better than other people.

"Out of love," he continued, "has to come simple justice. Love in isolation doesn't mean anything. It must be applied to other people to change their lives for the better through . . . simple justice, compassion, redressing of grievances, . . . recognizing that the poor are the ones that suffer the most."

Carter's senitivity to the less fortunate was first developed from his mother's example and from intense study of the New Testament, particularly Matt. 25:40 where Jesus said, "Inasmuch as you have done it unto one of the least of these [the hungry, the thirsty, the naked, the sick, the prisoners], you have done it unto me." He also was affected by tragedies among relatives. He has a nephew in prison, an adult first cousin on his mother's side in a home for the retarded, and a first cousin on his father's side in a nursing home after spending time in the Georgia state mental hospital.

He came to further understand the quandaries of the outs of society while governor. He related two such experiences to a Law Day audience at the University of Georgia on May 4, 1974:

I was in the governor's mansion for two years, enjoying the services of a very fine cook, who was a prisoner—a woman. One day she came to me, after she got over her two years of timidity, and said, "Governor, I would like to borrow $250 from you."

I said, "I'm not sure that a lawyer would be worth that much."

She said, "I don't want to hire a lawyer; I want to pay the judge."

I thought it was a ridiculous statement for her; I felt that she was ignorant. But I found out she wasn't. She had been sentenced by a superior court judge in the state, who still serves, to seven years or $750. She had raised, early in her prison career, $500. I didn't lend her the money, but I had Bill Harper, my legal aide, look into it. He found the circumstances were true. She was quickly released under a recent court ruling that had come down in the last few years.

I was down on the coast this weekend. I was approached by a woman who asked me to come by her home. I went by, and she showed me documents which indicated that her illiterate mother, who had a son in jail, had gone to the county surveyor in that region and had borrowed $250 to get her son out of jail. She had a letter from the justice of the peace which showed that her mother had made a mark on a blank sheet of paper. They paid off the $250, and she has the receipts to show it. Then they started a five-year program trying to get back the paper she signed, without success. They went to court. The lawyer who had originally advised her to sign the paper showed up as the attorney for the surveyor. She had put up fifty acres of land near the county seat as security.

When she got to court she found that instead of signing a security deed, she had signed a warranty deed. That case has already been appealed to the Supreme Court, and she lost.

. . . This bothers me; and I know that if there was a commitment on the part of the . . . attorneys in this state, to search with a degree of commitment and favor, to eliminate many of the inequities that I've just described, . . . our state could be transformed in the attitude of its people toward the government.

He tried to apply some of his ideas while governor, but apparently did not convince an overwhelming number of his fellow Georgia Baptists that Christian ethics can be effected by executive order. They cheered when he stood with them against misuse of alcohol, legalized gambling, and pornography. They booed when he did not go their way on such matters. But when he proposed to meddle in welfare reform and court procedures, some shook their heads and questioned whether neighbor love should be stretched so far. And when he quoted questionable theologians such as Niebuhr and Tillich, many fretted that he was on the broad, liberal road to destruction.

As the president of the United States, who happens to be a Southern Baptist, he faces much greater complexities in effecting his programs and explaining his rationales. And he has a much larger and far more pluralistic congregation looking to him for leadership than he had in Georgia.

He has gained respect for devoutness and devotion to his family. When he says that government workers should quit living in sin and get married, Americans know he is deeply serious behind his smile. They also know that he will be more understanding than most moralists.

But when he says, "The most important thing in my life

is Jesus Christ, and I just don't believe there is a conflict there with my commitment to my family, neighbors, and fellowman," there is wonderment.

Wonderment about how the centrality of Christ in the life of their president will be expressed in government policies.

Wonderment about what it will mean to have in the White House a lay preacher, deacon, and Sunday school teacher who reads the Bible every day and prays throughout the day.

His thirteen million Southern Baptist kinsmen are wondering, too. Their preachers, teachers, and writers produced him and launched him into the world. They wonder what their protégé will become.

Whatever judgment history places on his presidency, good or ill or mediocre, Southern Baptists will have to accept at least a share of the responsibility. They have helped to mold and make him the man that he is.

12

«‹« »»»

Religious Experience:
The Key to Understanding
Jimmy Carter

PEOPLE, INCLUDING political experts with long experience, find Jimmy Carter enigmatic and unpredictable. He is mystic and technician, preacher and pragmatist, conservative and liberal, all in one bundle of seeming contradictions.

He is rigorously self-disciplined and almost puritanically moral, but tolerates the behavior of swingers. He asks that free food stamps be given to the welfare poor yet opposes federal payments for poor women to have abortions. He hard-lines the Kremlin and soft-lines the use of marijuana. He goes by no one's traditional alphabet. He is (a) liberal, (b) conservative, (c) radical. He zigs and zags across the political spectrum. By contrast, previous presidents were all but predictable.

Why is he so puzzling to so many? How can he be understood?

We submit that the enigma rests largely in the eyes of the beholders. They try to chart Carter from traditional secular and relativistic mindsets. All the while, the president proceeds on a course that flows from a spiritual base and is shaped by his religious experience.

The nation that once rested on religious moorings is now

awash in the sea of secularism. The much-touted evangelical resurgence, dramatized by the sensational conversions of such disparate disciples as Eldridge Cleaver and Charles Colson, has had little effect on the planners and pacesetters in education, government, entertainment, and journalism. As secular guru Arthur Schlesinger, Jr., put it: "Religious faith hardly seems a living option for us today."

The most astute religious leaders concede this. "We [Christians and Jews] are an influence in society," says Billy Graham, "but not the dominant influence."

". . . Religion has been put in such a second-class status [in public life] that people begin to think it really doesn't count," adds Rabbi Emanuel Rackman, an authority on religion and education in American life. "Religion no longer has a chance to be a force in our secular state, as do other movements or idealisms."

Along comes Deacon Jimmy Carter to bring the ship of state back to dock. Judging from what he has done and said prior to assuming the presidency, no one should be surprised. Georgians remember him saying, "I have considered myself in full-time Christian service every day I have been governor." Campaign supporters recall his declaration, "Christ has set the standard I am to attain as his representative. I try to pattern my life after his life." He is on the record with scores of similar statements. He has unabashedly clotheslined his born-again beliefs at the laundry of public opinion.

One particularly revealing incident should be noted. In March 1974, after he had already decided to run for president, he attended a small prayer meeting in Atlanta with then Senator Harold Hughes, newspaper editor Reg Murphy, and a few others. Hughes had recently decided to leave the Senate and devote the rest of his life to Christian counseling. According to Carter's subsequent accounts, "Hughes argued there was an irreconcilable difference between the life of a completely dedicated Christian, on the one hand, and a businessman or a politcian on the other. Hughes said he wasn't trying to judge others, but in his own analysis being in political life was interfering with his full-time commitment to Christ. . . . I happen to disagree with him."

Plainly, Carter believes deeply that his calling to government is as lofty as a call to the ministry—which is Baptist teaching.straight out of the New Testament. By no coincidence, the president once taught a book at Plains Baptist Church titled, *God Calls Me*.

Consider just two of the so-called Carter enigmas in the light of his faith.

1. His rigorous self-discipline versus tolerance of conflicting behavior in other people.

His self-discipline is often attributed to his military training, exemplified by Admiral Rickover's now famous challenge, "Why not the best?" He has, we think, been more challenged and energized by his highest ideal, Jesus Christ.

Carter's Jesus is not the haloed, harmless, meek and mild teacher pictured in religious fiction, but the virile, strong-willed Lord who never deviated or flinched from his God-sent purpose to bring redemption to believers. This Jesus, whom Carter has studied intensively and with whom he walks mystically, calls on his followers to deny the baser instincts of self and take up their crosses of single-minded commitment to his cause and follow him. Jesus expressed the idea in paradox: "For whosoever will save his life shall lose it; but whosoever will lose his life for my sake, the same shall save it" (Luke 9:24).

How can this be reconciled with Carter's acceptance of others whose behavior is less saintly than his own? Bob Dylan and Dylan Thomas are usually cited, but Carter's closest aides are not especially known for their devoutness. Jody Powell, for example, can be downright irreverent.

"Jody's always backslid," says a minister's wife, who has known him all her life.

Again, Carter is showing himself to be a follower of the one who gave his sternest lectures to self-righteous religious persons. Jesus accused them of faithfully keeping the rituals of Judaism, while omitting "weightier matters" such as "justice, mercy and faith" (Matt. 23:23).

Carter's choice of advisers is enigmatic to his Baptist minister friends. "I know his inner circle," says Reverend Nelson Price. "They have high ethical standards, but I regret that none are evangelicals. I'll keep praying."

Carter didn't choose them for their devoutness or frequency of church attendance, but for their expertise and loyalty. Jesus also chose his inner circle from outside the religious establishment. They were all young (most, if not all, in their late teens), inexperienced in religious work, and rough-edged. One, Peter, was so inclined to violence that when an arrest party converged on his master, he swung his sword and clipped off a man's ear.

Another possible insight is in one of Jesus' parables, which Carter frequently quotes in church talks:

> Two men went up into the temple to pray, one a Pharisee and the other a tax collector. The Pharisee stood and prayed thus with himself, "God, I thank thee that I am not like other men, extortioners, unjust adulterers, or even like this tax collector. I fast twice a week, I give tithes of all that I get." But the tax collector, standing far off, would not even lift up his eyes to heaven, but beat his breast saying, "God, be merciful to me a sinner!" I tell you, this man went down to his house justified rather than the other; for every one who exalts himself will be humbled, but he

who humbles himself will be exalted (Luke 18:10-14, *RSV*).

Carter is also aware that Jesus was not a killjoy who kept himself aloof from merrymakers and low-class persons scorned by the religious establishment. Carter's Ideal performed his first public miracle at a wedding reception by turning water into wine. When he visited Jericho he took a festive meal with the town's most notorious sinner, the tax collector Zacchaeus. On many other occasions he drew fire from religious leaders for associating with the less-than-righteous.

Some members of the president's home church have still not forgiven him for participating in late Sunday afternoon softball games with press and staff during the election campaign. They played in a vacant lot catty-cornered across the street from the church, with the games often continuing past the time for Baptist Training Union. It was galling to those arriving at the church to see Carter, a deacon and Sunday school teacher, sporting with common sinners during churchtime. The church members apparently did not consider that Jesus frequently violated the Sabbath with the explanation that the Sabbath was made for man and not vice versa.

2. His softness toward the less privileged versus his opposition to federal funding of abortions for welfare mothers.

Carter has meditated upon Jesus' practice of "doing good"—healing the lepers, giving sight to the blind, feeding the hungry. Carter has a good personal track record in this regard, as did his father before him. Almost everyone in Plains, particularly blacks, has a story about Earl or Jimmy Carter's generosity. Upon becoming governor, Jimmy Carter said, "We must have a Christian approach to people who feel alienated and alone." And, "Every adult illiterate, every school dropout, every untrained retarded child is an indictment of us all." When he left the mansion, he re-marked to a Southern Baptist editor, "I guess if I have any one thing for which I am most grateful during my term as governor, it is that I have seen my state develop a clearly discernible conscience about the need to help the many underprivileged groups of Georgians who had been for-gotten in other years."

As president he continues this humanistic concern. Two examples are his support of legislation to free the handi-capped from discriminatory practices and to exempt wel-fare mothers with children under fourteen from having to work.

How can this be squared with opposing federal aid to poor women desiring abortions? He admitted at a press conference that this could discriminate against poor women. He bluntly added, "There are many things in life that are not fair," and that the government should not try to equalize where a moral issue is involved.

His answer infuriated many in the women's liberation movement who saw his stand on abortion as inconsistent with previous actions. They shouldn't have been surprised for two reasons: (1) He said during the campaign, "I don't think the government ought to pay for abortions. This is a belief that I've had for a long time." He is genuinely trying to keep campaign promises. (2) He sees abortion as a bibli-cally based moral issue that transcends any financial dis-crimination.

There is no enigma here if Carter is analyzed from the standpoint of his Baptist upbringing. Baptists and other evangelicals, along with conservative Roman Catholics, are almost unilaterally opposed to abortion, in harmony with their belief that children are conceived "in the image of God." For Baptists, abortion is also a church-state issue, and Carter is consistent here. As much as he believes abortion to be wrong, he will not back a constitutional amendment that will make the government a ruler of conscience.

On less clear-cut matters the president is less predictable. Take the "gray" question of quotas on imported clothing and shoes. Without quotas, unemployment increases in the textile industry. With quotas, textile goods cost more, making it harder for poor people to properly clothe themselves. The man who has on his desk Truman's reminder "The Buck Stops Here" is caught in the dilemma of trying to decide which is the lesser of two evils or which is the greater of two goods.

What does Carter draw from his spiritual life for help in making such a judgment call? He prays for wisdom as Solomon did. He follows his sensitivities and "leading of the Spirit." And after making the decision, he accepts the consequences in the calmness of having done God's will as far as he is able to discern it.

What about decisions where he feels no deep sensitivities and leadings? He moves pragmatically to advance immediate and long-range goals—winning public support for a second term in office, for example.

Does Jimmy Carter, then, see himself as a son of destiny, a twentieth-century Oliver Cromwell ordained to set things right, a messiah to "set the prisoners free" in the kingdom of this world?

Not in the sense that he envisions making a perfect world. Contrary to *Time*'s assessment of his first six months in office, he does not believe in the perfectibility of man. He does hold, as he has often quoted theologian Reinhold Niebuhr, that "the sad duty of politics is to establish justice in a sinful world."

Justice, he believes from studying the Bible, cannot be attained in a society caught up in a materialistic fever. It can only be established as the transcendent spiritual values that make human existence meaningful are treasured and pursued, values that were the fiber of America before the age of secularism. National Security Adviser Zbigniew Brzezinski believes that his boss passionately desires to "infuse" the country and international affairs with the "new spirit" of his inaugural address.

In sum, Jimmy Carter is caught up in a passion felt by the apostle Paul, who wrote to the Christians at Philippi: "I count not myself to have apprehended [achieved]: but this one thing I do, forgetting those things which are behind, and reaching forth unto those things which are before. I press toward the mark for the prize of the high calling of God in Christ Jesus" (Phil. 3:13,14).

Paul's high calling was to spread the Christian message throughout the first-century Gentile world. Jimmy Carter's vocation, which he also sees as a calling, is to exemplify that message in his personal life while striving to create "a just and peaceful world that is truly humane." He may be seen as an inconsistent conservative in liberal clothing or as a Don Quixote flailing at windmills in the bureaucracies and fiefdoms of politicians. But his words and actions should be judged in the light of his aspiration to be God's man in a secular world.

«««   »»»

Appreciations

THE HUNDREDS who made this book possible include members of the Plains Baptist Church, Carter relatives, (particularly Alton and Jeanette Carter Lowery), and other citizens of Plains; former pastors at Plains (especially Reverend Bruce Edwards) and relatives of ministers deceased; prominent Baptists of Georgia; national leaders of the Southern Baptist Convention (including the present SBC president, Dr. Jimmy Allen, and five former presidents); executives and editors from SBC agencies, particularly Walker Knight, editor of *Home Missions* magazine, Dr. Thomas W. Hill, director of communications for the Foreign Missions Board, Floyd A. Craig, director of public relations for the Christian Life Commission; Catherine Allen, assistant to the executive director for public and employee relations for the Woman's Missionary Union; Dr. W. C. Fields, assistant executive secretary and director of public relations for the executive committee of the Southern Baptist Convention; and Lloyd Householder, director of the office of communications for the Sunday School Board.

Also Helen Thomas and Wesley Pippert, UPI White House correspondents; Mrs. Florence Jordan, widow of

Clarence Jordan, founder of Koinonia Farms; librarians at Lake Blackshear Regional Library in Americus, Georgia, as well as librarians at Mercer University, the Chattanooga (Tn.) Public Library, and Red Bank Baptist Church (Tn.).

Special thanks must go to Jack U. Harwell and Robert E. LeFavre, editor and associate editor, respectively, and other staff members of *The Christian Index* for providing extraordinary research assistance, as well as lending many photos for this book. The additional special person who must be recognized for his invaluable research assistance is Reverend Waldo P. Harris, director of missions for the Georgia Baptist Association and a leader in the Georgia Baptist Historical Society. For permission to quote Clarence Jordan's "Cotton Patch Version" of the Good Samaritan, we thank Association Press, N.K., publishers of *The Cotton Patch Version of Luke and Acts*, © 1969 by Clarence Jordan.

These and other unnamed persons contributed graciously without insisting that any of their own viewpoints be asserted. Interpretations, speculations, and conclusions presented in the book cannot be attributed to our sources. For good or bad, the degrees of correctness, can only be assigned to the authors.

Finally, we acknowledge with gratitude the labors of Jane Wilson, who transcribed some seventy hours of tapes and typed a portion of the final manuscript, and Fay Parks, who prepared the balance of the manuscript for publication.

Index

58407